DIGITAL
TECHNICAL
THEATER
SIMPLIFIED

T0303360

DIGITAL TECHNICAL THEATER SIMPLIFIED

HIGH-TECH
LIGHTING, AUDIO, VIDEO, AND MORE
ON A LOW BUDGET

DREW CAMPBELL

**Allworth
Press**
New York

Allworth Press books may be purchased in bulk at special discounts for sales promotion, corporate gifts, fund-raising, or educational purposes. Special editions can also be created to specifications. For details, contact the Special Sales Department, Allworth Press, 307 West 36th Street, 11th Floor, New York, NY 10018 or info@skyhorsepublishing.com.

25 24 23 22   5 4 3 2

Published by Allworth Press,
an imprint of Skyhorse Publishing, Inc.
307 West 36th Street, 11th Floor, New York, NY 10018.

Allworth Press® is a registered trademark of Skyhorse Publishing, Inc.®, a Delaware corporation.

www.allworth.com

Cover design by Mary Belibasakis

LIBRARY OF CONGRESS CATALOGING-IN-PUBLICATION DATA IS AVAILABLE ON FILE.
ISBN: 978-1-58115-855-7

Printed in the United States of America

For Divine, who puts up with me.
Mahal na mahal kita, palangga.

Contents

Acknowledgments

My thanks go out to all my professional colleagues who shared their immense knowledge and experience with me.

I would especially like to thank all those who allowed me to interview them at length about their professional projects, including Brendan Quigley, Drew Dalzell, Edward Marks, John Huntington, John McKernon, Vikram Kirby, and Martin Coster.

A big shout-out also to Tad Crawford, Claire Abramowitz, and the rest of the ever-patient staff at Allworth Press.

Also, my sincere thanks to my professional partners, Jay Soo and Doug Trueblood, for their constant support, and the staff at Moving Bits Pte. Ltd. for lending their professional expertise and letting me use the printer.

Intro: Welcome to the Digital Stage

Ever play Telephone as a kid? This is the party game where you whisper a phrase to the person sitting next to you. Then, without asking for repetition or clarification, that person must then whisper the phrase they heard to the next person, who whispers it to the next person, and the next, and so on, around the room, until the last person whispers it to the first one, at which point you compare the two phrases—the one you started with and the one you ended with—to see how different they are.

I used to play this game with my high school classes, where I once saw "Canada is the home of the moose" become "Can Andy take Homer shoot me loose?"

One day, I tried an experiment and asked my students to play the same game with numbers. The first person whispered five single-digit numbers to his neighbor, and then off it went around the room. After fifteen or so people, the number came back to the start, completely unchanged. Hmm, interesting.

So I began to challenge my students, asking them to try six numbers, then seven. How about double-digit numbers? We began to do it under pressure of time. Time and again, they were able to whisper numbers around a circle flawlessly. When they did mess up, it was almost always because of a memory error—they just couldn't remember all the numbers that had been whispered to them—rather than a comprehension error. "Twenty-seven" never became "forty-one" or "eighty-five" because someone didn't hear clearly. Eventually, they could pass eight two-digit numbers around the circle, a total of sixteen whispered digits, with almost flawless accuracy.

The exercise showed the precise nature of numbers, and, while it is a weak analogy for digital communication, it is a perfect example of two kinds of transmission: one that is highly vulnerable to distortion, interference, and signal loss, and one that is not.

But let's go back a bit.

"Digital" means fingers. The word "digit" is from the Latin "digitus," meaning a finger or a toe. It might have meant nothing more than that, except that some forward-thinking person in India realized we could keep track of sheep or beads or jars of olive oil if we counted them on those fingers. The Hindus (not the Arabs) came up with the set of "numerals" to do this around 500 CE, and anyone who believes that there is no relationship between the number of numerals and the number of fingers is hereby awarded an honorary membership to the Flat Earth Society. If you are ever curious why our numbering system is "base-ten"—that is, based on groups of ten numbers—hold your hands up in the air and count your digits.

"Digital," then, has come to mean a system that is based on numbers, and numerical information. A digital system breaks the world down into pieces, and assigns each piece a number.

One way to understand the difference between digital and analog is to use your eyes as an example.

Your eyes are open most of the time. True, they do blink now and then just to stay moist, but practically speaking, if you are awake, your eyes are open continuously. They are continuously taking in what they see and feeding it to your brain as an unbroken, constantly varying, electrical signal. Your eyes are *analog*.

Imagine, however, if your eyes began to blink really, really fast, like thousands of times per second. And imagine if, every time you opened them for a fraction of a second, a tiny camera inside your eye took a picture. Then, a computer attached to this camera took the picture and cut it up into millions of tiny pieces. Then, imagine that the computer looked at each and every piece and assigned it a number based on what color it was. The resulting stream of numbers would be a *digital* representation of what your eyes were seeing. Analog devices send a constant, unbroken signal. Digital devices convert all signals to a stream of numbers.

For the first half of the twentieth century, all electronic devices were analog. Radio, television, videotape, stereos—they all used analog circuitry. The digital age began with the invention of the microchip, a device that allowed vast amounts of information to be stored electronically and retrieved instantly. The microchip wasn't built to store analog information—it didn't store a continuous, unbroken stream. It stored numbers, or digits.

Because of the microchip's ability to handle large amounts of numerical information, the first place it landed in the theater was where large amounts of numerical information were being used every night: lighting. With all those numbers to keep track of—circuits, channels, filters, levels, cues, etc.—it was logical to turn the noncreative parts of the job over to a tool that could keep track of numbers without fail. The first digital devices in widespread use in the theater, therefore, were computerized lighting boards.

Getting back to that game of Post Office, digital devices have one major advantage over analog devices: They can transmit huge amounts of data much more accurately than analog devices, whose constantly varying signal is subject to all sorts of interference. In a word, digital is *cleaner*.

The advantages of digital don't stop there, however. Because it is stored in random-access memory (RAM), it can be accessed, um . . . randomly. This means that you can get at any piece of it at any time, making it much easier to edit, change, rearrange, recombine, and otherwise mess with it. We will see later how enormously useful this is.

As the computer entered our society, it entered the theater the same way—by degrees. The kinds of jobs that a computer could take on were determined, to a large degree, by how much information the job needed. Early computers had no trouble with five hundred or so dimmer levels, but they couldn't handle the amount of information in a photograph. The size and storage capacity of computer chips has continued to evolve, however, and soon, a photograph could be easily scanned, processed, and stored. After that, the next milestone was recording high-quality sound, and a few years after that, a moving video image.[1]

The other hurdle to overcome was cost. Theater has never been the richest of arts (are there any rich arts?), so technology had to be financially accessible as well as technically accessible.

These days, it is simply ridiculous how much computing power you can put on your desk, or, with the advent of smartphones and tablets, in your pocket. Sophisticated computers are available to just about anyone, especially if you are willing to forgo the latest and greatest model. Digital technology is now widely available to the masses, unwashed or recently showered.

Somewhere along the way, the computer stopped being just a calculator or a spreadsheet and started to become a creative tool, another form of paintbrush, carving knife, or musical instrument. Today it is an essential part of any theater artist's life, from e-mailed scripts to moving lighting to 3-D previsualization to pixel-mapped LED video screens.

Theater, like everything else, has gone digital.

---

[1] The growth of computer chips is actually fairly predictable, as demonstrated by Gordon E. Moore, one of the founders of Intel, who predicted in 1965 that the capacity of computer chips would double every two years. This trend, known as Moore's law, has held true ever since, allowing microchips to take on ever larger amounts of data and ever more complex jobs.

How to Use This Book

This book is not intended to make you a digital theater expert. If that were the case, it would need to be ten times bigger (and would only be distributed digitally). Each of the fields we are covering, including digital lighting, audio, video, and show control, are filled with astounding amounts of technical detail. The intent of this book is to give you a broad introduction to the next generation of technical theater, an introduction that will help you talk to today's digital technicians. If one of these areas piques your interest, take a look at the list of books in the appendix or just dive in online. Throughout the text, I have suggested Google search terms that you can use to find more information about the topic of your choice.

The Internet is an indispensable resource for any kind of technical knowledge, whether you are scratching the surface or diving deep. This book will give you the general terminology and overall perspective to understand each area of digital theater; but change is rapid, products come and go quickly, and techniques are reinvented and improved every day. If you want to use digital technology, get used to turning to your search engine of choice whenever you have a question. To become an effective user of any technology, you must plug yourself into the collective brain of developers, manufacturers, and users.

Of course, the first time you look into a new area online, you will almost certainly be overwhelmed with the amount of information available. Start slow, concentrate on what you know, and build your knowledge.

At any point in any technical process, if you have a question or problem, type the problem into a search engine, being sure to include the product or computer platform involved. The chances of you being the only person on the Internet with this problem are effectively zero.

A Word About Data

Digital information is composed entirely of numbers, but they are not "base-ten" numbers. Computer chips are composed of millions (if not billions) of transistors, which are just microscopically tiny switches. These transistors can only do two things: They can turn on, or they can turn off. When they are turned on, they represent the number "1." When they are turned off, the represent the number "0." Computers, then, can really only handle two numbers: 1 and 0. Hence, they convert all numbers into "binary" numbers, also known as "base-two."

Each one of these numbers, each one of these 1s and 0s, is called a **bit** (short for binary digit), and it is the fundamental form of information in computers. Bits commonly come in sets of eight, which is known as a **byte**,[2] which has become the most common way of measuring data. While there are exceptions, in general, it takes 1 byte, or 8 bits, to make one character of text. When measuring larger amounts of data, byte is preceded by a prefix that multiplies it, as in

Kilobyte (KB)	One thousand bytes
Megabyte (MB)	One million bytes
Gigabyte (GB)	One billion bytes
Terabyte (TB)	One trillion bytes

Note that each of these sizes is one thousand times bigger than the one before. This is important to keep in mind when comparing sizes of things, as 500 MB is *a lot* bigger than 500 KB.

Just to make things a bit more squirrelly, data is measured slightly differently by software manufacturers, computer manufacturers, and storage manufacturers. You will commonly find that the hard drive you are using will hold slightly less than the advertised value. A 100 GB drive, for example, actually holds about 93 GB. The bigger your storage device, the bigger this discrepancy. The drive manufacturer is not trying to rip you off. He is just measuring the number of bytes differently.

---

[2] Note to the quibblers: I know, I know, I know, there are different sizes of bytes out there, but the most common one, the one that most people know, is eight, so just let it be.

Part 1: Audio

CHAPTER 1

Audio: An Introduction

Like lighting, you will need to have a general understanding of theatrical audio practice in order to understand what follows. If you feel like you've already got this knowledge in your pocket, skip ahead to chapter 2. If you aren't sure if you are ready to enter the realm of high-tech audio, try the following sentence:

"I want to put a microphone into the mixer, but the only available channels are for line-level signals and don't have XLR inputs."

All clear on that? If not, read this chapter before you skip ahead.

There Is No Sound Without a Source

An audio system is composed of a string of devices, all of which add up to form a **signal chain**. The beginning of that chain, like the beginning of a great river, is the source.

Sources come in three varieties: microphones, everything else analog, and digital. Let's do microphones first.

Microphones

Sound, when it is traveling around the real, nonelectronic world, is composed of waves of vibration in the air. If there is no air, there is no sound. That is why "in space, no one can hear you scream." That's not a scary thought, it's just a practical one. Sound needs air.

When I slap my hand against the table, the impact of my hand causes the table to oscillate back and forth very quickly. When the table moves away from my hand, it creates an area of low pressure in the air immediately next to the table. When the table rushes back toward my hand, it squeezes the air, creating an area of high pressure. As the table continues to oscillate back and forth, it creates waves of differing air pressure that travel outward from the table, filling the room, just like throwing a stone into water creates ripples that travel outward, filling the pond. The ripples are composed of peaks of high water level separated by valleys of low water level. The sound waves are composed of peaks of high air pressure separated by valleys of low air pressure.

When those waves of pressure run into something, they cause that something to move. The high-pressure waves cause that thing to move away from the air. The low-pressure waves cause that thing to move back toward the air. In this way, the vibration of the table is carried through the air until it meets another object. If that object is very dense and heavy, like a concrete wall, it will vibrate very little. If that object is very light, like your eardrum, it will vibrate quite a bit. This is how we hear sounds. Our eardrum is extremely light and susceptible to the vibrations caused by air movements. When the waves of air pressure strike our eardrum, it vibrates at the same rate as the wave of air pressure. The eardrum, in turn, is attached to a number of nerve cells, which pick up those vibrations and transmit them to the brain, which figures out that you just "heard" something.

Think about that for a moment. When a week-old kitten across the room from you lets out a tiny little "meow," the vocal cords of that newborn animal are vibrating a tiny amount of air and creating minuscule waves of air pressure that travel across the room and strike your eardrum, which is sensitive enough to not only register them but also pick out the pitch, timbre, and direction of the sound so that the brain can put them all together and conclude "kitten." Truly, the human ear is a marvel.

That's one reason why a microphone is designed a lot like a human ear. In essence, a microphone is an artificial ear, but instead of an eardrum, it has a tiny little strip of material called a **diaphragm**, which vibrates when struck by pressure waves in the air. The diaphragm is attached to a magnet, which moves whenever and however the diaphragm moves. The magnet, in turn, is floating inside a wire coil. The movement of the magnet inside the wire coil creates tiny fluctuations of electrical current, which are sent down a wire into an electronic device of some sort which "hears" the sound.

Microphones come in a dizzying variety and entire books are dedicated to this piece of technology alone.[1] For our immediate purposes, you need to know that the electric signal produced by a microphone—known as a **miclevel signal**—is extremely weak, and requires amplification before you can do anything with it. Hence, if you are going to plug it into a mixer or other audio device, you need to make sure that the device has a mic-level

---

[1] I particularly recommend *The Microphone Book*, by the late John Eargle, both because it is a very good book and because the audio engineer who wrote it has "ear" in his name.

input, where the signal can be pumped up to a useful level by a **preamp** a small amplifier that raises the mic-level signal up to a **line-level signal**, the common signal strength that is used inside sound systems.

All microphones from midlevel on up use a three-wire cable and a three-pin plug, known as an **XLR**. Don't use a mic that has any other kind of plug on it—it is low quality and will cause you problems sooner or later. Those other plugs, and the cables that go with them, have many uses, but mic signals are not one of them.

Mics use XLR cables because they can run **balanced** signals. Basically, a balanced output splits the audio signal into two signals, then flips one of them over, making a "negative" version of the original. The balanced output sends the two signals, one positive, one negative, through the cable in side-by-side wires. If some kind of interference, like a stray electrical signal from a power cable, hits the wire, it distorts both the positive signal and the negative signal equally. When the signals get to the other end, however, the balanced input flips the negative signal back to the right way, thus reversing the effect of the distortion. When the two signals are added back together, the distortion in the positive signal is cancelled out by the flipped-over distortion in the (previously) negative signal. Result: a clean signal.

Always use XLR outputs, cables, and inputs with microphones. This ensures that you are using a balanced signal. Otherwise, those tiny little mic-level signals will get wiped out by interference.

Line-Level Sources

Mics are not the only things that produce sound, but they are the only things that produce mic-level signals. Everything else that produces sound—CD players, iPods, DVD players, electronic keyboards, computers, cable boxes, and any other electronic device—produces a **line-level signal**.

Line-level signals use several different types of plugs, but the **phono plug** is most common. This is a long, barrel-shaped plug that comes in 1/8" and 1/4" versions. That plug on the end of your iPod headphones is an 1/8" phono plug. Also common is the **RCA plug**, which is often used for consumer electronic equipment like your DVD player. The RCA plug has a round collar, about 1/4" wide with a stubby little pin in the center. It is used for both audio and video at the consumer level.

Line-level signals can and sometimes do use XLR plugs, particularly on pro-level gear.

Both mic-level and line-level signals are actually not a single level; these terms refer to a range of levels. A high mic level is still less powerful than a low line level. Think of it this way: A high school teacher's salary may fluctuate up and down over the years, but it is still in the range of high school teacher salaries. The CEO of General Motors has a much higher salary, which may also fluctuate up and down. The range of the teacher's salary, however, will never be anywhere near the CEO's. Which is just wrong, by the way.

Digital Sources

All of the items listed above, including microphones and all the line-level devices, produce **analog** audio, even though the devices themselves may be digital. Your MP3 player is actually storing and playing a digital music file, but the last thing the player does before it sends the signal to the outside world is a **digital-to-analog conversion**, where it turns the stream of digital 1s and 0s into a continuously varying, analog electrical signal. This is the signal that goes into your headphones.

There are an increasing number of devices, however, that put out a signal that is still fully digital. This kind of a signal won't do you any good in your headphones (your ears are analog, after all), but it is a good way to pass a signal to another device without losing any signal quality.

Digital signals do not have a level—they are just a stream of 1s and 0s—so mic level and line level don't apply. We will discuss the various types of digital signals in chapter 5 on digital gear.

Sources Must Be Mixed

Now that you have some sound, whether analog or digital, you usually have to combine, or mix, several sources together. Enter the mixer.

Of any piece of audio gear, the one that seems to inspire the most reverence (among technicians) and confusion (among nontechnicians) is the mixer. With its seemingly endless rows of buttons and knobs, the mixer can look fairly intimidating.

Mixers are primarily described by the number of inputs and outputs that they have. A twelve-by-two mixer has twelve places to plug something in and two places to take sound out. Any source that has stereo sound will require two inputs for left and right. A microphone takes a single input.

On a decent mixer, the microphone input will be an XLR and will be equipped with an input level control, which allows you to adjust how much **preamplification** the mixer will do to turn the mic-level signal into a line-level signal.

Line-level inputs will be phono jacks or the oh-so-clever combo jack, which can take either an XLR or a phono plug. Digital signals must plug into digital inputs—we'll get to that in chapter 5.

Each input feeds into a **mixer channel**. Each channel has its own string of controls that allow you to change various aspects of the sound. Depending on the size and quality of the mixer, it can perform various operations on a signal, but it all really breaks down into four things:

Level

A mixer can change the volume, or level, of each channel. It can do that by changing the input level, by changing the channel level, and by changing the master level. You use the input level to get all the channels to be in the same general area. Then, you use the channel level to create the mix of sound that you want. Finally, you use the master level to control the overall level of sound coming from the mixer. At the channel level, there is usually a mute button to quickly shut the channel off and a solo button to shut all the other channels off, so that you can hear one channel all by itself.

Equalization

In the world of audio, the frequency of the audio wave—whether it is waves of pressure in the air or waves of electrons in a cable—determines its pitch. Every sound, except very pure "test tones," is composed of a collection of different frequencies. Equalization, or EQ, got its name because it was originally designed to balance out or equalize all the frequencies of a sound, so that you had equal amounts of energy across the audio spectrum. What we really use it for is to adjust the "timbre" or "color" of a sound, increasing or decreasing various frequencies. There is a very simple form of equalization on your stereo: the bass and treble controls. The bass controls the lower frequencies, while the treble controls the higher frequencies.

A mixer channel will almost always have at least two EQ controls: high and low. The more expensive the mixer, the more EQ controls it will have. A very good mixer might have five or more controls, each of which can be set to increase or decrease a particular set of frequencies.

Routing

A mixer channel will often have the ability to send the signal to an **auxiliary send**, also known as an "aux" or a "send." This is another output from the mixer, separate from the master output, which is used to send a portion of the signals somewhere else. Sometimes the signal is sent away for good, so that it can feed a monitor speaker, headset system, or other devices. Sometimes it is only sent away temporarily, to be processed by another device like an effects processor. In that case, it comes back into the mixer through a **return** and is added back into the mix. This is called an **effects loop**.

Signals might also be gathered together into a **submaster**. This is useful if you want to gather together a certain group of signals to control their collected volume. Rock-and-roll mixers for example, might gather together all the signals from the microphones that are pointed at a drum set. That way, they can control the entire drum set volume with one slider or knob.

Pan

We have two ears, so audio signals are frequently divided up into a stereo pair with one signal intended for each ear. The **pan** control on a mixer channel determines the relative strength of the channel output in the left and right outputs. If you pan the signal left, you increase the strength of the signal that is going to the left output, while decreasing the right one. Pan the signal to the right and you get the opposite effect.

The reason that mixers are covered in a blanket of knobs is that all of the controls for one channel are duplicated for all of them. You may, in fact, only be able to do a few things to an input, like change its level, pan, and basic EQ; but when you duplicate those knobs for twelve or twenty-four or forty-eight or eighty channels, you've got an awful lot of knobs. If you ever start to feel intimidated by a mixer, just remember, it's a lot of the same thing, over and over.

Mixer outputs will either be line-level signals with phono or XLR jacks or (if your mixer is digital) digital signals, using one of the variety of digital formats and jacks that, you guessed it, we'll talk about in chapter 5.

The Signal Might Need Processing

All of the other steps in the signal chain are mandatory, but this one is optional. As the signal passes through the chain, you may wish to alter it in some way. We've already covered some of those alterations, like level, pan, and EQ, but there are others that are not performed by the mixer. Instead, they are performed by outboard gear—that is, gear that is not built into the mixer.

Processors may be placed before or after the mixer in the signal chain, or they may be inserted in effects loops, which leave and then return to the mixer.

Dynamics

Ever go to an amateur night and listen to a bunch of people who don't really know how to use a microphone? As they sing or speak, their voices may get louder or softer. They may pull the mic away from their mouth, causing the sound to die away, or push it too close, making it boom out like Moses. An overexcited performer might yell into the mic, causing the sound system to overload and distort. **Compression** and **limiting** help audio people to deal with these problems (which occur with professional singers as well).

A compressor and a limiter are two different versions of the same thing. Both devices follow the sound level and, when it climbs above a certain volume, pull it down. Compressors use a ratio to determine how much to reduce the sound. If they are set at 4:1, for example, then they drop the volume one decibel for every four decibels it goes over a preset limit. A limiter is less subtle: You give it a volume level and it prevents the sound from ever getting louder than that level—it is an audio "line in the sand." Because they reduce the really high sound levels, compressors and limiters help guard against overloads. This means you can bring the overall volume up without worrying about distortion ruining your speakers. The softer voices will be more audible and the louder voices won't be so annoying.

Because they are so similar in function, compressors and limiters are often built into the same unit.

Reverb

If you've ever sat in a large church or a well-designed concert hall, then you've experienced reverb in its natural state. Reverb is just sound bouncing around in a space—caroming off hard surfaces and coming at your ears from all directions. The more places it has to go, and the fewer absorbent places in the room, the longer the sound bounces around. This effect can be recreated electronically by an **effects processor**. The sound is fed into the processor from the mixer, and the circuitry inside the box processes it according to complicated formulas, adding the echoes that would normally be created by the sound bouncing around a room. When the sound comes out, it sounds as though the original sound were created in another kind of space. Most processors let you choose what kind of space you would like to imitate, both in size and quality. It might have options like small room, ensemble hall, or concert stage, as well as warm, dark, or rich. By adjusting the processor, you can choose what kind of reverb you want.

Equalization

Anyone who has ever made a tape at home and then played it back in the theater will understand the need for EQ. The tape sounds different in different spaces. Acoustically speaking, every room in the world is different, depending on the textures it has (carpets, furniture, paneling, and so on) as well as the shape of the room itself. Every room will kill certain frequencies and accentuate others.

But wasn't there EQ in the mixer? Yes, there was, but only a few controls. A true equalizer is a separate unit that lives outside the mixer. It has a long row of sliders or knobs that increase or decrease the amount of sound at each frequency. It takes time and experience to set up, not to mention a certain amount of trial—and error. It also takes a sharp-eared technician. Once the sound is optimized for a space, you should put a lock on that EQ and leave it forever, or at least until you get different carpets.

Besides this kind of colorization, EQ also provides an important function in getting rid of feedback. The shape of the room will cause some frequencies to feed back more than others. Because EQ allows you to decrease those specific frequencies, it can allow you to push the overall volume up higher. Live music depends heavily on EQ for this reason.

The Signal Must Be Amplified

The line-level signal that leaves the mixer is still an electronic signal—it's not audible. In order to hear it, we have to use that electric current to move some air. The line-level signal, however, is not strong enough to move anything, so the next step is to pump it up with some amplification.

Remember how I said that mic-level signals are teacher's salaries and line-level signals are CEO salaries? Well, compared to those signal levels, the next level—**speaker level**—is like the budget of the Pentagon.

We use an **amplifier** to boost the line-level signal up to speaker level. Like mixers, amplifiers are rated first by the number of channels of amplification they offer. If you have two different channels of audio, then you need at least two different channels of amplification. Fortunately, an amp with two channels, known as a stereo amp, is quite common.

In many cases, you will need more than two channels of amplification, however. It depends on the number of speakers you have. One channel of amplification can generally power one or two speakers, depending on the amp and the speaker specifications. A large theater sound system might have five to ten (or more) amps to drive all the speakers.

To Hear the Signal, We Need Speakers

Finally, we arrive at the end of the signal chain and we are ready to rumble. Or purr or tweet or sing or gasp or rock out.

A **speaker** is like a microphone in reverse. You remember that inside the microphone, the wave of air pressure moved the tiny diaphragm back and forth, causing a magnet to move inside a coil of wire, creating an electrical signal.

Inside the speaker, the now-amplified electrical signal does the opposite as it runs through a coil of wire, causing a magnet to move back and forth. The magnet is attached to a curved lightweight **speaker cone** that moves with the magnet, creating waves of air pressure that we know as sound.

Sound systems can get enormously complicated, but they all follow this signal path through the four main elements: source, mixer, processing, amplification, and speakers.

CHAPTER 2

Why Audio Went Digital

I remember my first kiss, but then, doesn't everyone? I also remember my first Krispy Kreme doughnut, plucked warm from under a shower of sugary glaze, and the first time I played a video game. It was Pong, so you know I've been around awhile.

That list of memorable firsts, however, would hardly be complete without the first that I experienced in a New York City apartment around Christmastime in 1984. That was the night that I put on a set of headphones and heard my first compact disc. It was Chaka Khan's "I Feel For You," and dude, I felt for her too.

Without descending into a I-walked-three-miles-to-school-in-the-snow diatribe about the difficulties of predigital audio, let me just say that life was tough for the audiophile in the days of the vinyl record and the cassette tape. We had a lengthy ritual for playing a record that involved spraying it with cleaning fluid, wiping it (always in a circle, following the grooves), holding it gingerly by the edges as we placed it on the turntable, then carefully lowering the cartridge arm down until the needle gently kissed the vinyl. If the music got people dancing, you had to worry that the jumping bodies would cause the needle to skip across and, heaven forbid, *scratch the record*. After we were done playing, we would stand the record up to dry before carefully sliding it back into the plastic sleeve, followed by the cardboard album cover. To say we were picky would be understating the issue. I once had a terrible fight with a college girlfriend because she left some records stacked in a pile, rather than sliding them into a shelf where they could stand vertically.

So, yes, we were picky and annoying, but frankly, you had to be, if you wanted to preserve the pristine sound that was carefully imprinted on those vinyl grooves. Unfortunately, it was a losing battle—no matter how careful you were, dust and scratches were the inescapable fate for a vinyl record. Furthermore, only the highest-quality turntables could hope to avoid the inevitable wobbles and changes in speed that created "wow," "flutter," and all the other bastardizations of the original performance.

When cassette tape appeared, we had a medium that we could carry around and abuse a bit more, but the loss in fidelity was crushing. Cassettes were full of "hiss" and devoid of the highest and lowest frequencies, especially if you copied from one cassette to another. The phrase "second generation" was like a curse word. Playback speed was even more variable on tape than on records, plus the tapes stretched, broke, and got entangled in the decks. Everyone remembers those moments when you would pull the cassette tape out, only to discover the tangled spaghetti inside the deck where your "Summer '78 Awesome Mix" used to be. Oh, the humanity.

When I put those headphones on back in New York, the first thing I was expecting to hear was the first thing that you always heard when listening to tape or vinyl records: noise. The hiss of the cassette tape, the scratch of the needle, the popping of tiny imperfections in the record, these were the normal experiences of hearing a recording. What I heard when I put on those headphones was . . . *nothing*. Digital reproduction was virtually silent, and that silence was music to our ears. The fact that you didn't have to treat the media with such paranoid care was even more remarkable. Knowing my standard record-playing rituals, my friend delighted in rubbing his fingers all over the disk before casually tossing it into the player with all the sensitivity of a four-year-old tossing bread crumbs to pigeons.

And then Chaka Khan came on in all her noise-free glory and I blissed out for seventy minutes. I passed out and woke up in a stereo store, where I broke my first credit card buying into the digital age.

So, the first reason that audio went digital was fidelity. While CDs are not bombproof (or toddler-proof, as my brother discovered the hard way), the digital file that is embedded in the disk will play back the same way, over and over, for many years, despite being dusty and covered with fingerprints. Compact disc recover much better from scratches, do not change pitch, and, most importantly, have no perceptible hiss (unless it was there from the original recording).

Times change, of course, and a backlash was inevitable. There are still purists out there who claim that digital recording can never capture all the nuances of true analog sound and they may be right. I have a DJ friend who spins vinyl records all night and claims that his ears are far less tired after a night of analog vinyl than a night of digital CDs. To most people, however, the cost of dealing with analog media like records and cassettes was the loss of quality, caused by abuse to the media, and the loss of love, caused by well-meaning girlfriends who have had enough of your stupid rules.

Of course, fidelity isn't just an issue for geeky audiophiles; it matters for theater as well. Technicians refer to that hissing sound in a recording as the **noise floor**, because, like the floor, it just sits there under everything. If the noise floor is fairly loud, it can create a lot of problems. If you amplify sound, you amplify everything, including the noise. If the sound you are trying to amplify is very quiet, like a quiet passage of music or a gentle sound cue, then the noise will be quite obvious. Many a tender scene onstage has been mangled by a hissing sound cue played back on a creaking cassette tape.

Audio people talk about the **signal-to-noise ratio (SNL)**, which tells you how much louder the signal (i.e., the sound you are listening to) is than the noise floor. If your signal is really loud, like a pounding rock song, then you've got a lot of distance between your signal and your noise floor and you are not going to hear the noise very much. However, if the signal is soft, then your SNL is small and you will hear the noise. If your playback mechanism is digital, then the noise floor is much lower and you have a much better SNL. Of course, no system is noise-free (amplifiers are prime culprits for creating noise), but going digital at the start gives you a much better chance of keeping your SNL big enough so that when George and Lennie bed down in the clubhouse and those crickets start chirping on the prairie, there won't be analog hiss playing along with them.

Fidelity is hardly the only reason to go digital in the theater, however, and it may not even be the most compelling.

There's convenience, of course. Playing an actual vinyl record in the control booth was never practical, so we recorded cues onto tapes. Now, however, we can create those cues on a computer and burn them to a CD so we have a more convenient playback medium.

It's more convenient because digital media allows us to have random access to our sounds. When using tape, we were stuck with fast-forwarding the entire tape if we wanted to get at a cue towards the end of the show. You could have a separate cassette tape for every cue, but then you had this enormous stack of tapes, and you still didn't have access to a particular place in the cue without searching around. Digital media allows us to access any moment in any cue at any time, something that is incredibly useful for rehearsals or one-off events.

More than either fidelity or convenience, however, going digital with theatrical audio allows us to create more complex cues than ever before, change them at a moment's notice, and control them in unusual, innovative, and useful ways.

Let's first look at the digital process: how analog audio becomes digital. Then we'll look at the most significant application for theatrical users: digital playback. Finally, we'll take a look at other digital gear and how it all plugs together.

CHAPTER 3

How Audio Becomes Digital

So, we've discussed *why* audio went digital, but *how* does this happen? How does an analog audio signal, composed of an electrical voltage, become a digital signal, composed of 1s and 0s?

It all comes down to one word, probably the most important word in digital audio: **sampling**.

As we talked about in chapter 1, a microphone takes waves of air pressure and converts them to a continuously varying electrical signal. The key phrase here is "continuously varying." An analog signal is continuous. It is not broken up into increments of time.

Digital signals, however, are broken up into chunks of time. When a digital recording device is fed an analog signal, it must perform an **analog-to-digital conversion**, often called an A-to-D conversion. What the digital device does is look at the analog signal for a tiny fraction of a second—a small "sample" of time—and measure the strength of the signal. The digital device looks at that tiny sample of time, measures the average strength of the signal during the sample, and assigns it a numerical value. Once the device is done with that sample, it moves on to the next one. Thus, the continuous analog signal is broken up into a series of numbers, or digits (hence the term "digital").

Of course, this sampling process is happening in real time, and very, very, *very* fast. A typical sampling device can sample an incoming signal and assign a new number more than forty thousand times per second. The speed of the sampling is known as the **sampling rate**, and that number is critical for determining the quality of the sampling.

As you might imagine, the more samples you take every second, the more accurate your digital signal is. Remember that the pitch of a sound is determined by how fast those waves of sound are changing from low pressure to high pressure. The speed of the change, known as the frequency, is measured in cycles per second, or hertz (Hz). Higher-pitched sounds have higher frequencies. Think of a very small bell. Because of its lighter weight and smaller size, it can vibrate faster, which produces a high-pitched sound. A larger, heavier bell will vibrate more slowly, producing a lower pitch. A healthy young human ear that has not been listening to death metal at full volume can hear from about 20 Hz to about 20,000 Hz. A thousand hertz is known as a kilohertz, so 20,000 Hz is known as 20 kHz.

In other words, human hearing spans a range from 20 Hz to 20 kHz.

Because of something called the Nyquist–Shannon sampling theorem, we know that accurately capturing a particular frequency requires a sampling rate that is at least twice as high as the frequency you want to capture. Thus, to sample a wave of 20 kHz, we need a sample rate that is at least 40 kHz. That is one reason why two of the most common sample rates are 44.1 kHz and 48 kHz.

Compact disks use a sample rate of 44.1 kHz, but the generally accepted sampling rate for professional work is 48kHz. Pro audio gear can generally accept either one, and somewhere in the software, there is always a setting where you can choose. The current crop of consumer video cameras usually uses 48 kHz as well.

In their constant attempts to make digital audio closer to reality, many equipment designers now give you the option of doubling the sampling rate, up to 96 kHz. This does give you more resolution, but always keep in mind that the sample rate that the audience will hear is the last one in the system, so there isn't really too much point in recording at 96 kHz if you are playing back at 48 kHz.[1]

The single most important thing you need to know about sampling rate is this: It must be the same throughout your system. If you create your files at 44.1 kHz, then you have to play them back at 44.1 kHz. Quick, what will happen if you take a 44.1 kHz file and play it back at 48 kHz?[2] What will happen if you play a 48 kHz file and play it back at 44.1 kHz?[3] Check the notes for the answer, but if all your files sound too low or too high, you probably have the sampling rate set wrong somewhere.

_____

[1] Fights will break out in audio geek bars when they read this, of course, as some engineers passionately insist that there is still a benefit to sampling at 96 kHz, regardless of what happens afterwards. "Okay, man, just put down the thumb drive and we can talk this over like reasonable people . . ."

[2] It will have a higher pitch, because you are playing it faster than it was recorded.

[3] It will have a lower pitch, because you are playing it slower than it was recorded.

When creating digital audio files, sampling rate is one of two important numbers. In order to understand the second one, let's take a look at the number that the sampler is assigning to the incoming signal some forty thousand times per second.

The most fundamental type of data inside a computer is a bit, and there are only two types of bits: a 1 and a 0. All other numbers in the computer's memory are represented by 1s and 0s through something known as a binary numbering system. What you need to know about binary numbers is that the more bits you use, the more numbers you can represent. The numbers from 0 to 7 for example, can be represented by 3 bits.

If the sampling device was using 3 bits, it could only judge the strength of that incoming electrical signal, and thus assign it a value, on a scale from 0 to 7 where 0 would mean silence and 7 would mean as loud as possible. That is quite a small range of values for the entire signal level spectrum. In fact, it's basically useless.

The scale starts to get useful at 8 bits, when the computer has 256 different values to choose from. The first generation of samplers operated at 8 bits, which wasn't great, but it was a place to start.

The most common samplers these days use 16 bits, which means that they can represent that signal using numbers from 0 to 65,535. In other words, the sampler has 65,536 possible numbers to choose from when assigning a value to a sample. The number of bits that a sampler uses is known as the **bit depth**.

How much bit depth do you need? Unfortunately, in this case, we don't have physical realities like the range of human hearing or the Nyquist–Shannon theorem to play with, so it's a bit more subjective. More is usually better, of course, and everyone pretty much agrees that anything less than sixteen bits—the standard for compact disks—is unacceptable. As of this writing, twenty-four bits are fairly common in audio devices. Unlike sample rate, you don't have to worry so much about making sure that your bit depth settings are the same throughout the system. A sixteen-bit file will play fine through a 24-bit audio card, for example, and the reverse is also true—a 24-bit file will play through a 16-bit card, although it might not sound as good as when it is played through a 24-bit card. Still, it's a good idea to settle on 1-bit depth for all files that you create for a particular project so the equipment doesn't have to take the time to do a lot of conversion.

So we've got sample rate and we've got bit depth. These two numbers form the foundation of digital specifications. As I said, CD-quality sound is 16-bit, 44.1 kHz.

The combination of sample rate and bit depth tell you one other important piece of information: file size. After all, both of these numbers represent a huge amount of 1s and 0s and all that data starts to add up pretty quick. At CD quality your computer is recording or playing back 44,100 numbers per second, and each one of those numbers has 16 bits. A newer, higher-quality audio interface might be playing back 24 bit numbers at 96,000 per second. It adds up, and it becomes a problem when you are trying to store a large amount of material on a small drive, like a portable music player, or download audio files over an Internet connection.

It also becomes a problem when you are trying to send a lot of material over a network, whether an internal network in your theater or the Internet. When sending a file from one place to another, it is often helpful to know the **bit rate**, the amount of data that has to flow per minute to keep up with the playback. Bit rates are measured in megabits per second, or Mbit/s.

Take a look at the comparative sizes of these different formats.

BIT DEPTH	SAMPLE RATE	BIT RATE	FILE SIZE OF ONE STEREO MINUTE	FILE SIZE OF A THREE MINUTE SONG
16	44.1 kHz	1.34 Mbit/s	10.1 Megabytes	30.3 Megabytes
16	48 kHz	1.46 Mbit/s	11 Megabytes	33 Megabytes
24	96 kHz	4.39 Mbit/s	33 Megabytes	99 Megabytes

You can see how raising the bit depth and sample rate to the state-of-the-art 24/96 level actually triples the bit rate and the size of the files! These numbers would have been prohibitive a few years back, but hard drives and processors have now gotten so big and so fast (respectively) that we can now enjoy this higher level of quality with no guilt on our desktop computers. Generally speaking, however, these files are still too big for portable music players and Internet downloads.

Note also that the bit rate is measured in mega*bits* per second, while the file sizes are measured in mega*bytes*, which are about eight times larger. One byte generally contains 8 bits. Therefore, A 4.0 Mbit/s data connection does not move a 4.0 MB file every second. A megabit does not equal a megabyte.

Audio File Formats

Once an incoming analog signal has been sampled, the data needs to be arranged in some kind of format that a computer can read. You can have a lot of books in your library, but until you have them in some kind of order, you'll never find what you are looking for.

In order to help the computer organize and play back the data, the sampling device arranges the sound in one of many **audio file formats**. While there are dozens of formats out there, we are really only concerned about a few for the theater, so this section isn't as long as it could be.

Formats are divided into two basic groups, depending on whether they are compressed or not, and right there we have our first big confusion.

If you read the opening chapter, you know that compression is one of the types of processing that a sound system can do to a sound. (If you skipped that chapter, then you already knew that, naturally.) A compressor reduces the dynamic range of a sound by turning it down when it reaches a particular level, or threshold. But compression has another meaning in the world of computer file formats—it is a way of reducing the size of the audio file. Before we get into that particular piece of alchemy, however, let's talk about

Uncompressed File Formats

The kind of audio that we have been talking about so far is uncompressed. The computer slices up the audio as it comes in the door, assigns a value to each slice, and arranges those values in a line so they can be played back and turned back into audible sound. The sampler writes down all the numbers very faithfully, without skipping any or scrimping on detail.

The two most common file formats came from the two biggest computer software makers: Microsoft and Apple.[4]

Microsoft came up with the Windows Audio File Format and then invented the V that stands for "File Format" so they could call it a **WAV** file (pronounced "wave"). I guess WAFF didn't have the same ring to it. Apple, in turn, invented the Audio Interchange File Format, but ignored Microsoft's innovative V-for-FF swapping technology and just called it an **AIFF** file, (pronounced "A-I-F-F").

In point of fact, both WAV and AIFF files will play on many applications on Windows and Apple computers. Both files are used in both professional and personal arenas, and they actually play back exactly the same data, bit for bit. The difference comes in how the data is stored, not in how it sounds. And yet, you will still find people who swear on Bill Gates's future grave that one or the other is better. They are not. Bit for bit, a WAV file and an AIFF files are playing back the exact same information. They are, however, *storing* the information differently. To return to our library analogy, think about two libraries—one organizes the books by title and one organizes them by author—and you will have a sense of how WAV and AIFF are different.

Both WAV and AIFF files can store audio information in just about any combination of sampling rates and/or bit depths.

---

[4] Neither company did it alone, just for the record. Microsoft worked with IBM and Apple worked with Electronic Arts, so you audio geeks can just cancel that e-mail you were about to send me.

While they are acoustically identical, there are small, inaudible differences. AIFF has the ability to carry **metadata**, which is data about the data. Metadata might include the date of recording, the type of recorder, and information about how it was recorded or processed. The European Broadcasting Union got so whipped up about the lack of metadata in the WAV file that they actually created a version of it that *did* have metadata, the **BWF** file, which stands for Broadcast Wave Format. This format has become the go-to format for digital recording devices on film and TV sets, where it is useful to time-stamp each audio file. This info helps the lab technician sync up the audio file to the film or video footage that goes with it.

You can always tell what kind of files you are dealing with by looking at the extension, those characters at the end of the filename. AIFF files will end with ".aif," while WAV files end with ".wav." Want to guess what a BWF file ends with?

You clever people.

I would venture to say that, in the normal life of a theater sound person, the only uncompressed audio formats you will encounter are AIFF and WAV. You may, on occasion, have to deal with a .cda file, which is the native file format for CDs. Look in chapter 5 for more info about dealing with compact disks.

Compressed File Formats

Compression, like LEDs in lighting and virtually everything in video, is a form of magic that was invented by gray-bearded wizards who live beyond the last mountain and who only visit every seven years to give us a new file format.

Okay, not true, but it might as well be. Compression depends on very finely tuned mathematical formulas called algorithms, which pick apart an audio file and discard information that is thought to be beyond the capability of the human ear, a process known as "perceptual coding." By getting rid of sounds that your ears supposedly can't hear, compression algorithms make a file much smaller.

How those algorithms are written is a dark art, however, and nothing to be trifled with. Better not to ask how it came to be, but only how to use it.

Perhaps the most famous form of audio compression is known as MP3, which was standardized by the Moving Picture Expert Group, an organization that we are going to hear a lot from in the video chapter. Their first video standard, known as MPEG-1, had a section of the specification—Part 3—dedicated to audio. MPEG-1 Part 3 became shortened to MP3 and went on to rule the world of portable audio players, even when the video standards moved on to MPEG-2 and then MPEG-4.

And why not? With little loss of quality, converting a file from an uncompressed format to an MP3 can make it one-tenth of the size. Like magic, 90 percent of the file size just disappears, allowing you to put ten songs in the space you used to use for one.

Here's a bit of geek trivia for you. When one of the designers of MP3, Karlheinz Brandenburg, a postdoc working at AT&T Bell Labs was tuning up his algorithms, he heard someone down the hall playing Suzanne Vega's song "Tom's Diner." Karlheinz realized that Vega's nearly monophonic, a cappella recording, so dependent on her subtle vocal inflections, would clearly reveal any flaws in the compression. He listened to the song over and over again to test the algorithm. Some people jokingly refer to Suzanne Vega as the Mother of MP3.

You might think that, no matter how good the algorithm, there is no way that you can cut away 90 percent of the data and not hear the difference, and I would agree with you. If you play a song as an uncompressed AIFF or WAV and then play the same song immediately afterwards as an MP3, most people are going to hear a difference, if their speakers are any good. However, this isn't how people listen to music. They don't play two different formats back-to-back and their speakers aren't always that great. My teenage stepsister listens to music all day using the speaker on her *phone*, for Pete's sake, and there's no way that she will hear MP3's limitations on that tiny, quarter-inch speaker. Unfortunately, there are more people in the world listening to music on small low-quality speakers than huge expensive ones, so MP3 has been more than good enough to become, for a time, the portable musical format of choice.

Those days are ending, however, courtesy of the biggest thing to hit pop music since the haircut: iTunes.

More specifically, the iTunes Store. You see, when you sell ten billion songs in seven years, you have some influence on the Next Big Thing. By throwing its support behind Advanced Audio Coding, Apple made the AAC format hugely popular for downloading and storing music. AAC was designed to be the successor to MP3, and it has been a very successful successor, reducing file size just as much as MP3 but with better sound quality. How? I don't know, I don't care, and neither should you.

The MP3 format is patented, which means that anyone who creates software for it has to pay a royalty to the owners. For obvious reasons, Apple didn't want to pay that fee, plus, they were looking for a higher-quality format. AAC was perfect on all counts. Apple took the AAC format and added digital rights management (DRM) capability in an ill-fated attempt to protect their content from piracy and illegal copying. After getting reams of bad publicity, Apple relented and started selling DRM-free music in 2009.

AAC can also handle up to forty-eight tracks of audio, as opposed to two tracks in MP3.

I only mention AAC because you may be considering using content from iTunes for your show. While I don't recommend using MP3 for music onstage, you can get away with using content that originated in AAC, if you have to. Many of digital playback programs that we will be studying in the next chapter, however, don't support the format, so you will have to use iTunes or another audio conversion program to convert those AAC files to AIFF or WAV before you put them into audio editing or audio playback programs.

Google me
Audio format conversion software

All of the compression programs I have mentioned so far are **lossy**—that is, when the file is compressed, some of the data is gone for good. That's why it doesn't improve the quality of an MP3 to convert it to an uncompressed AIFF. When that file became an MP3, the data it threw away is gone for good.

There is, however, such a thing as **lossless** compression. If you refused to believe that compression was actually a magic spell before, lossless compression will make you a believer. Somehow, those gray-bearded wizards figured out how to cut an audio file size in half without throwing anything away. I use the **Apple Lossless** format to download my CDs into iTunes and I'll be a horn-tooth warbler if I can hear the difference, despite watching a three-minute, 10-MB song become a three-minute, 5-MB song. They are wizards, I tell you! Wizards!

Despite the higher quality of AAC and the uncanny nature of lossless compression, I still maintain, as a general rule, you should avoid using compressed audio to build up your sound cues. One reason: it's hard to predict what will happen when you start mixing compressed files together in a multitrack audio editing program. One never knows if the compressed files will play well with others. It's better to start with a full-blown WAV or AIFF file, and don't compress it unless you really have to. In these days of tiny drives with massive space, audio compression is a bullet we have to bite a lot less often.

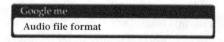
Google me
Audio file format

CHAPTER 4

Digital Audio Playback

Let's be fair. My favorite audio playback device is in my pocket right now. It's an iPod. Apple isn't the only company that makes portable playback devices, but the iPod does have the advantage of a strong output signal, a good interface, and compatibility with many file types, including the most common output formats: WAV and AIFF. Most MP3 players, however, can put out good-quality digital audio. They can be reloaded or rearranged on any computer and can be easily hooked up to any audio system with a cable adaptor. If you are a traveling company, you can carry all your files on it (with a backup on your laptop) and plug it into any mixer in the world. Simple. Reliable. High quality. Done.

But let's say that you want to do something beyond just playing a single file. Let's say that you want music to play through an entire scene while, at a specific moment, a car horn honks from outside. Or maybe you want music coming from a speaker in a radio onstage, plus wind whistling through the audience, plus a car horn honking from stage left. Or how about that Halloween maze that you created, the one where you want creaking doors and mysterious knocking to play for eight solid hours without stopping? Or, what about those planes flying over and trains chugging past? How about the sound of a man running around the theater, knocking on every door?

The iPod is good, but it isn't *that* good.

When you are ready to be truly flexible and creative with audio, you are ready for PC-based playback. Putting your digital audio files on a PC allows you to access them randomly, mix them, send them to different outputs, and change them all in real time without driving your operator completely stir-crazy.

PC-based playback has four parts:

- The computer
- Audio hardware interface
- Audio playback software
- digital audio workstation software

The Computer

All of the things I've listed above exist for both Macs and PCs, as well as Linux machines if you have a software geek among your students or staff.

You will, however, have to pay close attention to the specifications of your audio playback software. Depending on the software, it may specify

- Platform (Mac, PC, Linux)
- Operating system
- Other supporting software (such as QuickTime)
- Processor speed (in MHz or GHz)
- Disk space (on your hard drive)
- Memory (in MB)
- Video RAM (in MB) and/or graphics card
- Screen resolution

Generally, entry-level users will start by deciding which of the two major computer platforms they either own or are comfortable with. Then, they choose the type of software they want to use to play back the audio. That software package will specify some or all of the list above. Following those specifications, you can outfit your computer appropriately.

For example, let's say that I am more comfortable with the Mac computer platform. I want an entry-level software package, so, after a bit of Google and website research, I settle on the QLab software program (currently in version 2.0, as I write this), which is made by the company figure 53. Having decided on a software program, I immediately do what every software user should do: I start to scan the product website. No matter what software you use, you should start early to get familiar and comfortable with the support website. Software is so fluid that it is almost a living thing. New versions of software create new quirks, problems, and solutions. Furthermore, the community of users are the best resource that you've got when using any technology. Get used to hitting that support button and just looking around at the resources that are available online. Don't worry if a lot of things don't make sense. There are always more newbies out there than you think.

In this case, I go to the Support part of the website, which contains a promising-sounding link called Documentation. Sure enough, the very first thing listed on that page is Requirements.

As it turns out, QLab is pretty easy to support, and, according to the Requirements list, the software only requires version 10.5.2 or later of the Mac operating system, QuickTime version 7.3 or later, plus, for the video features, a video card that supports two aspects of the Mac Operating System: Quartz Extreme and Core Image. Because I have no idea what those last two things are, I follow a helpful link to the Apple website and spend ten minutes learning about them. After that, I go back to the QLab website and look through the different versions of the QLab software, each of which has slightly different features. After looking through the list, I decide to start with the "Free!" version, which will help me learn the software and try it out. Finally, satisfied that I have found a compatible product and that my computer is up to the job, I download the free version of the software to try it out.

Remember that this is only an example! This information may change in five minutes or next week or in a year. That's why, when engaged in a digital effort, you must, must, must become familiar with the online support websites. They can give you up-to-the-second information.

Another example: Let's say that you are a Windows person and you are looking for an entry-level program. After some Googling, you decide to look into "SFX," which is made by Stage Research Inc. You check the website, and right there on the Products page is a link called Requirements.

As is typical of the Windows environment, the list of requirements differs depending on which version of Windows you are running. For example, if you have Windows XP Home Edition, the list of requirements looks like this:

- Pentium 233-megahertz (MHz) processor or faster (300 MHz is recommended)
- At least 64 megabytes (MB) of RAM (128 MB is recommended)
- At least 1.5 gigabytes (GB) of available space on the hard disk
- CD-ROM or DVD-ROM drive
- Video adapter and monitor with Super VGA (800 × 600) or higher resolution

A quick look through the informational control panels on your machine will tell you if your computer is up to the job. Don't know where this information is? Time to find out. Use Google, your computer support person, or a fourteen-year-old to help you find them.

Note that the requirements listed above for both Mac and Windows are the **minimums**. The number of cues that you can run simultaneously, the speed with which your computer responds, and its relative stability will improve as you add more memory, processing speed, and better video cards. The best upgrade is almost always memory, known as RAM. It is never wrong to have more memory.

Any audio software will also have requirements for the audio interface, so let's look at that next.

Audio Hardware Interface

If you are using your computer to create the audio content, then you need a way to get audio into it. If you are using your computer to play back audio in the theater, then you need a way to get content out of it. If you are using the same computer for both, then you need an interface that does both.

Almost any computer on the market today comes with an audio interface— that is, a way to get audio in and out of the computer. They are known as the mic and headphone plugs. My advice: ignore them.

The mic and headphone plugs are rarely good enough for theatrical use. Relatively speaking, they are fairly low-quality interfaces, suitable for inputting voices for online chats and outputting music to earbuds. The mic input can't take a balanced signal, which is particularly important if you are going to be recording from microphones, and the output doesn't have the clean, powerful signal that you need. If you are going to be amplifying your audio to fill a theater, you need better quality. Audio interfaces also have higher-quality preamps (to pump up those mic-level inputs to line level) and additional features like a headphone jack that lets you monitor the input directly. The built-in headphone jack will only allow you to monitor the sound after it has passed through the computer hardware and software.

Furthermore, your computer only gives you a single mono input and a single stereo output, and trust me, you will outgrow that in a heartbeat.

The audio interface is sometimes referred to as a **sound card**, because some of them are designed to fit into a card slot in a desktop computer. The higher-quality interfaces still work this way, but this doesn't work for a laptop, which lacks those card slots.

Many interfaces, however, are actually external devices, known as "plug and play." These devices plug into your computer's USB or FireWire port, so they work fine for laptops. Opinions rage about whether FireWire or USB is better, but the cooler heads will tell you that they are quite similar, as long as you are using the new USB 2.0 standard (as opposed to the USB 1.0). As we go to press with this book, Apple has just released its "Thunderbolt" input/output technology. It is quite possible that this will become another useful standard for theatrical audio.

When shopping for an audio interface, pay attention to what platform it supports. Macs can use most PC interfaces, but frankly, it's best to get an interface that is specifically designed for your platform. Pay attention to how many and what kind of inputs and outputs it has, and how it plugs into your computer.

If you are using the same computer for both content creation and playback, then the interface will have to serve two masters. When shopping for the interface, have the specs for both your audio playback software and audio creation software (also known as a digital audio workstation or DAW) available. If you are using two different computers—you have one computer dedicated to your venue and another dedicated to a recording studio—then you can buy audio interfaces for each one separately.

In order to buy that interface, you have to know a few things about the software, so let's look at that. First, the content creation software: the digital audio workstation.

Digital Audio Workstation Software

A good audio production system, known as a digital audio workstation or DAW, allows you to perform the following:

1. Import sound from CDs or other forms of digital media.
2. Record sound from external sources, such as microphones, guitars, and electronic gear.
3. Assemble and edit these sounds in multiple tracks on a timeline.
4. Alter those sounds using filters, plug-ins, or other effects.
5. Mix the sounds together.
6. Create finished files in a range of different formats.

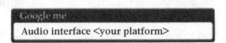

Google me

Audio interface <your platform>

DAW software is like a very flexible multitrack tape deck. Typically, the screen is set up with multiple tracks running from left to right. Audio is represented by colored blocks, often with a visible sound wave running through them. You can move these blocks of sound around, slice and dice them, change their pitch and speed, and apply many kinds of processing to them, like dynamics, EQ, reverb, and lots of other effects. DAW software is where you take raindrops and combine them with traffic, thunder, and children's voices to make the effect of a city school yard during a thunderstorm. It is like an artist's canvas and paint box for the audio designer.

Many audio hardware interfaces will come with their own DAW software, but that doesn't mean that you have to use it. You can make your software decision independently of your hardware decision.[1] There is an incredible amount of software out there.

Many companies put out freeware or shareware products, either because they are ongoing projects supported by a community of users (like the current program Audacity) or because they want to entice you to try the product so that you will eventually pay to upgrade to a version with more features. Either way, there are a lot of good products out there for little or no money, as long as you are willing to deal with fewer features and less support. You do get what you pay for, but if you are new to producing digital audio, freeware and shareware give you an inexpensive way to experiment.

For years, the only name in town for professional digital audio production was Pro Tools. Even today, if you walk into a professional postproduction studio, the chances are very good that you will see Digidesign's industry-leading software.

Pro Tools rose to its position partly because, from the beginning, it was designed as a digital version of a multitrack tape deck. Unlike a regular analog tape deck, however, engineers could manipulate that audio in a "nondestructive" way. In other words, any change that you made to any bit of audio could always be removed, because the original file would always be stored in its original form.

Other DAWs were born as tools for electronic musicians. Cubase (by Steinberg) and Digital Performer (by Mark of the Unicorn) are two examples of DAWs that started as **MIDI sequencers**, programs that were designed to control musical synthesizers. Over time, they added the ability to record and manipulate actual audio. In turn, Pro Tools added the ability to control MIDI instruments, so the features of the programs converged. In the minds of many users, however, Cubase and Digital Performer were for music, while Pro Tools was for film and video production.

Apple has gotten into this world on both sides, developing Soundtrack to provide an audio component for their Final Cut Studio suite of media production programs, as well as Logic Studio for professional music applications.

---

[1] Until very recently, there was one big exception to this: Avid's "Pro Tools" software, which previously required an Avid hardware interface in order to use their software. In November of 2010, however, they finally relented and released version 9 of their software which will run on almost any hardware interface.

Besides these complex professional programs, there are many other software programs for creating your content. Here is a list of things to consider when choosing your software:

Platform compatibility

First and foremost, check to see which software will work on your platform of choice. There are good programs available for both Mac and PC as well as the Linux platform. Personally, I believe that you should use applications on the platform they were originally created for. Applications that have been "ported" over to another platform don't necessarily work as well.

External hardware

As I said above, many interfaces come with their own software, so it's really best to be making this decision hand in hand with the decision about the hardware interface. As I said, Pro Tools software will *only* run with a Pro Tools hardware interface attached. This is how Digidesign keeps people from copying their software. You have to buy the hardware in order to make the software work. Other software packages are more forgiving.

Ratings and reviews

There are lots of sites where reviews are written about both software and hardware. Besides Googling, look at the websites for the major industry magazines: *Mix, Sound on Sound, Electronic Musician,* and the magazines dedicated to your computer platform of choice (*Macworld, PC Magazine,* etc.).

Personally, I take both professional and user reviews with a grain of salt. Sometimes, the pros are concerned about features that don't affect theatrical production, and users can sometimes get on personal rants or raves that are not well considered. I try to scan lots of reviews from different sources and look for general trends, like ease of use, sound quality, and stability. No one review can persuade or dissuade me, but if three different people say that a program is "buggy and unstable," I feel justified in moving along. The most important comments are reviews coming from people in the theater industry.

Features

This is where the rubber hits the road. What can it do? Will it do what I need it to do? Here's a list of important features for a DAW for creating theatrical content.

- Live recording: Recording audio through an audio interface
- Multichannel recording: Recording multiple tracks at once

- Monitor level: Being able to see the level of the audio input while recording
- Import WAV, AIFF, and MP3 formats
- Import restricted formats, like AAC and WMV
- Export to AAC (M4A) for podcasting
- Nondestructive editing with Cut, Copy, Paste, Trim, Insert, etc.
- Unlimited undo
- Large number of tracks (at least sixty-four)
- Ability to alter pitch and tempo
- Filters to remove noise from recorded tracks
- Filters to alter equalization (EQ)
- Ability to control dynamics (Compressor, Normalize)
- Other effects (Reverb, Reverse, Chorus, Echo, Phaser, etc.)
- Support for VST plug-ins—a high-quality format for software "tools" that can be added to existing DAW programs
- Ability to create WAV and AIFF files
- Ability to burn to CD
- Software instruments and MIDI: essential for those who wish to use the DAW software to compose music
- DJ-style controls: important for people who want to use this software for live performance, like, um, DJs

Drivers

In this context, a driver is a piece of software that connects the audio editing/playback software with the interface hardware. In Windows software, there are several pieces of system software that control audio. These various layers of software tend to slow down the signal as it passes through the computer, introducing a delay that geeks call "latency." One way around this is to use a driver that essentially hijacks the audio signal and steers it around all this other software, like a good publicity agent steering a celebrity past the paparazzi. This driver is known as ASIO.[2] If you are working in Windows, make sure that your software is compatible with ASIO or suffer the curse of latency.

In the Mac world, the software was designed to pass audio through quickly, using a driver known as Core Audio. If you are in the Mac realm, make sure that your software and interface both use it.

_____

[2] Audio Stream Input/Output

Where to Find Content

People always ask me, "Where did you find that sound?" and the answer is always different. As a professional sound designer, I collect sounds for a living. I am rarely without a portable recording device (I am partial to the Zoom H4 at the moment), and I am constantly annoying my friends by whipping it out to record rain, street sounds, machines, restaurant interiors, and so forth. My library of sounds is constantly growing and developing, but it hardly begins to fulfill all the various needs I have. When faced with a new sound design, I generally break it down into two lists: make and download.

For the Make items, I look around my environment. When I was designing *Macbeth* at the University of Texas, I needed the sound of a tribal people dancing and shouting while preparing for war. Fortunately, UT has a great dance company, and they rehearse in a big, wide-open studio with a cavernous roof, so I asked the choreographer to let me borrow them for an hour. I set up four microphones: a stereo pair close to the dancers and another stereo pair at the other end of the studio to capture the reverberations. For an hour, I asked them to stomp, scream, chant, and wail, recording dozens of different versions which I later tweaked and mixed into the bed of tribal worship that I needed.

For recording these kinds of sounds, I use a portable Pro Tools interface plugged into my Mac laptop. It has four inputs, so I can have four different mics all recording at once.

The best sounds are almost always the ones that you find and make yourself, because you have very specific control over what they sound like, so that's always my preferred way of getting what I need.

That takes time, however, and it doesn't work if the sound you need is something specific and exotic, like the bear I needed for Shakespeare's *The Winter's Tale*, a play which, as everyone knows, contains the best stage direction ever written: "Exit, pursued by a bear."

In this case, and in many others, I turned to the vast resources of the Internet. There are, of course, a zillion places to get free content, but again, you get what you pay for. I frequent several pay sites (like SoundDogs and SoundEffects.com) because they have well-maintained, easy-to-understand catalogs that allow me to quickly find what I need; plus, the quality of the sounds is generally far better than what I can find for free. They also allow me to download sounds in multiple formats, which is very useful.

Wherever you get your sounds, be aware that those sounds may be copyrighted. If you are buying sounds, you generally are also buying the right to use them however you want. If you are downloading free sounds, look for royalty-free versions that can be legally used. If you are using commercially distributed music, then make sure you know what constitutes fair use. Mostly, it will depend on the size of your house and whether you are charging admission. If you are working in a commercial theater or large, visible academic institution, check with your legal staff to see how they are dealing with this issue. Some institutions, like my former employer Universal Studios, have blanket agreements with the international artist-rights management organizations ASCAP and BMI. These organizations exist to make sure that artists are properly compensated for the use of their art. Don't assume that you are beyond their control. Check first.

Audio Playback Software

In a few cases, like some Pro Tools setups, you might be using the same software to both create and play the audio, but generally, you will be using a separate piece of software to create the show. Most users of DAWs don't need specialized playback, because all they want to do is play a single audio file. For the theater, however, we need a lot more flexibility and features.

Audio playback software breaks down into two rough groups:

1. Timeline-based
2. Cue-based

We are going to go deeper into these concepts in the show control chapter, but, for the moment, this is what you need to know: Timeline-based programs are based on a clock of some sort, and they are designed to run all the cues at specific times. This is useful if you have a preprogrammed show that always runs exactly the same way, like a show in a theme park, museum, fountain, video wall, etc.

Cue-based programs operate more like what we are used to. In these programs, you can assemble a series of audio (and, in some of them, video) "events" that will happen when you hit the GO button. Both of the programs I mentioned above, QLab and Stage Research SFX, are cue-based.

In general, all cue-based playback software programs work in a similar way. The user imports an audio file (often by just "dragging and dropping") into a **cue list**. The cue list is a list of events that will happen in sequence during the show. Files can be programmed to happen when the operator clicks on a GO button on the screen, when a certain amount of time has expired, or when the computer receives a signal from another device.

Cue lists are very flexible. Audio files can fade up or down, loop, and start or stop at any point in the file. Multiple files can play simultaneously or be daisy-chained so that one file begins playing when another is finished, or after a certain amount of time. Cue lists can be instantly changed as well, if you decide to add, delete, or reorder cues in the middle of rehearsal.

Many programs allow multiple cue lists to play at once, which is very useful if, for example, you have one set of sounds that plays throughout a presentation, while other things come and go.

These programs are capable of sending these cues to lots of different outputs, bounded only by the number of outputs in the hardware interface. You might, for example, set up your system with an output to the main speaker cluster over the stage, two more to the left and right speakers, another one to a speaker in the very back of the house, and yet another to the speaker in the radio on the set. To organize the multiple output channels, audio playback software has a **matrix**, which allows each audio file to be assigned to any number of outputs in any given cue.

Let's go back to that production of *Macbeth* for a real-life example. In the opening scene of the play, a group of soldiers are reporting the news of Macbeth's victory on the battlefield. The director wanted the reports from the battlefield to feel as though they were being shouted from hilltop to hilltop, as the news of the battle was being relayed back to the king. At the same time, he wanted the witches to be crawling onto the stage, accompanied by whistling wind, unearthly screeching, and that tribal pounding and wailing I talked about earlier. Then, at the exact instant that a witch raises her arms to the sky, he wanted a bolt of lightning and a huge clap of thunder.

Obviously, this was not going to work with a CD player.

First, I brought all the soldiers into the studio and recorded them shouting their lines. I made each shouted line into a separate audio file. Then I created new sound effects files for the other noises. I found the wind and the thunder at an online sound effects site, recorded the dance company, and convinced some actress friends to scream bloody murder (which was surprisingly easy). I took the screams into my DAW (Pro Tools) and "dirtied" them with various filters and pitch shifters.

I created separate files for the tribal background, wind, thunder, witch screeching, and each line that a soldier shouted.

Once I had all the files, I cranked up my audio playback program.

First I created cues for the background sounds: the wind and the drums. Because I was cueing them separately, I could precisely adjust the volume of each one, in case the director wanted more or less of either one. The shouted voices were all separate cues, so I could use the matrix to assign each one to a different speaker in the theater, giving the sense of voices shouting from all sides. The screeching of the witches was programmed to automatically happen after each set of shouts, but through a different set of speakers.

When it came time for the bolt of lightning, I programmed my audio console to send a MIDI command to the lighting control board.[3] With the

---

[3] I will show you how to do this in part 4.

cooperation of the lighting designer, that MIDI command triggered a lighting cue that simulated a bolt of lightning. A fraction of a second later, my peal of thunder rocked the theater. Because both the lightning and the thunder were being triggered by the same device, they always came exactly together. The entire sequence was triggered by a single GO command on the computer, with an additional GO that was taken as a visual cue when the witch raised her arms.

Like I said, you can't do that with a CD player.

Because theatrical audio playback is more specialized than content creation, it does not attract the wealth of choices that DAW software does. When choosing software, consider the following:

Platform

There are good products available for both Mac and Windows, but they do not cross over. Macs and Windows handle audio quite differently. Mac software will be based on the Core Audio program, while Windows will generally be based on ASIO.

Audio interface

Make sure that your software will support the **audio interface**, or **sound card**, that you will be using. Check the website for a list of interfaces that have been successful for others. The maker of the software usually won't guarantee that a particular interface will work, so pay attention to the comments of other users.

Features

All of the features that I have described above will be supported by any decent audio playback program. At a minimum, your software should be able to handle the following:

- Multiple simultaneous playback of files
- Multiple cue lists
- Volume adjustments (including timed fades)
- Loops
- Matrixing inputs and outputs
- AIFF and WAV formats
- MIDI input and output

More complex programs will offer more features, like the following:

- Support for video playback and/or live camera inputs

- Support for live audio inputs
- Additional output channels
- Support for sending audio over computer networks
- Show control functions, like controlling external devices, accepting triggered inputs, or following time code
- Scripting of custom functions

Some playback programs, like SFX and QLab, come in more than one version, allowing you to get the level of features that you need, without paying for stuff that you don't.

User Interface

Some programs have predesigned interfaces that are easy to understand. Other programs that are designed for permanent installations will have the tools to create your own on-screen interface, while others will be controlled by text commands. For nonpermanent applications (like stage productions), the friendly, predesigned interfaces are the best.

CHAPTER 5

More Digital Audio Gear

Digital playback was just the beginning. Once the digital ball started rolling, it never stopped. Almost every piece of equipment in the audio toolbox went digital, and all for the same reasons: Going digital meant less noise, distortion, and signal loss, plus it gave designers more options.

We are still, however, a long way from a completely digital sound system, and we may never get there. In fact, there is a determined group of people out there who still adamantly argue for the superiority of analog equipment, saying that it is warmer or easier to listen to over time. These voices have faded a little as digital sampling rates and bit depths have gotten higher; but opinions are opinions, and in the end, it may come down to personal preference.

Digital equipment does allow more features than analog, and it is always getting cheaper, so expect the growth of digital equipment to continue. Here are some of the pieces of equipment that have made the leap.

Digital Mixers

Besides the audio quality, digital mixers have several advantages over analog. The biggest one is that the controls can be "soft"—that is, any button or knob on the front panel can be assigned, through software, to any function. That means, for example, that you can have a forty-eight-channel mixer but only have twenty-four-channel sliders. Push a button and the sliders control channels 1 to 24. Push the button again and they control 25 to 48. Push the button again and they control your sends or your returns or your effect loops or your Nintendo. Whatever! When you are controlling the signals through software, instead of through hardwired analog pathways, you have more flexibility. This generally means smaller control surfaces can control more things.

Note that some audio engineers don't like this trend toward soft controls, particularly in live situations (as opposed to recording studios). In a live theater, problems happen quickly, and an audio engineer wants to be able to quickly scan his console to isolate and solve the problem. In a panic situation, like a sudden burst of feedback or a dead microphone, he doesn't want to flip through pages of menus to call up the right control. That's why digital mixers for live, professional applications, like rock concerts, don't tend to use as many soft controls as those mixers designed for other applications.

Digidesign took the digital mixer to a new level by creating the Control 24 digital mixer, which is basically a Pro Tools DAW that is specifically designed to run live shows (while also recording them like a studio setup).

CD Players

The compact disc has now been around long enough to be tottering on obsolescence, but it still hangs on as a distribution and playback format. Hence, it is still useful to understand how CDs actually work under the hood.

The compact disk audio format was standardized in 1980 by something called the Red Book format.[1] The Red Book covers the CDs that you stick into your commercial CD player. There is also a Yellow Book that covers CD-ROMs, an Orange Book that covers recordable CDs, and a White Book that covers video CDs. They are all part of the "Rainbow Books," a collection of standards that define compact discs. (There is no rainbow book for DVDs.)

Among other things, the Red Book format determines maximum playing time (79.8 minutes) sampling rate (44.1 kHz) and bit depth (16-bit) as well as the format of the uncompressed audio files on the disk, known as .cda files. If you want to take files from a commercial CD and put them on your computer, you have to "rip" them off the CD using software designed for that purpose, like iTunes, the Windows Media Player, or many others. These programs will look at the .cda files and convert them to a format that works on a computer, like AIFF, WAV, or MP3. The native .cda files will do you no good by themselves. They have to be converted as they are "ripped." Likewise, if you want to burn a CD in Red Book format, you need software to convert your other file formats to the .cda format.

This can create some confusion if you are working with compressed audio files, like MP3s. A standard CD is 700 MB, which gives you about seventy minutes of uncompressed stereo audio. If you are converting AIFF or WAV files to put them onto an audio CD, then it's no problem. Seventy minutes

---

[1] There are also Yellow, Blue, Orange, White, Green, Purple, Scarlet, Black, and Beige books, each of which determines the standards for a different type of disk-based storage medium.

of AIFF or WAV files is the same size as seventy minutes of .cda files: about 700 MB. Burn, baby, burn.

But let's say that you try to get clever about your audio files. Since MP3 files are about a tenth of the size of uncompressed AIFF or WAV, you could fit seven hundred minutes of compressed MP3 audio in about the same amount of disc space as seventy minutes of AIFF or WAV. When you try to burn the seven hundred minutes of MP3 files onto a CD, however, you will be disappointed, as the software will tell you in no uncertain terms that there is not enough space on that disk. That's because, in order to burn a Red Book CD, the software is converting your compressed MP3 files back into uncompressed .cda files, which can only fit about seventy minutes of music on a CD.

Now, it is possible to put seven hundred minutes of MP3 files onto a compact disc, but not in Red Book format, which means that it won't play on a standard CD player. In this case, you will be creating a "data disk," not an "audio disk." This works fine for passing files from one computer to another, plus, there are some CD players out there that will actually play a data disk full of MP3s. They are the exception, however, not the rule.

In general, however, CDs are on their last legs. In the world of 16-gigabyte thumb drives and terabyte hard drives, 700 MB just isn't what it used to be. For one of my recent projects, the sound designer actually delivered all the audio files on iPod Nanos, giving the producers a convenient way not only to carry the files but to preview them.

Digital Audio Networks

Compact discs may be fading away, but digital networks are coming on strong, and for good reason.

One of the biggest places where analog audio loses fidelity and signal strength is in long cable runs, like from mixers to amps. If you are operating a large venue, you may have cable runs in the hundreds of feet, which can really eat into the fidelity of a signal, due to electromagnetic interference, loss of high frequencies, and voltage drops over long distances. You can address the situation by running fatter cables, of course, but copper is expensive, especially if you need to run a separate cable for each discrete output.

Besides wanting to send audio over long distances, audio system designers wanted to have a simple way to send audio to lots of different locations at once. For example, look at a museum with lots of exhibits. It is really nice in this sort of a setup to run all the audio for all the different exhibits from one place. It allows you to quickly start up and and shut down the whole system at the beginning and end of the day; plus, it allows you to "take over" the system if you want to broadcast announcements, like upcoming tours, special events, and emergencies.

For both of these reasons (and others), the search was on very early in the digital revolution for a way to send audio digitally over a network, just like computer data. The big problem, of course, is that audio is *extremely* time sensitive. If it pauses *at all* to wait for data to catch up, then there will be a break in the program, and that is simply not a possibility when dealing with audio—it absolutely must be continuous. Sudden bits of silence are not going to cut it.

In this sense, Ethernet, the standard network that runs all over our houses, offices, and yes, theaters, is poorly suited for audio. It doesn't generally provide time-stamped data, so all those bits of data running through the cable are a bit like the White Rabbit in *Alice in Wonderland*: worried about being late, but having no idea what time it really is.

In 1996, a Colorado-based company called Peak Audio came up with a solution, which they called CobraNet.

CobraNet operates over a standard Fast Ethernet network (100 Mbit/s), just like a computer network. It can carry up to sixty-four channels of uncompressed audio, which is a huge savings in hardware, when you consider the size and cost of sixty-four different analog audio cables. Of course, you have to spend some additional money for the devices that package the audio for the network and unwrap it at the other end.

CobraNet keeps all the audio in sync by electing one of the devices on the network as the "conductor" device and designating all the other devices as "performers." The conductor device is just like the conductor of an orchestra—it keeps time by broadcasting a steady beat that the other devices must follow. If something happens to the conductor device, the CobraNet network instantly chooses a different conductor, who picks up the beat instantly, often without any break in the sound at all.

CobraNet isn't something that you will see in a medium-sized theater, but it is currently running in thousands of large venues, like hotels and stadiums.[2]

CobraNet isn't perfect. It does suffer problems with **latency**, which means that a certain amount of delay can creep into the system. This delay, however, is measured in milliseconds, or thousandths of a second, so it is manageable for anything but the most exacting installation.

CobraNet allows system designers to take the audio from the mixer and drop it onto the network as a digital signal. Then, anywhere that network goes, they can plug in a network-capable amplifier, set that device to receive a particular

_____

[2] In fact, one of the first uses of CobraNet was for Super Bowl XXXI, in 1997.

signal on the network, and poof, that signal is converted to analog and pumped up to speaker level. Plug in a normal speaker and you've got sound. For an even cleaner link, they can use a network-friendly **powered speaker**, which has the amp built right into the speaker cabinet. The signal arrives at the powered speaker over the network, is converted inside the unit and only travels a matter of inches as a vulnerable analog signal. Sweet audio goodness.

CobraNet is a solution that allows designers to put audio signals on a standard Ethernet network. In some cases, particularly large permanent installations and professional sound studios, the system designers will forgo putting the audio on the standard Ethernet network and instead use a dedicated audio network that does nothing else. A good example is the MADI system (Multichannel Audio Digital Interface), which, unlike CobraNet, is an industry standard that does not need to be licensed. MADI provides up to sixty-four channels of digital audio over coaxial or fiber optic cables, with resolutions up to 24 bits, and that, ladies and gentlemen, is some high-quality audio.

Plugging It All In

So, how do you know if a signal coming out of a piece of audio equipment is an analog or digital signal? First, by looking at the labels on the connections and at the specifications of the equipment, and second, by the type of plug on the back of the unit. The following are the common types of digital connections that you will currently find on audio gear. If your connection is not listed here, it is probably analog.

AES/EBU: Originally created by the Audio Engineering Society and the European Broadcast Union, this has become an extremely popular digital format. It carries two channels of audio and generally uses an XLR connector.

S/PDIF: Believe it or not, this is pronounced like it looks, "SPI-diff."[3] This format was created as more of a consumer format, as opposed to AES/EBU, which was for the pros. The two standards operate in a very similar way, but they use different plugs. S/PDIF, in an attempt to make the cables cheaper, uses RCA coaxial cable or optical cable with a special plug called a Toslink plug. The other major difference is that S/PDIF can only go 10 meters (33 feet), while AES/EBU can travel up to 100 meters (328 feet).[4] If you are

_____

[3] It stands for Sony/Philips Digital Interconnect Format, Sony and Philips being the two primary forces behind it.
[4] This is with a balanced, unshielded cable and XLR connector, the more common configuration. The pros sometimes use an unbalanced, coaxial cable and a BNC connector to stretch this up to 1,000 meters (3,281 feet).

reading a specification sheet, S/PDIF is sometimes known by its International Electrical Code designation, IEC 60958.

Both AES/EBU and S/PDIF show up on CD players, MiniDisc players, DVD players, cable boxes, and digital video recorders like TiVo. In order to make use of it, you have to have an amplifier or a mixer that has a matching input.

ADAT: When Alesis created their eight-channel digital tape deck, the ADAT, in 1991, it was a revolutionary piece of equipment that brought digital recording to bedroom studios everywhere. That deck is long gone, but the digital interface that it used, the ADAT Lightpipe is still with us. ADAT uses the same Toslink plugs as S/PDIF, but that's where the similarities stop. ADAT can send up to eight channels of digital content, whereas S/PDIF can only send two.

You will find ADAT connections on multi-track digital playback devices (like Alesis's own HD24 hard disk recorder), computer audio cards, digital mixers, and other audio devices that are handling more than two tracks of audio at once.

Are you confused? No? Then you're not paying attention! All these abbreviations can be mind-numbing, so let's look at a real-life example.

Let's say that you are setting up a sound system for a live theater application. After doing some research, you have settled on a Yamaha 01V96VCM mixer, which has the features you like, even if its name is perilously complex.[5] You look at the specs and see that the mixer has the following digital inputs:

Terminal	Format	Connector
• 2TR IN DIGITAL	IEC 60958	RCA pin jack
• ADAT IN	ADAT	OPTICAL

So what does this tell you? Well, you know that it has a two-track input that is in the IEC 60958 format and, because you read this book, you know that is a S/PDIF input. Furthermore, it has an RCA jack on it, so all you need is an RCA coaxial cable from the audio store.

Secondly, you can see that this mixer has an ADAT input which is, not surprisingly, in the ADAT format. The plug is optical, so that means a Toslink cable, also available at your neighborhood audio store.

You have also decided to use the SFX playback system from Stage Research, which runs on a PC. You have equipped that PC with a sound card

---

[5] I am old enough to remember when this mixer first came out and was simply titled "Yamaha 01V." Later, Yamaha upgraded it to 96 kHz so they tacked that on. Finally, they added something called "VCM effects," so the name reached its current length. By the time you read this, it may have gotten even longer.

from AudioFire Pre 8 sound card from the Echo company. In addition to its analog outputs, it has the following: ADAT. Digital Output, optical connector, eight channels of ADAT.

So you know that you can get eight channels of audio from your computer via an ADAT optical cable.

Finally, you have chosen a professional-level CD player, the Tascam CD200. One of the reasons you chose it is because it has the following spec: S/PDIF digital out on coaxial and optical jacks.

Could it be any easier? You've got two channels of audio coming out of the CD player via a S/PDIF cable with either coaxial or optical connections. The mixer input was coaxial, so that makes that decision right there. You already have the RCA coaxial cable.

The bottom line is, with one ADAT Toslink cable and one RCA coaxial cable, you can plug in all of your digital sources to your digital mixer digitally. That way, the signal never leaves the digital realm until it is on the way out to the amplifiers. Fewer analog-digital-analog conversions means less noise and distortion. It's a beautiful digital thing.

Of course, this is just one example of how to read specification sheets and shake out information about digital connections. You may use entirely different equipment, but the process is the same.

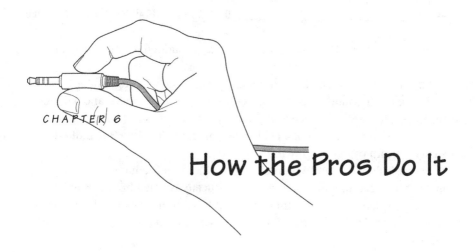

CHAPTER 6

How the Pros Do It

Swimming with Speakers: Creating Audio for *The House of Dancing Water*

When Belgian-born theater director Franco Dragone was brought in to direct the new show at the just-finished City of Dreams resort in Macau, there was no doubt about the scale of the show. Dragone was already known for directing mystic fantasies on an epic scale, first for the Cirque du Soleil and later for his own company, Dragone, and he was no stranger to spare-no-expense, casino-funded entertainment, having helped to establish the Cirque in Las Vegas seventeen years earlier with the cutting-edge *Mystère*.

Besides *Mystère* (and the epic Celine Dion show), Dragone is also famous for two aquatic Las Vegas shows, *Le Rêve* and *O*, both of which take place in, around, and over giant, million-gallon water tanks. *The House of Dancing Water* would also happen over water, but this is Macau, the land of "We do it bigger than Vegas," so the water tank became a water *lake*. By some estimates, the *Dancing Water* tank is five times bigger than that of *O* (which was the biggest theatrical pool in the world when it opened).

Even with this massive watery stage, the show producers wanted the experience to be as intimate as possible, so the audience seating is steeply raked and curls 270 degrees around the stage, almost surrounding it.

Like Dragone's previous shows, *Dancing Water* is a circus-style acrobatic show, which meant that a live orchestra would be necessary. Live circus acts require a live band that can respond instantly to sudden changes, like a performer who misses a trick and wants to try it again.[1]

So, let's review: We've got a show that takes place in a huge water tank, an audience in the round, live musicians, flying circus performers, and a director known for creating fantastical productions with mystical soundscapes. Depending on how much of a challenge you enjoy, it's either an audio designer's dream or his worst nightmare.

Francois Bergeron and Vikram Kirby of Thinkwell Productions started by making sure that the musicians were acoustically isolated from the audience. As Kirby explains, "If, for example, you put the drummer where the audience can hear him directly, then when he hits the snare, *bam*, you've lost control of that sound."

The problem is timing. Sound actually travels fairly slowly, so once the drummer hits that snare, the sound will take its time meandering through the audience. Every member of the audience is going to hear it at a different time, depending on how far away they are. The difference might be as much as one hundred milliseconds (one millisecond is one/thousandth of a second), which might not sound like much, but your ears are fully capable of distinguishing between two sounds that arrive twenty milliseconds apart. This becomes a problem in the theater if the sound of the snare is also being amplified by speakers in the rear of the auditorium. The sound from those speakers gets there through electrical wiring, traveling almost at the speed of light, so it arrives well ahead of the sound from the stage, which is traveling through the air at the speed of sound. The combination of the early-arriving amplified sound and the late-arriving live sound produces a mushy mess that confuses the audience's ears. Before you know it, there are several snare sounds and none of them match the guitar or the vocal.

In a traditional proscenium theater, the audio designer solves this by delaying the sound that goes to the rear speakers, as well as lowering their volume, so that they match the live sound that is traveling directly from the stage. If a live sound takes eighty milliseconds to reach an audience seat, then the speaker sitting next to that seat will have an eighty-millisecond delay. Presto, the two sounds arrive together and the audience ear is blissfully un-

---

[1] There are a few circus-style shows out there that do not use live music, like the Cirque du Soleil show *Love*, which uses a recorded soundtrack mixed together from Beatles songs. In this case, however, the sound technician is armed with multiple versions of the songs and various "stall" tracks, all of which can be instantly accessed (via a computer-based playback system, naturally) to cover unexpected events. It is a difficult and imperfect solution, however, and live bands are still considered the best way to go with circus acts.

aware that the live sound from the stage is being amplified by a speaker just a few feet away.[2]

The sound coming from each speaker is delayed depending on the distance from the stage to that speaker. If the speakers are different distances from the stage, then the times will be different. The process of setting all these times is called delay tapering because the farther you go from the stage, the longer the time. In this way, the sounds are "tapered."

Furthermore, in many modern theaters, the main speakers are stacked up in line arrays, tall stacks of speakers that hang down in front of the proscenium like giant Js. The lower speakers point steeply down and serve the front of the audience. The rest of the speakers are stacked in a curve, with each successive speaker pointed farther up and back. Each speaker in the array is given its own volume setting (audio engineers call this a "gain" setting), so that all the seats hear the same volume. This process is called gain tapering.[3]

With a theater-in-the-round setup like *House of Dancing Water*, however, this problem becomes immensely more difficult. With the drummer sitting to one side of the audience, that snare sound will arrive at a different time to each section of the audience. The line array speakers must be numerous, pointed in a host of different directions, and narrowly focused, and the rear speakers must have complex delay programs: a difficult and expensive solution.

What the designers want to do is create a time-zero point: a place on the stage where the audio can appear to "start." The time-zero point can then be used as a reference point for timing all the audio arrival times for all the audience members. In a sense, the sound should appear to emanate from this time-zero point, regardless of whether the musician is actually sitting there. With an audience in the round, the best place for this time-zero point is dead center, right in the middle of the circular stage, the same distance from each pie-shaped section of the audience. Unfortunately, this being an acrobatic show, we can't very well suspend the band over the middle of the stage where the flying performers go. Thus, the production went to plan B: Put the band somewhere else entirely, isolate them acoustically, and then feed the sound through speakers over the stage.

---

[2] If you are ever setting up delay times, here's a tip: Sound travels at 1,126 feet per second at sea level with moderate temperature and humidity. In the theatrical realm of "close counts," you can use one foot per millisecond, so measure the number of feet to the stage and set your delay at that number of milliseconds. Fifty feet equals fifty milliseconds. Done.

[3] If you ever get a chance to watch a big rock show load in, watch the engineer when he is setting up the line arrays. Often, he will attach a laser beam to each speaker and use it to aim the speaker at a particular section of the audience.

In *House of Dancing Water*, the musicians were placed behind the audience in a glass-enclosed space, where they can see the stage (and thus respond to the changing performance) but not be heard directly. Instead, the sound of the band is carried to the audience through a carefully designed sound system.

The main speakers at *Dancing Water* are eight sets of line array speakers, suspended from the main grid over the water, high enough to be out of the way of flying bodies. Above the main line arrays are three more arrays of subwoofers for low frequencies: one cardioid and two line arrays. Using the computerized playback system, the signals to all these speakers are time- and gain-tapered to match the time-zero point. The net effect, when all the speakers are turned on and working together, is a perception that the music is coming from out over the water, from the time-zero point.

Besides the main speakers, the *Dancing Water* system also uses a very large surround system, placed in three tiers: high surround line arrays, low surrounds, and rear speakers that are actually behind the audience.

There are a few live microphones onstage for speaking characters, but the vast majority of the sound in those speakers comes from that audibly isolated band.

By the time you add up all the guitars, keyboards, drums, vocals, and other instruments, the band produces 112 tracks, which would mean an awful lot of copper wire running between the band, the monitor mixers, and the front-of-house mixing position. Instead, the *Dancing Water* system uses two digital streams based on the MADI protocol to gather up all these signals. The signals that start digital, like keyboards and computer sequencer playback, go directly into the MADI streams, while the analog signals from microphones, guitars, and other instruments are digitized first, then fed into the stream. Once the signals are in the stream, they stay digital all the way through the system. "Our philosophy," says Kirby, "is only digitize once." The two streams, each of which can carry up to sixty-four channels, are routed to the front-of-house and monitor mixing positions as well as to a multi-track recording station, so that the music can be recorded and played back for mixing sessions and cast rehearsals.

The monitor station actually contains two monitor consoles: a DiGiCo mixer that creates a mix for the band and a Yamaha mixer for the underwater speakers used by the divers and performers waiting for entrances.

The FOH mixing is done on an LCS Matrix3 Audio Show Control System (by Meyer Sound Laboratories), which contains a 200 × 200 matrix of inputs and outputs, allowing the designers to put any sound anywhere in the theater, using the same time- and gain-tapering process that they used to line up all the arrival times. Want to make a twittering bird float back and forth over the audience? No problem.

Besides the live band, *Dancing Water* also uses a digital playback system for various nonmusical sound effects. In rehearsal, the designers used a QLab playback system, but when the design was ready to be committed to a more permanent solution, they moved the sound to an LCS Wild Tracks system that was integrated into the Matrix3, which gave them greater flexibility for routing and cueing.

Even though the music was being provided by a live band, there are lighting effects that are cued with some additional clips of recorded audio, so the audio system does generate LTC time code, which links the audio playback with the lighting consoles. There is also a custom-designed sync with the video servers, using the Art-Net protocol, which allows the video servers to call up their own soundtracks from the Wild Tracks hard drive.

And if all that weren't enough, *Dancing Water* also makes use of Constellation "Electroacoustic Architecture" technology, also by Meyer Sound. The Constellation system uses dedicated microphones and speakers, scattered throughout the house, to imitate the acoustics of different kinds of spaces. By "listening" to the audio in the theater through its own microphones, processing that sound with reverberation and delay, and then rebroadcasting it out through a special set of speakers, the Constellation system can instantly expand or collapse the apparent size of a space, taking you from a cathedral to a quiet country church faster than you can say . . . too late, it's done.

All of these systems and standards are in constant development and flux. The world of digital audio is moving so quickly these days that, with a large-scale project like *House of Dancing Water*, one that is several years in the making, the designers must sometimes make educated guesses about what will be available when the show finally opens. As Kirby says, "Sometimes you have to commit to standards and hope that the gear is available by the time you install the show."

In this case, their commitment to MADI and the LCS Matrix3 paid off nicely, as the entire system came together as planned for their summer 2010 opening in Macau.

Part 2: Lighting

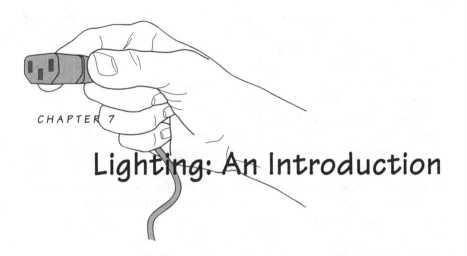

CHAPTER 7

Lighting: An Introduction

In order to get a handle on digital lighting, you will need to have a general understanding of theatrical lighting practice. If you already have this knowledge, you can skip over this chapter and get into chapter 8.

Not sure if you should read this chapter? Try this sentence on for size.

"I want to three-fer those 1000 W ellipsoidals into circuit 24, but it's rated at 20 amps, so I'll use two circuits and combine them into a single channel at the console."

If you understood that sentence, feel free to skip ahead. If not, let's dig in.

There Is No Light Without Power

Before you can have anything digital, or anything electronic, or anything electrical, you have to have power. In the digital world, it is electricity that makes the sun come up.

Electricity is provided by the power company, who generate it by burning coal or splitting atoms or trapping water from waterfalls and using this energy to turn great big magnets inside even bigger coils of copper wire. Turning a magnet inside of a wire coil creates electricity. True, it's a bit more complicated than that, but only a bit, and you don't really need to know much more because, basically, electricity is magic. And neither you nor I really need to know how the magic works. What we *do* need to know is how to measure the magic and how to use it safely.

My favorite analogy about electricity involves the fish tank at the Seattle public market. They have these long tanks full of live fish, and whenever somebody wants one, the sales guy reaches in with his bare hands, yanks one out, and tosses it over the heads of the surprised tourists (or the smug locals) right into the hands of another guy by the cash register, who wraps it and sells it, singing in Sicilian the whole time. It's pretty impressive, but even more so when you consider that this is how electricity works.

Imagine a long tank full of fish. I mean, really full. Imagine a tank so full that you could not put one more fish into it. Absolutely jammed. Now imagine that the sales guy down at one end reaches in and pulls one fish out. With one fish removed, there is room for another fish. Now imagine that there is a fisherman who pulls up to the other end of the tank with his catch of the day. He sees that there is room for one more fish in the tank, so he dumps a fresh one in. Only he does not stop there. He keeps trying to force more fish into the tank. No matter how hard he pushes, though, he will not be able to get another fish in the tank until the sales guy down at the other end pulls one out. The fisherman keeps trying, though, and every time the sales guy pulls a fish out, the fisherman succeeds in getting a new one in. Sometimes, the fisherman pushes so hard that, when the sales guy reaches into the tank, he comes up with not one fish but two, or three. In fact, if the fisherman pushes really, really hard, the sales guy might be overwhelmed by fish when he reaches into the tank.

This is electricity.

Confused? Never fear! Okay, the fish are electrons, and they are swimming around inside the fish tank, which is a cable. The fisherman is the source of the electricity, which means that he is the power company. The sales guy is the load—the thing that is using the electricity. He could be a stereo, a toaster, a clothes dryer, or a theatrical lighting instrument. It does not matter. A load is a load. The load (the sales guy) is pulling electrons (fish) out of the cable (tank) while the power company (fisherman) is pouring them in the other end. This is the flow of electricity.

The analogy breaks down in one critical place, however. For electricity to truly flow, it must have a round-trip ticket. The load cannot simply take in all those electrons and not let them go again. Electricity must follow a complete circular path from the source to the load and back again. There are two possible ways back to the source, and because electricity is lazy and impatient, it will always take the easiest and quickest one. Take a look at an electrical outlet. Unless you are in a very old building, you will see three openings. If you are in the United States you will see two vertical slots and a U-shaped hole. One of the vertical slots is the "hot" line that is carrying power from the electric company. The other vertical slot is the "neutral," which is carrying the power back to the electrical company when you are done with it.[1] The other U-shaped

---

[1] Quibblers will complain that this description is not exactly accurate, and they are right. Because our power is distributed in AC, or alternating current form, the electrons are actually switching directions in the cable, sixty times a second. Therefore, they are traveling to and from the power company on *both*

hole is the "ground," which carries the power straight into the earth itself, if necessary. More about grounds in a minute.

Let's go back to the fish tank. In order to make good use of electricity, it is frequently necessary to measure how much there is of it, so let's go back to the fish tank. There are three terms that are necessary to understand and use electricity: wattage, voltage, and amperage.

Wattage

The amount of fish that the sales guy is pulling out of the tank is the **wattage**, and it is measured in **watts**. Anything that uses power, from followspots to electric toothbrushes, is measured in watts. This is a measure of how much power the device uses when it is turned on.[2] A computer uses about 100 watts. A standard-sized lighting instrument uses from 500 to1000 watts.

Voltage

The amount of force that the fisherman (the power company) is using to push the fish into the tank is called the **voltage**, and it is measured in **volts**. When the sales guy (the load) reaches into the tank, he can feel how hard the fisherman is pushing, and it affects how many fish come out. The sales guy is only equipped to handle a certain number of fish at one time, just like your toaster is only equipped to handle a certain number of electrons. In fact, all electrical devices are rated to accept a particular voltage—one that that is in use in the country where they are sold. In the United States and Canada, power is officially delivered at 120 volts, although in practice, it averages around 115 volts The United States is in the minority in the respect—most of the world runs their power at 220 to 240 volts which allows for smaller cables, fuses, and circuit breakers. It is very important that electrical devices be fed the voltage that they are designed for. If you take a 120-volt hair dryer to Paris and plug it in without

lines, switching directions every 1/60 of a second. The power is provided from the power company on the hot line, however, and this matters sometimes, which is why plugs and outlets often have one blade and one slot bigger than the other one, just to make sure that you plug it in the right way.

[2] Many electric devices actually continue to use power when they are turned "off." This is because they are not really off—they are in a "standby" mode. This is true of televisions, DVD players, computers, and many other electronic devices. They are designed this way so that the internal circuitry stays warm and comes on faster when needed. This "standby" mode uses a significant amount of power, however. A 1998 study by the Lawrence Livermore Laboratory found that "standby power" was responsible for 5 percent of all the electricity usage in the United States the equivalent of the output from eighteen standard power plants. If you want to save this power, plug the device into a power strip and turn the strip off when you're not using it.

an adaptor, you are going to get a puff of smoke and a little sizzling sound as the motor burns up. Too many fish. If you plug a 220-volt hair dryer into an American outlet without an adaptor, the motor won't burn up, it will just run very slowly (or not at all). Not enough fish.

Fortunately, these days, many devices have "smart" power sources that automatically detect the incoming voltage and adapt to it. This is true of many laptops, as well as iPods and many cell phone chargers. Before plugging your device into a strange power source, however, it is *imperative* that you check the voltage that it is designed for. This is not hard. Look on the back of the device, generally around where the plug comes out. If your device has a "wall wart" or a squarish block somewhere in the cable, look there. Looking for where it says "Input Voltage" and a range of numbers. For example, it might say "Input Voltage 100–240v." In this case, the device can handle between 100 and 240 volts, which basically means that you can plug it in anywhere in the world. If it says "Input Voltage 100–120v," then you are restricted to an outlet that is providing the lower voltage.

Of course, any electric device can be adapted to a different voltage by plugging it into a voltage regulator that converts the local voltage into something your hair dryer can use.

Note that your electronic device may also have an "Output Voltage," which is the actual voltage that is being fed into the device, once the power plug gets through converting it from whatever is coming out of the wall. Electronic devices actually use lower voltages internally, generally from 5 to 12 volts so that wall wart or cord brick is converting the source voltage into something that the device can actually use. If your wall wart ever gets lost or broken, you can replace it. Just make sure that you get a converter that provides the same output voltage as the original one.

Amperage

The number of fish per second that are flowing through the tank is the **amperage** (sometimes called the **current**), and it is measured in **amps**. Cables, fuses, switches, plugs, and anything else that power passes through when going from the power company to the load are rated in amps.

The amperage depends on two things: how hard the power company (the fisherman) is pushing and how hard the load (the sales guy) is pulling. Bigger loads pull harder, meaning that they require more amps. Bigger voltages have the opposite effect; because the power company is pushing harder, the load doesn't have to pull as hard, so the amperage actually goes down.

These three terms—watts, voltage, and amperage—are the key to understanding, measuring, and using electricity, and they are related by the "West Virginia" law:

Watts = Volts × Amps

Or . . .

W=VA

If you are trying to figure out how to plug in your electrical devices, this law is the key. Remember:

Electrical loads are measured in **watts.**

Electrical sources are measured in **volts.**

Everything that connects loads to sources is measured in **amps.**

Let's try an exercise. Let's say you have three 500-watt lights (a total of 500 watts) and you want to know if you can plug them into a single circuit. You are in the United States, so your power is coming in at an average of 115 volts.

In this case, you want to know how many amps these lights will use. Then you can see how many amps your circuit is rated for.

Plug the numbers into the West Virgina formula:

1500 watts = 115 volts × amps

Using your best high school math, solve the formula for amps.

$$\frac{1500 \text{ watts}}{115 \text{ volts}} = \text{amps}$$

Whip out your calculator and do the math.

13.043 amps

So, your lights are going to use just a tad more than 13 amps. A standard household plug is 15 amps, so you are safe plugging them into your living room outlet. Most theatrical plugs are 20 amps, so you're even safer there.

Bottom line: go ahead and plug those lights into your circuit.

But, you ask, isn't there an easier way to figure this out? And the answer is, yes, a little bit easier.

When we did the above example, we used 115 volts as the voltage, which creates a lot of ragged numbers like 13.043 amps. However, if you round off the voltage to 100 volts, things get a lot easier. This is perfectly safe to do in daily life (not a good idea if you are designing a nuclear power plant), and it actually creates a safety cushion. By assuming a lower voltage, your amperage numbers come out a little high, giving you a little margin of safety. Look at what 100 volts does to the problem above:

1500 watts = 100 volts × amps

$$\frac{1500 \text{ watts}}{100 \text{ volts}} = \text{amps}$$

15 amps

Much easier. In fact, you don't even have to do math anymore. Just add up
your loads and then move the decimal point two places to the left. Thus,
1500 watts becomes 15 amps without even reaching for the calculator. And, as I
said before, your amperage number is actually a little high, which is not a bad thing.

Two more things that you need to know about electrical power: AC versus
DC and cycles per second.

AC versus DC

When electricity was first being sent across power lines in New England, a
War of Currents broke out between the two major electrical companies of the
period and their owners: Thomas Edison and George Westinghouse.
Edison ran his systems on direct current (DC), which sent all the power running in a single direction through the wires. Westinghouse, assisted by his
chief engineer Nikola Tesla (who had worked for Edison previously and
defected after his ideas were ignored), ran his systems on alternating current
(AC), which reversed the flow of power many times per second. The War of
Currents got nasty, mostly because Edison was fighting a losing battle on electrical standards, and he did not want to lose his market share.

The primary problem was transmission loss, the amount of power that
would be lost as the electricity was sent over long distances. In Edison's DC
system, the tranmission loss was so high that power generating stations had
to be less than a mile away from the load, meaning that a huge number of
power plants had to be built to supply the growing demand. This was fine
with Edison—he was in the business of manufacturing power plants—but it created a huge expense for consumers.

One of the ways to reduce transmission loss is to send power out of the
power plant at a much higher voltage than you will actually need. In an AC
system, this is very easy to do using **transformers**, electrical devices that can
change the voltage of incoming power with no moving parts. In fact, that wall
wart on your cell phone charger is doing exactly that. Changing the voltage in
a DC system is much more difficult, requiring expensive machinery with lots
of moving parts, requiring extensive maintenance.

By using an AC system, Westinghouse and Tesla could build fewer, larger
power plants, push the voltage up to tens of thousands of volts, and send it all
over the countryside. When that power got to the houses where it would be used,
it went through another transformer that brought it down to a usable voltage.

Westinghouse won the War of Currents, and Tesla's system is still in use
today to bring power from generating plants into your house.[3] Somewhere

---

[3] It got ugly before it was over, though. Edison claimed (falsely) that AC power was more danger-
ous than DC and even had his film crew shoot the electrocution, by Edison employees, of a circus

in your neighborhood, there is a transformer (if you have power poles, it is probably hanging from one of them) that is "stepping down" the high voltage from the power company to something you can use.

DC power is still in wide usage, however. It just doesn't come out of the walls. Electronic devices and many motors use DC power internally, as does your car, which is why you have to be careful where you attach the jumper cables when you jump-start it. Positive to positive, negative to negative! If you send the power in the wrong direction, you will blow the fuses. Anything that uses a battery is using DC power. That wall wart we talked about before is most likely changing the household AC power into the DC power that your cell phone prefers.

The power that comes out of the wall, however, is alternating current.

Cycles per Second

So how fast is that alternating current alternating? In the United States, it is changing directions sixty times per second, or 60 hertz, generally written as 60 Hz. Internationally, just about everything I said about voltage applies to hertz: The United States is in the minority (most of the world is operating on 50Hz); plugging your electric device into the wrong number of cycles can damage it; most electronic devices are smart enough to realize that; and you can confirm whether your device can handle the local voltage by reading the fine print on the back. An internationally safe device will say "50–60 Hz."

Power Supplies

We've already talked a bit about the external power supply, or "wall wart" that comes with many electronic devices. Of course, it is always best to use the power supply that came with your device, but if you damage or lose that power supply, you may need to replace it, so let's talk about what it actually does. Besides, once you understand power supplies, you can really freak the guy at RadioShack out.

Let's talk about an external power supply that you use every day: your cell phone charger.

As I said before, the external power supply is lowering the voltage from the wall socket to something that your device can use.

An Apple iPhone, for example, requires 3.7 volts of power to charge its battery. If you feed it 110 volts out of the wall (in the United States), you are giving it almost thirty times more power than it can handle. Pop! Poof! And we're

_____

elephant that had killed three men. Harold Brown, the inventor of the electric chair, was secretly paid by Edison to design the chair to demonstrate the dangers of AC power, all as part of Edison's publicity campaign against Westinghouse.

off to the Apple Store to buy another iPhone. The external power supply takes that toxic 110 volts of AC and safely converts it to 3.7 volts of lovely, organic DC.

If you look at the fine print on most power supplies (not Apple ones, unfortunately), you will see two sets of numbers: "input power" and "output power." The input power tells you what kind of power the device requires from the wall. As I said previously, most power supplies these days are capable of handling a wide range of voltages, which will be stated on the device. Look for something like "110–240v." It will also have an amperage number, which tells you how much current (how many amps) the device is actually using.[4]

For "output power," there will also be a voltage listed. This is important, because you need to feed the proper voltage to your device. Close does *not* count. If your device wants 12 volts, you need to give it 12 volts. Check the back of your electronic device. Next to the place where you plug in the power source, there should be some numbers, telling you the required voltage.

There should also be an amperage listed on your device, generally in milliampere-hours, abbreviated as mAh. One ampere-hour is the electric charge transfered by a steady current of one amp per hour, so one milliampere-hour is the charge transferred at the rate of one *thousandth* of an amp per hour. That's not very much, but it adds up. That Apple iPhone, for example, uses about 1400 mAh.

Remember that voltage is a measurement of how much power is being *provided*, while amperage is a measurement of how much power is flowing through a device. If you feed a device too much voltage, it may damage it. However, if your charger is rated for more milliamp-hours than your device requires, that's okay. Voltage is *pressure*. Apply too much pressure, and you can break something. Amperage is *capacity*. If your charger has too much capacity, it's like having a room that's bigger than you need. It doesn't hurt anything. If you have a charger that is rated for 2000 mAh and your device only requires 1400 mAh, you're all set.

The other way around, however, is a problem. If your device needs 2000 mAh and your charger can only provide 1400 mAh, then it's like that salesman trying to pull fish out of the tank faster than the fisherman can put them in. In the world of electronics, that leads to blown fuses and burned-out power supplies.

---

[4] Note that Apple's external power supplies do not contain this information anywhere on their glossy white bodies. This is because the Apple power supplies are built to handle just about anything that comes out of any household plug in the world, so Apple, in its typical "technology for non-geeks" approach, doesn't clutter up their clean design with confusing statistics.

Bottom line: When selecting a power supply, voltage must match exactly. Amperage must equal or exceed the requirement of the device it is powering.

Incidentally, laptop computer power supplies have another wrinkle. They supply power at several different voltages. That's why, if you look at the plug at the end of the power supply, you will see a bunch of different pins. Some of those pins have power at 3.3 volts or 5 volts or 12 volts. When buying a replacement power supply for a laptop, make sure that the power supply you are buying is specifically designed for the make and model of your computer so that all the pins match.

To Control Power, You Need Dimmers

Once you have enough power flowing into your theater, the next hurdle is getting less of it. Simply put, you don't want all your lights on, at full brightness, all the time. Enter the dimmer.

When I wrote my first book about technical theater in 1992, the standard dimming technology was called the **silicon-controlled rectifier** or SCR. At that time, the conventional wisdom was that SCRs were definitely better than what came before—they were lighter, smaller, and easier to control than their predecessors—but they would soon give way to something even better. After all, despite the improvement to stage lighting technology, SCRs were far from ideal: They still took up a lot of space, gave off a lot of heat, and, most disturbingly, made a lot of noise.

Keep in mind, this was 1992, before the Internet, cell phones, or laptop computers were in common usage. I didn't even have a *pager* in 1992. Considering the scale of technical innovation that has swept the world in the last twenty years, a major breakthrough in dimming technology would look like a no-brainer.

The fact is, it hasn't really happened. While the major manufacturers have all come up with other technologies, there has not been a groundswell of need for them. Consequently, they remain specialty items that are only used for specific applications. Thirty years after they became mainstream technology, SCRs are still king of the theater.

In order to understand the pros and cons of SCRs, let's take a look at how they work.

The *R* in SCR means "rectifier," a type of very fast electronic switch.

Although AC power is switching direction quickly, it doesn't do it instantaneously. The effect can be shown by a sine wave graph, where the ebb and flow of power can be clearly seen. The flow of power in the positive direction steadily decreases until it hits zero, whereupon the power begins to flow in the negative direction. The negative flow increases until it hits the maximum amount of power, then begins to decrease until it hits zero. Power then begins to flow back in the positive direction until the maximum is reached and the cycle begins again.

In order to decrease the amount of power flowing through the circuit, the SCR shuts off every time the power crosses the zero point, then turns on again after the appropriate amount of time has passed. The amount of time it stays off determines how much the power is reduced. So, for example, if the dimmer is set at 50 percent, then the SCR switch stays off for 50 percent of the wave. The lower the dimmer setting, the longer the SCR stays off.

This process reduces the amount of power flowing in the circuit without wasting any of the electricity. Lower dimmer settings simply use less power. This was a grand step forward from the older resistance dimmers, which simply reduced the amount of power flowing to the lights by converting the extra power into heat.

SCRs are also not load dependent. In other words, they basically function the same no matter how much of a load is plugged into them.[5] Earlier dimmers had to be loaded up to capacity to work properly, forcing electricians to fill the pits of theaters with "ghost loads" of lighting instruments that were plugged into the circuits but never seen by the audience.

The problem with the SCR is that jagged edge on the waveform. Because the wave of power shoots up suddenly, it actually can cause the filaments in the lights to rattle, a phenomenon that electricians call "filament hum" or, for the musically inclined, "lamp sing." In addition, the dimmers themselves will hum, due to the jagged waveform's effect on various parts of the circuitry. In a noisy theater, particularly one with music playing, you won't hear it. But, in a quiet, dramatic scene, the filament noise can be clearly heard, particularly if the dimmers are at half power where the noise is most pronounced. In a highly reflective concert hall, it can cause major problems. The noise from the dimmers themselves effectively prevents system designers from putting the dimmers anywhere in the theater. They must be stowed away in a room of their own.

Filament hum effectively reduces the life of the lamps, particularly PAR lamps, because the wires in the filament are being shaken every time the power dims down.

The jagged waveform also creates problems for certain kinds of loads, especially fluorescent lights, neon, metal-halide, and any kind of motor, so plugging any of these into an SCR dimmer is not a good idea. Sometimes people

---

[5] Well . . . mostly. If you have a single light plugged into a circuit and you add another light to the same circuit, you may find that you have to adjust the dimmer level slightly to make the first light operate at the same brightness as before, but the adjustment will be slight and only visible to those with super-sensitive vision.

ask if they can plug any of these items into an SCR circuit if the dimmer is always kept at full. The answer is no, it's still not a good idea. You might get away with it, but an SCR circuit has an electronic device called a choke, which is actually there to help smooth out the power, but which creates an unnatural waveform that can damage circuitry. Bottom line: An SCR dimmer should only be used for an incandescent light. If you need a **nondim** circuit to plug in any of these other items, you should install a nondim module in your dimmer rack. This module will provide the clean power that your motor or nonincandescent light needs, while still allowing you to turn it on and off with your lighting control board.

Besides filament hum, another reason that everyone wants to see a next-generation dimming solution is because everyone wants to get the dimmers out of the dimmer room. Think about it: If you could attach the dimmer directly to the lighting instrument (or even build it right inside it), then you would no longer have to have all that complicated cabling running from the dimmers up to the circuits. You could simply provide generic power outlets everywhere, plug the lights in wherever it was convenient, then use a control network (or better yet, a wireless connection) to control the dimmer right there at the light. Less copper wire, lower installation cost, more flexibility, everybody is happy.

Various attempts have been made over the years to design a dimmer that overcomes this noise problem, and there have been successes, most visibly with sine wave dimming,[6] a technology that reduces the height of the entire wave, rather than cutting it into little bits. Besides overcoming the noise, sine wave dimmers create less heat, extend lamp life, and adapt to different voltages while being lighter and more efficient. They will also improve your social life, increase your income, and make you famous.

Seriously, they are a vast improvement over SCRs and you can buy them right now, from several different lighting companies. The problem, as always, is cost. As of this writing, sine wave dimming is still going to separate you from a somewhat bigger pile of simoleons than SCRs, and for general theatrical usage, it is still a hard case to make. SCRs are, simply put, good enough for most people. Without a huge demand for something better, neither sine wave nor any other kind of dimming has found the kind of large-scale market that would make it cheap enough for theaters.

The main market for these superquiet dimmers continues to be concert halls and other acoustically sensitive spaces where the cost is justifiable.

---

[6] Sometimes called "pulse-width modulation" or PWM dimming. Some companies market a version known as IGBT, or "insulated gate bipolar transistor," which is similar.

The rest of us theater shlubs, with tears in our eyes, give a deep sigh and order another rack of SCRs to install in our dimmer rooms, where their noise and heat can be comfortably contained.

To Control Dimmers, You Need Control Consoles

Now that you have all those dimmers, you will need a way to control them. Typically, you don't want to sit next to the dimmers when you control them, especially since they are generally hidden in a room backstage. Furthermore, you want to be able to control a lot of them at once, sometimes in complicated ways. While you may occasionally see small, portable, all-in-one dimmer packs with the controller attached directly to the dimmers, most dimmer racks are controlled by a **lighting control console**, connected to the dimmer racks by a thin control cable. The control console sits in the lighting control booth, usually with a clear view of the stage, while the dimmers are tucked away backstage somewhere.

We're going to talk about the inner workings of control consoles in much more depth later on, but here is what you need to know right now.

The control console talks to the dimmers using a language—actually, it's called a protocol—known as DMX512 ("DMX five twelve" or simply "DMX"). When you set a level for your lights on the control console, the console translates those numbers into the DMX512 protocol and sends them over the control cable.

To Bring Power from the Dimmers, You Need Circuits

Throughout the theater, there are boxes with outlets where lighting instruments can be plugged in. These are the **circuits**. Each circuit may have one or more plugs. If two lights are plugged into the same circuit, then they will be given the same amount of power at all times.

Each circuit is connected to a dimmer in one of two ways: directly, or through a **patch panel**.

If your circuits are connected directly to your dimmers, then you are one of the lucky people who have "dimmer-per-circuit." Each and every circuit gets its own lovely dimmer. End of story, morning glory.

If you have more circuits than you have dimmers, then you have a **patch panel**, a place where circuits are physically connected to dimmers. There are several different styles, including the **phone patch**, so called because it looks like those old-style telephone switchboard panels, with a forest of cords connecting circuits to dimmers.

Each circuit is rated in amps, and the combination of all the things plugged into that circuit cannot exceed that amp rating. It actually doesn't matter how many lights you plug into one circuit. What matters is how much total amperage you are drawing from the circuit. That's why we need the math that I laid out in the section on power above. Whenever you are plugging lights into circuits, it is essential that you figure out how much amperage you are drawing and then compare that to the amperage rating on the circuit.

Multiple instruments can be plugged into a single circuit through **two-fer** or **three-fer** cables, which have a single male plug and multiple female plugs. Like circuits, cables are rated in amps, so make sure that you are not overloading it. Cable ratings tend to be lower than circuit ratings.

Circuit Protection

If a theatrical system is going to be overloaded, it is most likely to happen at the circuits. There are two ways to cause problems: an excess load or a short circuit.

An excess load means that you have too many things plugged into a circuit. You have not added up your loads correctly and you have tried to pull too many amps out of a circuit. For example, you might have a 20-amp circuit and you have tried to plug in four 750-watt lamps. Four 750-watt lamps give you 3000watts, which, using our "100-volt West Virginia law" above, gives us 30 amps. Sound the buzzer, Johnny, that's too much!

If an excess load is allowed to continue, the wires will heat up and eventually melt, possibly causing a fire. The solution: a circuit breaker. This electronic device senses the amount of power passing through a circuit, and if the power stays too high, the circuit breaker shuts the circuit down by "tripping," or shutting off. If your circuit breakers are tripping, check what you have plugged into the circuit. Do the math again and see if you are asking too much.

A short circuit means that the power is traveling from the power company to the load, but is somehow sidestepping around the load and trying to go back to the power company through an easier route. A short circuit is exactly what it sounds like: a circuit that is too short—that is, a circuit that is not going through a load, like a lightbulb or a toaster or a video monitor. Power is always trying to get to the "ground," the big piece of metal that is stuck into the earth somewhere under the building, and it's lazy, so it takes the fastest, shortest path to that ground, preferably one that doesn't involve going through a load. If a wire breaks loose inside a lighting instrument, for example, and comes into contact with the metal body of the instrument, this will cause a short circuit; the power flows into the metal body and whatever metal is connected to it, always looking for the ground. If your body is available as a path, the power will take it. With all the salty water in your body, it makes a marvelous conductor and electrons simply love it. If your hand is on the instrument when that short circuit happens, you become the easiest path to the ground and you are going to get a visit from the Wicked Witch of the Electrons. Not good.

Fortunately, when a short circuit happens, the circuit breaker detects the sudden increase in current as the electrons, freed from their job of driving a load, go wildly in search of the ground, like toddlers on an Easter Egg hunt. Sensing peril, the breaker shuts down the circuit and, if you are the electrons' route of choice, prevents you from being electrocuted. Thanks, circuit breaker!

Lighting Instruments

So, the power comes to the theater and enters the dimmers, which are controlled by the channels in the control console. Then it travels throughout the theater via the circuits, where it actually starts to do something interesting: turn on the lights.

If you want to seriously increase your cachet with the tech people, don't call them lights. To a theatrical technician, they are **lighting instruments**, or **instruments** or **fixtures** or **units**. If you point to a light and say, "Where is that unit pointed?" you will let the technician know that you can speak his language, or at least that you are willing to. Language is important.

First, let's talk about the two general categories of lights:

Conventionals versus Moving Lights

For many years, theatrical lights were attached to a pipe with a **C-clamp**, focused where the designer wanted them, and left there throughout the show. It was good enough for me when I was a kid; why isn't it good enough for you?

Because when I was a kid, lighting was a lot less interesting, that's why. As we are going to explore in the chapter 11, lighting took a huge step forward in the 1980s, when lighting instruments developed the ability to spin, zoom, and change color.

That doesn't mean, however, that the good old stationary lighting instrument is gone Far from it. With a good moving light costing anywhere from ten to twenty to *thirty* times more than a stationary light, there will be a market for these reliable, simple fixtures for a long time.

Theater techs call the nonmoving lights **conventionals**. There are a few cases where manufacturers have simply mounted a conventional instrument in a moving yoke, but that means it isn't conventional anymore. If it moves, it's a moving light.

Moving lights are part of the digital revolution in the theater, so we are going to describe them in more detail in their own chapter. Conventional lights have been around since the early twentieth century and are pretty darn analog, so we'll just take a quick look here.

There is a wide variety of conventional lights, but here are the ones that you need to be able to recognize to survive backstage.

Fresnels

Conventionals break down into two general categories: hard-edged and soft-edged, depending on the beam of light they put out.

By far the most common kind of soft-edged light is the Fresnel (pronounced "fruh-nell"), named after the distinctive ridged lens invented by Augustin Fresnel, a French physicist who spent his life developing a number of important optical formulas and preparing the way for the theory of relativity.[7] You can always tell a Fresnel from any other kind of instrument by rubbing your hand over the outside of the lens. A Fresnel lens will have ridges in it. Anything else will be smooth. Fresnel actually developed his namesake lens for lighthouses.

Besides its impressive pedigree and unusual lens, the Fresnel has a number of other positive features. It is a cheap way to get a lot of light onstage and its beam has a nice soft edge that blends with the light from other instruments. The Fresnel beam is also adjustable in size, from a large circle to a small one. Making the beam larger is called **flooding** it; making it smaller is called **spotting**. These adjustments are made by sliding the lamp closer to or farther away from the lens.

Fresnels are designated by the diameter of the lens. An eight-inch Fresnel has a lens that is eight inches wide.

Ellipsoidals

When you need to have good control over the shape of the light beam, perhaps so you can cut it sharply off a wall or add a leaf pattern to it, you need a hard-edged instrument, and the most popular one is the **ellipsoidal**.

Ellipsoidals are actually capable of being either hard- or soft-edged, and all things being equal, I would usually prefer to use them over the less-controllable Fresnels. All things are not equal, however, because the ellipsoidals, with their more complex optics, are considerably more expensive to own and rent than their soft-edged counterparts.

Not that an ellipsoidal is some kind of rocket science. An ellipsoidal reflector spotlight is so called because (are you sitting down?) it has a reflec-

---

[7] There is a street named after him just around the corner from the Eiffel Tower.

tor shaped like an ellipse. This style of reflector has the useful property of focusing the light more precisely, making it easier to manipulate. After the light leaves the reflector, a lens system collects it and sends it out the front in a well-controlled beam.

Besides the reflector and lenses, ellipsoidals also control light with **shutters**, little metal blades that push in from the side of the instrument and cut off part of the light beam. Using the shutters, you can give the beam a sharp edge that, for instance, follows the line of a drape, the bottom of a flat, or the edge of a podium. You can also slide in a **template** (or **pattern**, or **gobo**, short for "go-between"), a piece of metal with a design cut out of it which allows the instrument to act as a sort of shadow projector, projecting whatever shape is cut out of the metal. Templates are a great way to get creative with lighting. You can cut your own simple patterns out of pie plates, or you can select from the constantly growing selections offered by several different companies. Ask your dealer for a catalog. Remember, though: If you are going to use templates, you must have an ellipsoidal spotlight. Fresnels cannot handle templates because the beam of light is not sharp enough.

I mentioned earlier that an ellipsoidal is capable of being either hard- or soft-edged. This is possible because an ellipsoidal has all of its lenses mounted in a movable barrel that can slide back and forth. If you want to make your ellipsoidal fuzzier—that is, get rid of the sharp line—just run the barrel forward or backward until you like it. Likewise, if you are inserting a template and you want the image to sharpen up, run the barrel back the other way.

Ellipsoidals are referred to by two numbers: the diameter of the lens and the **focal length**. The focal length is the distance between the lamp and the center of the lens system, and the only thing you need to know is that the longer the focal length, the narrower the beam that comes out the front.

There is also a class of ellipsoidals called **zoom ellipsoidals**. These handy instruments have an adjustable focal length, so you can make fairly radical changes to the size of the beam without hanging a different instrument. Why not use them all the time and have more flexibility? There are two trade-offs: cost (predictably, zooms are more expensive) and amount of light. Zooms tend to be less bright than the fixed focal length units, because they waste some light inside the instrument.

PARs

Finally, there's the instrument that has changed the face of rock and roll the **PAR can**. Basically an automobile headlight mounted in a metal can, the PAR can (it's written in all caps because it's an abbreviation—parabolic anodized reflector) be bright, intense, and durable. It is not a subtle instrument. It cannot be focused, spotted, or given any kind of sharp edge. Even so, many theater and dance designers have been lured to it by the intensity of the beam. It makes great sunlight, among other things. As I said before, most rock-and-roll shows are packed with PAR cans.

Boring but Important Stuff

All lighting instruments should use theatrical cabling and plugs. Do not use household wiring to run theatrical instruments. Most household wiring uses **Edison plugs**. They are easy to plug in, commonly available, and cheap. They lack toughness, however, and cannot handle a huge amount of power, so they are limited to lower wattages, like toasters and televisions.

You will occasionally see Edison plugs on small theatrical lighting instruments, but if they are not rental equipment, they really should be changed to one of the other types of theatrical plugs below.[8]

Most theater applications use either **stage-pin plugs** (also called the three-pin plug) or **twist-lock** plugs. They are easy to tell apart: Stage-pin plugs are rectangular and twist-lock plugs are round.

Stage-pin plugs are tough, durable, and can handle lots of power. I highly recommend taping stage-pin connectors together with gaffer's tape. Do not use duct tape or masking tape—it will melt, and then you'll have gooey glop all over your pretty black plugs.

In my opinion, the best kind of plug is the **twist-lock plug**. These are durable, can handle large amounts of power, and best of all, they do what the title says: They twist and lock into place, so they will not come apart. No taping required.

One caution about twist-locks: They did not come onto the market with the same degree of standardization that Edison and stage-pin plugs did, so there are several different kinds of twist-lock out there. If you are renting or buying instruments to use along with your existing equipment, make sure the plugs match. You may have to take one of your plugs down to the supply company to be certain. It is easy to get cynical about these kinds of compatibility problems until you realize how amazing it is that all the electrical outlets in all our different houses fit all the electrical plugs on the ends of all the different clock radios that are sold all over the country. Now that is something to be happy about. I can deal with the occasional odd twist-lock.

---

[8] Small equipment that is designed for film and TV use sometimes has Edison plugs. This is because film and TV crews are sometimes working in homes or offices and they need to plug into the wall. This is a special case, however, and I still recommend that all theatrical lighting gear use one of the two major types of theatrical plugs.

One final note about plugs and outlets: The end of the cable where the prongs of the plug stick out is called the male end. The end that has the holes that the prongs stick into is called the female end. The male prong goes into the female slot. That is what they are called—I did not invent it and I do not want to get any letters about it.

Regardless of what kind of plug you use, it is important to use appropriate cable. Theatrical cable should be extra-hard-duty SO-type cable that you buy from a theatrical dealer or wholesaler. Anything less is asking for trouble, and by trouble I mean failures, short circuits and fires.

CHAPTER 8

Why Lighting Went Digital

Some people say that it started with Tharon Musser, but even she knows that she was just another mile marker on the highway to the future. It was a big mile marker, though.

The year was 1975 and Tharon Musser was already an experienced, well-known lighting designer. She had won a Tony three years earlier for *Follies,* and at the age of fifty, she was already being called the Dean of American Lighting Designers.

She was, therefore, a good person to take a risk with. A big risk.

A Chorus Line was a show about Broadway dancers, known as gypsies. It tried to crawl inside the tender, complicated psyches of people who brutalize their bodies for difficult, frustrating, painful, and occasionally, mind-blowingly euphoric careers as chorus line dancers.

Based on a series of workshops with actual Broadway gypsies, the show presented the emotional roller coaster of a dance audition and, by extension, a dancer's life. It sought to portray, among other things, the internal monologue that dancers experience as they encourage, berate, and reassure themselves during the audition, while simultaneously trying to learn a new dance routine.

The sudden changes, from a full-blown dance audition with dozens of people hoofing across the floor, to private moments of personal revelation, are shaped by constant movement in the lighting, which required a dizzying number of cues.

Musser wanted to be able to pick out individual dancers on a stage of whirling bodies, giving the audience a chance to hear their inner thoughts: "I hope I get it." "God, I really blew it!" "I really need this show . . ."

That wasn't all she wanted. This was the age of disco, and dance floors were fast becoming whirligigs of spinning lights. The audience's visual sense was changing, and that had to be reflected in the look of the show. At times, the entire stage was divided up into blocks of brilliant color, putting each of the nineteen dancers in a personal shaft of saturated light.

For the finale, the dancers, now dressed in magical, glittering costumes, kick-stepped their way across the stage and into their dream of Broadway stardom.

And here was the really tough part. There was almost no scenery, just a wall of mirrors upstage that did little more than reflect the black floor of the audition hall and the line of desperate dancers. The stage picture was created almost entirely with lighting. Often, there was nothing *but* lighting.

To really appreciate the challenge, you have to understand what standard Broadway lighting was like at the time. The old Broadway theaters still operated with what were known as "piano boxes," rolling racks of resistance dimmers that were approximately the size and shape of upright pianos. The boxes had big Frankenstein-style levers that faded the dimmers up and down, and the only kind of "automation" available was to lock the handles together, which allowed you to dim all the lights at once. Most Broadway shows had three electricians, each of whom operated two piano boxes.

Clearly, this kind of arrangement wasn't going to work with the complicated cueing of *A Chorus Line*.

Looking for a new technology that would allow Musser the kind of flexibility and increased capacity that she needed, the producers turned to a company called Electronics Diversified in Portland, Oregon, who sold them a new board called the LS-8. What the good folks at ED didn't tell the producers is that the company hadn't really built it yet. They had bought a prototype lighting controller from a college technical director from Greensboro, North Carolina, but they hadn't made it into a new product yet. Without a product of their own to ship, ED had to send the prototype, along with the guy what built it, off to the Shubert Theatre in New York. And that's how Gordon Pearlman became a hero to TDs everywhere and Broadway got its first computerized lighting control console.

One of my early computer teachers got it exactly right when he said, "A computer is never going to make your life easier or save you time. It just lets you do more things." So it was with *Chorus Line* and so it is with all stage lighting. The producers initially dreamed that computerized lighting would save them buckets of money because they wouldn't have to pay three electricians to run the show. In the end, however, computerized lighting opened up so many possibilities for lighting design that the producers ended up spending all those savings on more lights and the labor to install and maintain them.

Lighting went digital because it allowed designers to do more things, to find ever more interesting and complex ways to tell stories through light. It also created an explosion of new products, all of which expanded the possibilities of lighting. In this section, we are going to look at how the digital revolution created massive change in the industry by doing four things:

- It allowed designers to create large numbers of complex cues through **computerized control.**
- It allowed designers to expand their visual palette and create new kinds of visual imagery through **moving lights.**
- It allowed engineers to create more efficient, longer-lasting instruments that converge lighting and video with **LED lighting instruments.**
- It allowed system designers to create new products that were universally compatible through **DMX.**

Although it isn't as sexy as those massive control boards or magic LED instruments, the DMX control protocol is so central to lighting these days that we are actually going to cover it first. Once we have the horse before the cart, we'll look at the consoles and the oh-so-sexy (and yet oh-so-practical) LEDs.

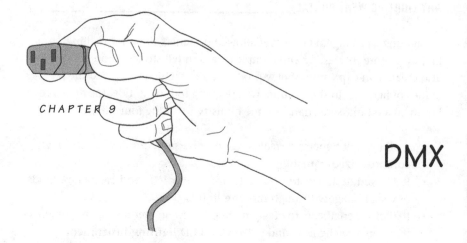

CHAPTER 9

DMX

Back in the early 1980s, a whole host of companies were designing and manufacturing stage lighting control consoles and dimmers, and all of them faced the same challenge: how to send reliable information from the control consoles, typically placed in a control room with a view of the stage, to the dimmers, which were stashed backstage. The problem was, all of those companies did it differently. The most common approach was a constant, low-voltage signal put out by the controller. As the operator moved the slider up, the voltage would increase. The dimmer would respond accordingly, going up and down as the control voltage went up and down. Even this simple approach, however, was handled differently by different companies. Strand's voltage went from 0 to +10 volts, for example, while Kliegl went the other way, from 0 to -10 volts. There was a booming business in adaptors that allowed one brand of console to talk to a different brand of dimmers, and a lot of grumpy customers who wondered, "Why can't they all just get along?"

Around this time, the world of electronics had been badly bruised by several high-profile disputes over formats, including the VHS versus Beta debate in video and a war over computer operating systems, so the time was ripe for some respected voices in the theater industry to suggest an industry-wide standard for control signals. Some companies were worried about giving up market share if their proprietary standards were thrown out, but in the end, the dominant stage lighting companies realized what audio, video, computer, and other equipment manufacturers have realized throughout the history of technology: *Standardization is good.* Having common standards allows for new products that would never see the light of day if everyone had to develop complete proprietary systems. Customers are a lot happier because they don't have to buy all their gear in one place. Everybody wins.

The result was the adoption, in 1986, of **DMX512**, a standard protocol for control of lighting equipment. In the beginning, **DMX**, as it is generally known backstage, was only envisioned for control consoles sending information to dimmers. For this reason, it is unidirectional—that is, information only travels one way on a DMX line. Control consoles can talk to dimmers, but the dimmers can't talk back. This was primarily a cost-saving decision, as it meant that users would only need a computer brain on one end of the line, the controller end. Dimmers could be "stupid"—that is, they didn't think about the information they were sent, they just did what they were told. Later on, as the cost of computer chips came down, system designers began to long for two-way communication, but more about that in a minute.

DMX is a way of sending out 512 channels of information at once. Each one of those channels carries a single piece of information, a number from 0 to 100.[1] Each of the devices on the network listens to a single channel of information and does whatever that channel tells it to do. In the case of a dimmer, it sets its own level based on the number it sees on its assigned DMX channel.

What Is Digital Multiplexing?

DMX stands for digital multiplexing. The protocol is digital because it sends numbers (digits) down the wire, instead of the continually shifting voltages of the analog world. Digital information is much more robust than analog, which means it doesn't get messed up as easily when it travels over cables. Multiplexing means that a single piece of wire is used to send multiple streams of information. Multiplexing is a very common technology—you use it every time you pick up the telephone.

When you pick up the phone in London to talk to your spouse in Minneapolis, your conversation is carried over a single piece of wire that stretches across the ocean (or gets turned into a radio signal and bounced off a satellite). You do not, however, get sole usage of this piece of wire. If this were the case, we would need thousands, if not millions, of wires stretching across the Atlantic Ocean to allow all the people there to talk to all the people here, all at once. What is really happening

---

[1] In fact, DMX sends a number from 0 to 255, but modern lighting controllers translate that 0–255 scale into the 0–100 scale that we are used to. For example, if you enter 50 percent into the controller, it will translate that into the 0–255 scale and send the number 127 over the DMX network. If you are dealing with automated lights, the manual will often list both numbers, the 0–100 "level" and the 0–256 "value." Unless your controller is specifically designed for automated lights, use the 0–100 "level."

is that you are sharing the wire with other conversations. The computer operating the phone line sends a fraction of a second of your conversation over the phone, then switches you off and turns on the next conversation for a fraction of a second, then switches that one off and turns the next one on, and so forth. When you are standing in London, talking to Minneapolis, you are actually not connected all the time. Although you can't hear it, your conversation is actually being turned on and off very quickly to allow other people to use the same piece of wire for their conversation. No one is aware of the line-sharing because the switching happens very quickly, thousands of times a second. This phenomenon is called multiplexing.

In the case of DMX, multiplexing allows hundreds of sliders on a lighting controller to talk to hundreds of dimmers, all at once, because all those connections are multiplexed. Without multiplexing, you would have to run an individual wire from each slider to each dimmer, and that's a lot of copper.

Plugging It In

DMX was designed to be daisy-chained. In other words, you run a cable out the back of the control board to the closest thing you want to control, then you run a cable from that unit to the next one, and so on. DMX-compatible devices will have a plug marked DMX IN and a second one marked DMX OUT or, in some cases, DMX THRU. All DMX cables should go from an OUT (or THRU) plug to an IN plug. The DMX standard supports up to thirty-two different devices in one chain. (A rack of dimmers counts as one device, regardless of how many dimmers it contains.) The last device on the line gets a "terminator" in its OUT plug. This specially designed DMX plug contains a small resistor that shuts off the signal at the end of the line. If your DMX network is behaving erratically, it might be because it isn't terminated. Some types of lighting equipment are internally terminated, which means that you don't need the terminator if that device is at the end of the line. Check the directions.

If you do need to split a DMX cable into two cables for some reason, it is possible. You cannot, however, just make up a DMX two-fer cable like you can with power cables for lighting instruments. You need an appropriately named **DMX splitter**, which is a small box of electronics with one DMX IN and two or more DMX OUTs. This is convenient if, for example, one part of your DMX universe is in the auditorium and one is backstage and you don't want to have to daisy-chain it all. Splitters are also necessary if you want to put more than thirty-two devices in one DMX universe.

While we're on the subject of cables, DMX uses two different kinds, or at least it used to. Let me explain.

The DMX protocol only requires three wires, two that carry data and one ground wire, but the original designers decreed that it would use plugs and cables with five wires. The purpose of this was twofold: First, they figured that someday, people were going to want a two-way flow of information, so they put in two extra cables for that; second, having a five-wire plug would keep people from using standard microphone cables, which are not designed for the higher signal voltages of DMX.

Furthermore, using five-wire plugs would keep someone from accidentally plugging a DMX signal into an audio line, which might be damaged by DMX's higher signal level.

Nevertheless, some manufacturers have included DMX plugs on their gear with only three wires, on the theory that, since we are only using three wires, we should only plug in three wires. This also allows the use of standard audio cable for our DMX systems. You can even buy an adaptor that will allow you to plug in a three-wire cable into a five-wire DMX plug. Many people have taken this as an invitation to use three-wire microphone cable to run DMX signals.

I don't recommend this.

It might work for a while, or it might work for a few units, but someday, my friends, there will be trouble. A higher signal strength requires a tougher cable. Invest in real DMX cable and use the five-wire plugs. You will have a much more reliable system in the end.

When the DMX protocol was recently updated,[2] the authors of the standard formally decreed that all DMX plugs shall have five pins and this time we really mean it.

Choosing Channels

DMX puts out information on a number of different channels—512 of them, in fact. This works just like your television set, where you use the channel selector to decide which channel to watch. For a DMX device, you have to tell it which one of the 512 channels to watch for its information. This is usually done either by punching in numbers on a small keyboard or by setting tiny switches, known as DIP switches, on the device. For units that require more than one channel, you will set the **starting channel** on the device. For example, let's say you are plugging in several dimmer packs on a DMX line and each pack has twelve dimmers. The first pack would be set to channel 1 as its starting channel and use DMX channels 1 to 12. The second pack would

---

[2] It is now formally called DMX512A and has been accepted by ANSI, the national nonprofit organization that oversees standards in the United States.

be set to channel 13, so it would use 13 to 24 for its dimmers. The third pack would be set to 25, and so on. For any device that uses multiple channels, the starting channel is the *lowest* channel number that it will use.

DMX Beyond 512 Channels

When the designers of DMX were deciding how many channels to support on their line, they picked a number that was both electronically convenient and high enough to handle an enormous dimmer rack: 512. Hence, the name DMX512. Once the standard was in place, however, equipment designers realized that it was useful for lots of different things that needed to talk to a controller, including smoke machines, special effects, and most significantly, the rapidly proliferating automated lights. All these different technologies started eating up DMX channels like a golden retriever going through a bag of liver treats.

Automated lights were the prime offender. These complex machines need a lot of information to be happy. Besides the intensity of the light, they may also want to know color, direction, shutters, zoom, and focus, as well as information about other mechanical devices and preprogrammed effects. A sophisticated instrument might need as many as forty different channels of information. Install a dozen of these data hoggers and 512 doesn't look like such a big number anymore.

The solution was to run more than one set of 512 channels, or more than one **universe**. A high-quality lighting controller may have the capability of running two, three, even four different universes of 512 channels. Generally, a lighting technician will assign these universes in some kind of logical way: universe A for the dimmers, universe B for the automated lights out front, universe C for the ones over the stage, universe D for special effects, for example. Each universe requires its own cable, so the back of the lighting control console will have one DMX OUT plug for each universe.

The Limits of DMX

DMX is unidirectional, meaning that information only flows one way, from the controller to the controlled device. Again, this limitation seemed fine in 1990, when system designers were primarily concerned with getting a slider to control a dimmer, but seems impossibly shortsighted in the plugged-in twenty-first century. The controller can talk to the instrument, but the instrument can't talk back? How will I know when the lamp has burnt out? How can the instrument confirm where it is pointed? How do I know that a smoke machine is at the right temperature or out of fluid? These are the things that keep engineers up at night.

And it gets worse. Besides having one-way communication, DMX also provides no error checking which means that, unlike the Internet connection you use to surf the web, there is no mechanism to make sure that the information that is sent is the same information that was received. (Unfortunately, there is still is no way to confirm that the information on the Internet is actually true.) Again, for its original use, this was not a problem. DMX sends information continuously, even if it hasn't changed. If an incorrect dimmer setting is sent, it isn't a big deal—there will be a new setting sent a fraction of a second later that will wipe out the mistake before anybody sees what happens.

The lack of error correction, however, is a larger issue where "momentary" commands are being sent. In this case, the command causes something to happen that cannot be undone. Let's say, for example, that you have a pyrotechnic effect that is loaded up and ready to go. If you used DMX to control the effect, you would run the risk of sending a false message to "fire!" In this case, the incorrect message would not be saved by a correction that arrived later. Once the powder is lit, that charge is going to explode.

This is one reason why *DMX is never used in any application where life safety is an issue.* Stage machinery and pyrotechnics, for example, should never use DMX to communicate, as an incorrect transmission could create an accident.

Saddled with one-way communication and no error correction, DMX has stayed inside the world of lighting, with a few forays into special effects. Modern smoke and fog machines, for example, will generally have a DMX port, allowing them to be operated from your lighting control desk.

With these limitations, why have people stuck with DMX for so long? Well, one reason is, the industry has had trouble getting an agreement on a replacement standard, but another reason is that DMX just *works.* Throughout the world, if you connect two pieces of DMX equipment, the odds are really good that they are going to work correctly, and continue to do so. In the language of engineers, DMX is robust, meaning that it can take a lot of physical and electrical abuse and still keep working. Although I wouldn't recommend it, a DMX cable can be stepped on a lot harder than an Ethernet cable and still keep working. Again, I don't advise you to do it deliberately, but you can run DMX cable around all kinds of electrical equipment (microwaves, refrigerators, fluorescent lights, etc.) and it will generally stay connected and working. You can also run a DMX cable about three times farther than an Ethernet cable. For these reasons, expect to see DMX equipment for a long time.

There have been various efforts over the years to produce a DMX standard that employs two-way communication, most notably with a standard called remote device management, or, with our slavish insistence on three-letter acronyms, RDM.

RDM was designed so that it would work over existing DMX networks, as long as the devices involved were RDM compatible. As of this writing, it has yet to gain a wide following, mostly because only the most sophisticated systems really need to send information both ways on a DMX network. Of course, adding RDM functionality to any device means more hardware, more programming, more testing, so, naturally, more cost. So far, the vast majority of the live entertainment industry hasn't been willing to pay for it.

Interestingly, despite the fact that the original DMX specification included an extra pair of wires to carry return communication, RDM actually works on the same pair of wires as the rest of the DMX signal, meaning that those other two wires are *still* not doing anything.

DMX Over Ethernet

While overcoming the limitation of one-way communication has not been a major priority for the industry, overcoming the limitation of 512 channels most certainly has. Using several different universes can help you gain more channels, but that means a lot of DMX cable, which is not cheap, strung all over the theater, not to mention other pricey bits of gear, like DMX splitters. To make life even more complicated, a sophisticated system might have several different controllers that are all "talking" at once to various devices. One lighting controller might be running dimmers while another is handling automated lights, both of which need to send signals to a video controller, fog machines, and a lightning machine. That's a lot of connections and a lot of headaches.

There have been a number of schemes developed to bring all this gear together on an Ethernet network, the same thing that brings your Internet signal to your computer. Ethernet can handle about forty times as much data as DMX, which means you can send all those DMX universes on one cable. Plus, the computer network industry is a lot larger than the theatrical lighting network, so all the equipment that Ethernet networks need—routers, switches, cable, plugs, etc.—are much cheaper and more easily available than DMX gear. If you are doing a permanent installation, building contractors are quite familiar with Ethernet networks and the "Category 5" wiring (known to the geeks as "Cat-5") that it uses. Ethernet also has a number of tricks built in to overcome physical obstacles, like wireless broadcasting and the ability to send signals over standard phone lines. Finally, the truly geeky among us love the idea of being able to control a lighting system remotely. Putting your lighting controller on an Ethernet network means that you can, in theory, control it from anywhere in the world.

In order to broadcast your DMX signals over an Ethernet network, you need to use one of several network protocols that are designed for sending lighting information. The three best known ones are the following:

- ACN, which was developed by a nonprofit industry group[3]
- ETC-Net, a proprietary system created by the ETC lighting company
- Artnet, which was created by Artistic License and then put into the public domain

Hang on, you say, I thought that DMX was a protocol! And isn't Ethernet a protocol? Why do we need another protocol?

Actually, there are many levels of protocol in any communication system. In order to allow communication between computers on the Internet, for example, the networks use the TCP/IP protocol, which travels over Ethernet cables when it reaches your home or office.

When the control information leaves your control console, it is organized into the DMX protocol. In order to keep the information properly organized when it hits the Ethernet network, however, it has to be reorganized into one of the three protocols listed above. This is because Ethernet doesn't really understand or care about your lighting information. Think of the Ethernet as the road your car drives on. There are rules that govern the layout of roads, but you also need traffic laws to control the cars that drive on those roads. DMX info is the car, Ethernet is the road, and the network protocols are the traffic laws.

Using this analogy, you can see why you can't use more than one of these protocols on your network. That would be a bit like using traffic laws from the U.K. and the United States on the same roads. Considering the fact that cars drive on opposite sides of the road in these two countries, disaster would ensue. The same is true of lighting control networks. Your network will be ACN or ETC-Net or Artnet, but only one of them.

With these competing standards rolling around, there is a lively debate among theatrical technicians about how best to put DMX information on Ethernet networks, or whether to do it at all. If you are thinking about setting up a network in your theater, you will need a qualified theatrical network person to help you design it.

In general terms, however, the scheme usually works like this: One or more lighting controllers puts out one or more universes of DMX through standard DMX cables. Those cables go into a DMX-Ethernet converter, which gathers all the DMX signals, converts them to one of the network standards,

---

[3] The Entertainment Services and Technology Association, or ESTA. www.esta.org.

and outputs them on a single Cat-5 cable, which goes to a central network server. The server then sends that information out on network cables that fan out all over the theater. At the end of each of those cables is a converter that changes the network data back to DMX. From there, a DMX cable goes to the device that needs to be controlled. That way, the long run from the controller to the device is over a single, cheap, fast Ethernet cable, and it only converts to the expensive DMX at either end.

In some cases, the signal can actually travel over Ethernet for the entire trip without being converted to DMX. Very sophisticated lighting controllers and lighting instruments sometimes have an Ethernet plug built right into the back. These devices can interpret data from one of the network protocols directly. This is particularly true for things like video walls that require massive amounts of channels and information that will quickly swamp the 512 channels of a DMX network.

So, do you want to put your lighting data on an Ethernet network? For small- to medium-sized, straightforward installations, the answer is no. Considering the robustness and plug-and-playability of DMX, you don't need anything fancier. Yes, it would be cool to control your lighting console from a sidewalk cafe two states away, but, dude, seriously, you and me and six other nerds at LightingGeeks.net are the only people who really think so.

For large, complicated systems, particularly those with multiple controllers, the answer is an absolute, unqualified maybe. It will depend on many issues that are specific to your installation, like the brand and type of your equipment, the particular needs of your facility, and the skill of your operators.

DMX from Your PC

It doesn't take any complicated network protocols to run your DMX system directly from your computer. Your PC is quite capable of replacing a dedicated, stand-alone lighting controller. The lighting controller is essentially a computer, after all. The only thing your lighting controller has that your PC doesn't is a port that outputs DMX data. This problem is quickly solved, however, by adding a **DMX dongle** to the USB port on your computer. This allows you to run a DMX cable from your laptop to a dimmer rack, moving lights, or any other DMX device. See the lighting control chapter for information on turning your computer into a lighting control console.

> Google me
> DMX lighting dongle

DMX Fail Mode

DMX is pretty robust, but no network is perfect, and a DMX network can fail. This might happen if a cable is broken, a plug gets pulled out, a device in the DMX chain goes down and fails to pass the signal through, or in the case of wireless signals, some kind of interference gets in the way. Some DMX devices will allow you to set what happens if the DMX signal fails. Choices include the following:

- **Fade to Black:** The light goes to a value of zero. Useful for a special effect light that you really don't want to stay on.
- **Hold Last State:** The device stays at whatever value it last received. This is usually good, unless the DMX fails right in the middle of a fade, which might leave you with some weird looks on stage.
- **Fade to Memory:** Some devices allow you to set up a set of levels (a cue, basically) that will happen if DMX ever fails. This is usually a general light cue, which makes things look half-decent and keeps enough light on for safety.
- **Fade to Sequence:** Some devices will let you fade to a sequence of cues if the DMX signal fails. This is useful if you want things to turn on or shut down in some order.

Wireless DMX

It is possible to run DMX without any wires at all. In this case, the one-way nature of DMX is an advantage, along with the relatively low amount of data and the fact that the data is sent continuously.

Wireless DMX is a nice thing to have if you have a large performance venue, if you are outside, or if your lights are on a moving platform, like a parade float or a scenery wagon. If you've got lights way up on top of a building, it's really nice if you can avoid running a DMX cable all the way up there. If your lights are on a parade float, you can't really have it dragging a control cable down the street.

To use wireless DMX, you need a transmitter and a receiver. After connecting the control console DMX OUT to the transmitter's DMX IN, power up the transmitter and follow the setup instructions from the manual. You run the DMX cable out of the controller and into the transmitter. Once you have set up the transmitter and the receiver to talk to each other (not difficult–read the instructions), the signal will travel wirelessly up to the receiver. Put the receiver close to the dimmer or the moving lights (whatever you are controlling), then run a DMX cable out of the receiver and into the devices, daisy-chaining them just as you normally would.

If your transmitter and receiver are set up correctly, you should be able to make changes on the console and see them happen at the devices.

These days, quite a few automated lights offer wireless DMX as an option. If you go this route, you don't need a separate receiver—it is installed in the lighting instrument itself. All you do is tell the light the name of the transmitter, tell it a DMX starting channel, and you're off! Make sure you pay attention to the broadcast range that is listed in the manual. Also remember that, as with all wireless devices, there may be interference from radio networks, microwave radiation, or other bits of stray energy, so test the network well before showtime. These days, the more sophisticated wireless DMX systems, like wireless microphone systems, use frequency-hopping technology that allows the system to continually search for the clearest frequencies and automatically switch to them.

Want to see how that works? Try this example:

Putting It to Work

Wireless DMX is a great way to control a lighting element when you can't (or just don't want to) run a cable to it. Try this example:

Let's say you have a scenery wagon with an office set. On the set is a desk; on the desk is a lamp. You want to be able to control this lamp, but, because you have multiple scenic wagons rolling around backstage, you would like to avoid having cable running everywhere. Solution: a battery-powered light with wireless DMX.

To do this, you need the following:

1. DMX-compatible lighting control board, which virtually all of them are
2. DMX wireless transmitter
3. Battery-powered DMX wireless receiver
4. Battery-powered, DMX-compatible dimmer
5. Low-voltage lamp
6. DMX cables (two)
7. Rechargeable battery, anywhere between 9 volts and 24 volts

One of the more popular wireless DMX systems at the moment is the SHoW DMX system made by City Theatrical (CTI). There are other manufacturers as well. Talk to your theatrical equipment retailer.

In a wireless system, the DMX data flows from the console DMX OUT to the transmitter's DMX IN, then through the air to the DMX receiver. Then, it comes out of the DMX OUT and travels to the dimmer's DMX IN.

The transmitter can be plugged into the wall, but the receiver is riding around on that wagon with no cords, so it will have to be powered by a battery. The nice thing about CTI's gear is that it doesn't care what voltage the battery is, as long as it is between 9 and 24 volts. CTI also makes batteries, if you are into one-stop shopping.

Choose a location for the receiver that is within range of the transmitter (check the manual for range information). Try to ensure that you don't have radio barriers between the transmitter and receiver. Radio barriers include metal, water, and some types of glass.

Connect the receiver by running a DMX cable from the receiver's DMX OUT to the dimmer's DMX IN. If the dimmer has a setting for "Internal Termination," turn it on. Otherwise, place a DMX terminator in the DMX OUT plug.

Hook up the battery to the receiver and the DMX dimmer with low-voltage cable. *Make sure that you have wire that is adequately sized for the power requirements of your dimmer.* Also, pay close attention to which cable is coming from the "+" side of the battery and which one is coming from the "−" side. It matters! Take a good look at the manual for both the receiver and the dimmer before you plug them in. This is DC power, not AC, so it only flows in one direction. If you plug the cable into the wrong side, you risk damaging your equipment. Read the manual and follow the instructions carefully.

Once everything is plugged, power up the transmitter and the receiver and configure them to talk to one another, following the instructions in the manual. Once you have a successful connection between the transmitter and receiver, set a DMX address on the dimmer. Make sure you have green lights on all the devices and then try adjusting the level of the DMX address at the control console. If all your configurations are correct, the lamp should respond. If it doesn't, go back and check that your settings are correct on all three devices. Also check that your battery is charged.

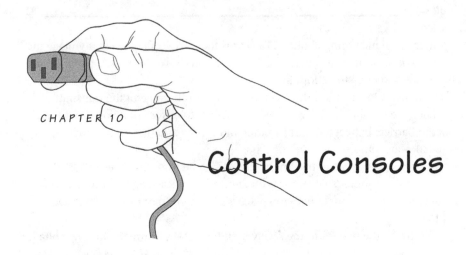

CHAPTER 10

Control Consoles

It is my personal belief that the designers of programmable lighting consoles are great fans of *Star Trek*. Every time I look at them, they seem to be more like the desk where Ensign Sulu sat while driving the starship *Enterprise* where no television show had gone before. Just as the design of the *Star Trek* communicators influenced today's flip phones, the consoles on the *Enterprise*'s bridge are reflected today in the sleek, futuristic style of lighting control boards. So sit down, slide your hands over that array of sliders, wheels, and buttons, and prepare for the creation of lighting magic at warp speed.

Before we talk about the hardware, let me cover one important concept in lighting control software.

The Channel

Lighting control boards do not control dimmers or lights or fog machines or any kind of physical equipment. They control **channels**.

The channel is the fundamental building block of lighting control. When creating a light plot, a designer will create a list of channels that is logically ordered in whatever scheme makes sense to him or her. For example, a portion of that list of channels might look like this:

Channel	Purpose
10	Low Pink Side Light
11	Low Blue Side Light
12	High Amber Side Light
13	High Blue Side Light
14	Amber Backlight

That list of channels only exists inside the brain of the designer and, after he enters it into the console, the brain of the console.

The actual dimmers that are controlling the lights on this list might have an entirely different set of numbers. Each dimmer in the dimmer is given a DMX address, which operates just like a post office address. When a dimmer level comes over the DMX network with that dimmer's address on it, that dimmer takes note and responds. To continue the above example, the list of DMX dimmer addresses might look like this:

DMX Address Purpose

21	Low Pink Side
25	High Blue Side
31	Low Pink Side
32	High Amber Side
43	Amber Backlight
46	Low Blue Side
47	High Amber Side
55	Amber Backlight
60	High Blue Side
74	Low Pink Side
89	Low Pink Side
90	High Blue Side
94	Low Blue Side
103	High Amber Side
127	Amber Backlight
128	Amber Backlight
141	High Blue Side

Much harder to remember.

For this reason, a modern control board allows you to **soft-patch** the list of channels to the list of DMX addresses. Using the soft patch function, you can assign specific DMX addresses to each channel and turn the above list into something like this:

Channel	Purpose	DMX Addresses
10	Low Pink Side	21, 31, 74, 89
11	Low Blue Side	46, 94
12	High Amber Side	32, 47, 103
13	High Blue Side	25, 60, 90, 141
14	Amber Backlight	43, 55, 127, 128

Much easier to remember.

Once you soft-patch the DMX addresses to the channels, the DMX addresses become invisible to the user, and all you have to worry about are the channels, which can be numbered and arranged however you want.

Just to create some confusion, the DMX address is sometimes called the **DMX channel**, but this should not be confused with the control channel inside the console.

DMX addresses are not only used for dimmers; they are used for any device that is being controlled by DMX, whether it is an automated light or a fog machine or a color scroller. All these devices must be assigned a DMX address, so that they can receive the information that is intended for them.

As I said in the DMX chapter, a group of 512 DMX addresses (or channels) is called a **DMX universe**, and some higher-end boards can control more than one universe. In order to do this, however, they need to have a separate DMX OUT plug for each universe.

In a simple setup with a single dimmer rack, the DMX address of the dimmer is the same as the dimmer number. With multiple racks, however, things get a bit more complicated. On a typical Broadway show, it is not uncommon to see at least six dimmer racks of ninety-six dimmers each. You can see that a single universe of 512 addresses won't be able to handle this. A large-scale show might use dozens of universes. The *Spider-Man* show on Broadway uses more than forty of them. Yikes.

Remember, however, that all these universes become invisible as soon as the soft patch is implemented. A designer may ask to see channel 238, but unbeknownst to him, the control console may be bringing up handfuls of dimmers in several different universes. The soft patch makes all those headaches go away.

The Back of the Board

Control boards are connected to dimmers (and everything else they control) in one of two ways: a direct, proprietary connection or DMX-512.

Direct connection is very rare these days, and you will really only see it in older systems. In these systems, there is a control cable that runs from the control board directly to the dimmer racks and is using some kind of proprietary control standard. Ever since DMX came into the theater in the early 1990s, virtually all manufacturers have adopted it, making these older proprietary systems happily obsolete. I only mention it because you may have inherited one. My advice: Throw that sucker out, have yourself a bake sale, and buy a new board and new dimmers with DMX control.

On the back of your DMX-compatible control console, there will be at least two DMX plugs: DMX IN and DMX OUT. If your board supports multiple universes, then there will be a DMX OUT plug for each universe, labeled universe A, universe B, and so forth. There may be both three- and five-pin DMX plugs. Use the five-pin ones.

If your board supports an external monitor, there will be a PC-style video outlet that accepts an RGB plug for a video monitor. Lighting control boards use standard PC monitors, just like your desktop computer. Some boards support multiple monitors, allowing you to see more information at once, which is quite useful. The *really* cool ones have touch screens. Nice . . .

Many control boards have a USB port which can be used to connect to a computer or an external drive. This is useful for updating system software as well as backing up your data.

There may also be a plug for a MIDI cable, which is used to send and receive show control messages from other equipment. More about that in part 4.

Some high-end boards will have an input and/or output for time code, which allows the console to track a time code stream from another computer. If there is an output, then your control console can generate time code as well, allowing other machines to follow it. Again, see part 4 for more info.

As I mentioned in the DMX chapter, lighting system designers will sometimes elect to send data over Ethernet. A few high-end lighting control boards actually have an Ethernet plug built right into the board, allowing you to put the control board directly onto the Ethernet network.

Finally, there may be inputs for a keyboard and a mouse as well as a printer port.

Backing It Up

It was one thirty in the morning at a large university theater and we were just finishing a long, difficult, but ultimately rewarding lighting rehearsal for an upcoming opera. The director and the designer had spent the evening in tense conflict as long-standing visual concepts, worked out long ago over endless coffee and beer and scotch and coffee again, were tossed out in a fever of new creation. The visuals that had worked in the renderings didn't work in reality. Cues were created, debated, thrown out, and redone. In the middle of the struggle, the frustrated director actually picked up the headset and talked directly to the operator, cutting the designer out of the conversation.

Enraged, the designer had shut down the headsets and pulled the director out to the hallway for a nose-to-nose debate. The department chair had been called. Lines were drawn in the sand, wiped out, then drawn again.

Now, with the battle over and their weapons sheathed, the director and designer stood in the aisle, joking about their misunderstandings and generally making up.

The stage manager had been up since 5:00 AM and, despite her carefully constructed facade of unflappability, had struggled to maintain calm through the last hour of rehearsal. Now that the end was in sight, she was ticking off her to-do list and calculating how many hours of sleep she could afford and still get the call sheet typed. The lighting design assistant was rolling up drawings and stashing paperwork in three-ring binders, swimming in that euphoric exhaustion that comes with a victory after a long campaign. He glanced over at the director and designer, so recently at each other's throats, now smiling and laughing as the debris of the rehearsal was cleared away around them. The assistant stage manager cleared the empty water bottles off the tech table and exchanged a roll of the eyes with the lighting assistant. Thank God *that's* over.

Meanwhile, up in the light booth, a young first-time light board operator was saving the contents of the control board memory onto an external disk. Or, at least, that was the idea.

When something really bad happens in the theater, even if it happens very quietly, there is almost a telepathic shiver that goes through the staff, as everyone suddenly becomes aware that something, somewhere is really, really wrong. And it usually starts when the paging light on the intercom turns on.

"Um, James?" said the control board operator to the lighting assistant, over the headset. "What does it mean when the screen says 'Show Not Found'?"

Turns out that this particular control board had a screen that let the operator choose between "Load from Disk" and "Load to Disk." If you were trying to save a show from the board's memory to the external disk, you would choose "Load to Disk." If you chose "Load from Disk," then the contents of the external disk would be loaded on top of your current show, erasing it.

Goodbye, show.

I just want to make it clear that I was not the operator.

In any case, at one thirty in the morning, after a twelve-hour lighting rehearsal, with one wrong keystroke, the entire night's work was gone. History. Puff of smoke. And while the light board's memory might have been erased, the light board operator's memory will never delete that moment.

These days, it's a bit harder to lose an entire show like that. Interface design has come a long way, for one thing, and most control boards allow you to save multiple shows, so loading a new one does not always delete the old one. Some boards also have an "autosave" function that keeps track of things as you go, giving you something to fall back on in case of a catastrophic failure.

Nevertheless, a good backup strategy is an essential part of computerized lighting control. Whenever you use a computerized board, make sure you know what your backup strategy is, and then use it religiously. Do a backup every time you take a break. Most boards have either a USB port where you can attach an external drive or a compact flash port where you can put a CF card.

Enough said? Probably not.

Back it up!

Types of Control Boards

There are an awful lot of control boards on the market, from dead simple to Starship *Enterprise*. They tend to fall into a few basic categories.

Manual Preset Boards

When lighting control was separated from the dimmers, the first major innovation was the preset board, so called because it allowed you to have one cue showing on stage while you preset the next one.

A preset board has a row of sliders or wheels that corresponds to the channels. The operator sets each slider to a number, which sends that number out on the DMX channel. If a dimmer is listening to that channel, it sets itself to that number. Simple as that.

What makes preset boards useful is that there is actually more than one row of sliders. Each row is known as a scene, and there will always be at least two. A two-scene preset board allows you to have one scene controlling the dimmers while you set the other one. Somewhere on the board is a large fader handle that allows the operator to fade from one scene to the other one. Sometimes that fader is actually a split fader, meaning that it consists of two faders right next to each other. Generally, one of the faders is reversed so that full is at the bottom and off is at the top. This allows the operator to grab them both together and simultaneously fade one scene from full to off while fading the other scene from off to full. This is where the term crossfade comes from—a simultaneous crossing of fades as one travels from 0 to 100 and 1 travels from 100 to 0 like two elevators passing each other as one heads for the penthouse and one goes to the basement. A split fader allows you to time the two fades at a different rate, perhaps bring up the next cue quickly as the previous cue slowly dies away. This is a useful trick when you want to bring lights up quickly in one part of the stage, while letting them die off slowly in another part.

Dipless Fading

When two-scene preset boards were first invented, they were "dippy." That is, when the operator was fading from one scene to the next, the lights had a tendency to drop in intensity halfway through the fade. To understand why this is, imagine you are fading between these two scenes, with these channel levels:

	Chan1	Chan2	Chan3
Scene A	100	0	80
Scene B	0	100	100

Channel 1 is fading from full to zero, channel 2 is doing the opposite, while channel 3 is making a slight adjustment upwards from 80 to 100.

As the crossfade happens, the fader for scene A is moving from 100 percent to 0 percent, while the fader for scene B is moving from 0 percent to 100 percent. As the fade happens, each channel in the scene would be sent through the fader for that scene, which would send out a certain percentage of that level, depending on the fader position. If the fader was at 50 percent, for example, then 50 percent of the channel level would be sent to the dimmer.

If a channel was set to a level in both Scene A and Scene B, then the control board had two different intensities for the same channel, one coming out of fader A and one coming out of fader B. Without a computer brain, the only thing a manual, noncomputerized board can do in this situation is send the higher of the two values.

Let's look at what happens to channel 1, as it fades from 100 in scene A to 0 in scene B.

CHANNEL 1

SCENE A FADER: GOING DOWN				SCENE B FADER: GOING UP				SENT TO DIMMER
Level		Fader			Level		Fader		Highest
100	×	100%	=	100	0	×	0%	=	0	100
100	×	80%	=	80	0	×	20%	=	0	80
100	×	50%	=	50	0	×	50%	=	0	50
100	×	20%	=	20	0	×	80%	=	0	20
100	×	0%	=	0	0	×	100%	=	0	0

If you look at the far-right column, you will see the number that is sent to the dimmer—the higher of the two channel levels. In this case, the dimmer does exactly what we want it to do: It executes a nice, smooth fade from one hundred to 0.

Channel 2 goes the other way, from 0 to 100. Again, it works just fine:

CHANNEL 2

SCENE A FADER: GOING DOWN				SCENE B FADER: GOING UP				SENT TO DIMMER
Level	Fader			Level	Fader			Highest
0	×	100%	= 0	100	×	0%	= 0	0
0	×	80%	= 0	100	×	20%	= 20	20
0	×	50%	= 0	100	×	50%	= 50	50
0	×	20%	= 0	100	×	80%	= 80	80
0	×	0%	= 0	100	x	100%	= 100	100

However, watch what happens when we try to fade channel 3, which is going from from 80 to 100:

CHANNEL 3

SCENE A FADER: GOING DOWN				SCENE B FADER: GOING UP				SENT TO DIMMER
Level	Fader			Level	Fader			Highest
80	×	100%	= 80	100	×	0%	= 0	80
80	×	80%	= 64	100	×	20%	= 20	64
80	×	50%	= 40	100	×	50%	= 50	50
80	×	20%	= 16	100	×	80%	= 80	80
80	×	0%	= 0	100	×	100%	= 100	100

Well, now we've got a situation. Instead of making a nice, smooth fade from 80 to 100 our channel is now dipping down to a lower level along the way. Take a look at a graph of the dimmer levels:

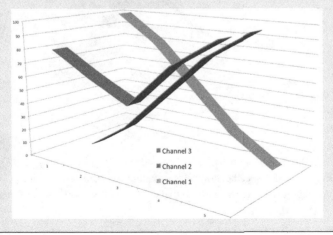

See the dip? By following the same HTP rules as the rest of the console, the fader actually lets the levels drop in the middle of the fade.

Enter the dipless crossfade.

Once console designers had a brain in the control board that could do some math, they created a new circuit that, rather than choosing between the two levels, actually added them together, producing a set of dimmer levels that made a smooth fade.

Watch what happens when we add the outputs of the two faders together:

CHANNEL 3

SCENE A FADER: GOING DOWN				SCENE B FADER: GOING UP				SENT TO DIMMER
Level	Fader			Level	Fader			Sum
80	×	100%	= 80	100	×	0%	= 0	80
80	×	80%	= 64	100	×	20%	= 20	84
80	×	50%	= 40	100	×	50%	= 50	90
80	×	20%	= 16	100	×	80%	= 80	96
80	×	0%	= 0	100	×	100%	= 100	100

Or, if you prefer a graph:

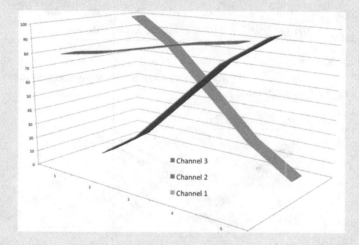

Much better.

When you see the specification "dipless fading" on control specs, it means that the console brain is doing the math to make these nice, smooth dipless fades.

A two-scene preset board is the most basic of lighting control boards, and it is quite useful if you just want to "turn on some lights." Preset boards are also useful for introducing the basic concepts of lighting control: cues, channels, and fades. It's getting harder and harder to find control boards without some sort of computer functionality, though. Even the most basic two-scene preset has some small memory functions, like allowing you to record a few standard "looks" or a few effects.

One common configuration for a preset board is a single-scene/two-scene setup that allows you to control a certain number of channels in two-scene mode and twice that number in single-scene mode. For example, a 24/48 preset board has two rows of twenty-four sliders each, allowing you to control twenty-four channels and fade between two scenes. If you turn on the single-scene mode, then you can use all forty-eight sliders together to control forty-eight channels. In this case, you lose the ability to crossfade between scenes. Some consoles overcome this limitation by using a hold function to freeze all the levels in place, allowing you to set up the next cue on the same set of sliders.

Besides the two rows of sliders, a two-scene preset board might also have the following:

Bump (or Flash) Buttons
These are buttons that sit right below each slider and serve as momentary on/off buttons. That is, if you push it, that channel turns on to full. If you take your finger off, the channel goes instantly to 0. Very useful for a quick rock-and-roll show. Bump buttons are sometimes controlled by a "bump master," which sets the level of the channels that are "bumped on."

Fade Timer
While a simple preset board will not allow you to create a cue, it will often provide a timer that controls how fast one scene fades to the other. As soon as you grab the crossfader and start fading, the timer starts. After that, the control board ignores the crossfader and fades the channels at whatever time is set on the fade timer.

Blackout Button
Blackout buttons are the object of my personal campaign to make life easier for everyone in the theater. I hate them! When pushed, these buttons force all the channels to 0 no matter what. When I was in the lighting rental business, we would field several calls a week from people who claimed their control boards were broken. "Have you checked the blackout button?" we would always ask. After the poor user released the blackout button and all the lights came on, they would always ask, "Why is *that* there?" Why indeed. Memo to all lighting equipment companies: Remove the blackout button!

Grand Master

This is a slider that allows you to fade everything smoothly to 0. Unlike the hated blackout button, this is actually useful as a way to provide a smooth fade to black at the beginning and end of the show.

Submasters

If you have a particular look that you want to use fairly often, you can assign those channels, at any level, to one slider. Then, if you want that look, you just push up that one slider. Very useful for rehearsal halls, work lights, houselights, etc.

Effects

On a preset board, an effect is basically a string of channel levels, programmed to play in sequence. If you put an effect into a loop, it becomes a chase.

Audio Input

Some boards can be set up to "listen" to an audio input and trigger certain channels with the audio input reaches a particular level.

You won't see them around much anymore but there used to be five-scene presets and even ten-scene presets, allowing the operator to work further ahead, setting up more cues. Now that computer memory chips are so reasonably priced, there really isn't any reason to spend large sums of money on hundreds of little sliders. I must say, however, back in the day, it was pretty fun to run a big show on a forty-eight-channel five-scene preset manual light board. Yessir, 240 little wheels, spinning as fast your fingers would go as you raced the actors to the next cue. It was never dull. It was also never the same show twice, which is the biggest argument for computer control.

A manual preset board is just what it sounds like: manual. In other words, there is no computer to remember anything for you, run cues for you, or otherwise bother or help you. There is no guarantee that the cue that ran perfectly in rehearsal will run that exact same way during the show. It is unforgiving of lapses in concentration. I personally saw a lighting operator fired from a first-class regional theater because, under the pressure of performance, he would sometimes set a string of levels one channel over from where they should have been, like a blind person who types with his hands one row up from the "home" keys.

The other problem with manual boards is that, despite my wife's ability to simultaneously feed a child, cook dinner, and remember the dance steps to "Nobody but You," the human brain actually doesn't multitask very well. It likes to concentrate on one thing at a time, and there are times when, in theatrical lighting, that isn't enough. Sometimes you want multiple things to happen at the same time.

In order to maintain consistency, handle complication, and multitask, you need to go digital, and that means you need . . .

Memory Consoles

There are times when it's a good idea to remove the human element. This is one of those times.

When computerized lighting consoles first appeared in the 1970s, they were pretty much just a way to automate the preset boards I talked about above. The computer would remember the levels of each of the cues, so you didn't have to set all those sliders every time. It also remembered how fast you wanted the cue to happen and recorded it. If you wanted to change a level, you could call up that cue, either "live" on the stage or "blind" on a computer screen and edit it. Pretty cool, at least at the time. (We were young. Remember, this was when mail was something you got at the post office, not something that appeared in a heads-up display on the inside of your eyeglasses.)

Times have changed. With the advent of huge dimmer racks, moving lights, multimedia, show control, and complex cueing, memory boards have developed into sophisticated control systems in a dazzling variety of styles, uses, and prices.

Every control board is good for something, and none of them are good for everything, so let's take a moment to cover some basic concepts that span most or all control consoles.

Cue Stacks

At its most basic level, a cue is an event that happens during a show. Usually, a cue happens when you push the Go button, but some boards have multiple ways of initiating an action. Some boards also accept input from other show control sources, so a cue may be triggered by an external command.

Many boards use the word "cue" to refer to a list of channel levels. By convention, cues are numbered, starting with cue 1. On the first pass, most programmers will number the cues using all the whole numbers: 1, 2, 3, etc. As the show develops, they may want to insert cues between these numbers, so they will number the inserted cues with decimals: Cue 1.5 would happen between cue 1 and cue 2, for example. Programmers may also decide to create certain cues with different numbers, like creating a cue 999 that brings all the lights to a low intensity for a lamp check.

Besides dimmer intensities, a cue may contain other commands, like sending new information to moving lights or external effects.

Cues are organized in a **cue stack**, which is a list of cues along with information about how they are timed and organized. The cue stack is run with the Go button, which runs the next cue in the sequence. Other controls for the cue stack include Pause, Back, and Go to. That last one can take you anywhere in the show and is used constantly in rehearsal, to back up or jump ahead.

By default, cues run in numerical order, from smallest to largest, but it is possible to force cues to run out of sequence.

Besides the cues themselves, a cue stack might also contain any of the following timing information:

Fade Times

Every cue has a number that describes how fast it will be run. If a cue is a crossfade from one set of levels to a new set, then there will be two times: an Up time and a Down time, so that you can control the outgoing levels and the incoming levels separately.

Wait Times

A cue can be told to wait for a certain amount of time before it runs. This is useful if you want to trigger several cues at once, but you don't want them all to start at the same time.

Autofollows

This function is used if you want a cue to start immediately after the previous cue has completed. It's also called "linking" cues. Very useful for a dramatic finish to a scene, where you want all the lights to fade down to just a single spotlight on our heroine, then a slow fade to black as we wonder if she is really going to take that poison.

More complex boards may have more than one cue stack, allowing you to keep multiple processes—media control, moving lights, conventionals, effects, etc.—separate.

Faders

In order for a cue to run, it has to be loaded into a fader. All consoles have at least two faders, so that you can do a crossfade: one cue fading up and one cue fading down. Most consoles, however, have multiple faders, so that you can run multiple things at one time. Want to have a beautiful sunset unfolding on the cyc while a scene is playing inside a house? Create the sunset cue and load it into one fader, while all of your cues inside the house—lights turning on and off, gentle shifts of focus from one side to the other—are running in the second fader.

Submasters

Sometimes, you want to pluck a group of channels and control them separately from everything else. This is particularly true when you are running a show live, with little or no preprogramming. Building submasters allows you to bring up groups of lights at any time, regardless of what the faders are doing. Running an awards show? Build a submaster with the lights for the podium. Anytime a presenter steps up, you bring up the podium submaster and bingo, no one's ever talking in the dark.

Presets and Sequences

Many boards will allow you to create preset "looks" which can be called up to create a cue. Having a library of preset looks makes programming easier, but it has other benefits. When you use a preset to record a new cue, some boards will copy the channel levels from the preset into the new cue, while others will only record the command to run that preset. The second option is great if you want to be able to adjust those levels in every cue where they appear. Imagine that you have a preset created for a living room scene with a sofa down right, and you've got a whole bunch of lights directed at that sofa. Then, one day, the director picks up the sofa and drags it three feet to the left. Now you have to adjust all the lights that were pointed at that sofa, but you only have to do it once, because your new sofa preset will run whenever a cue calls for it.

Some boards will allow you to create a sequence of cues that run automatically when triggered. This sequence can be placed in the cue stack as a single cue. If the sequence is looped and designed to run continuously, it is called a chase.[1]

Moving light boards sometimes allow a version of presets called a palette, which sets a value for one or more moving light parameters, like focus, color, zoom, etc. They are quick and easy ways to turn all the moving lights to Rosco 80 or focus them all on a specific spot or put a template in all of them.

Moving Light Profiles

As we will see in the chapter 11, every moving light uses a passel of different DMX channels to control all its settings and features. Furthermore, every light is different. It would be a huge waste of mental energy if you had to remember that channel 24 is the green dichroic filter in one light while 163 is the zoom feature in another. Furthermore, we really want to use big, round numbers when programming lights, like 0 to 100 not the 0 to 255 numbers that are native to DMX. When we are setting that green filter, we want to set it at 50 percent without having to figure out that means DMX level 127.

---

[1] Want a good firelight effect? Bury two or more lights in the fireplace and give each one a slightly different warm gel. Then use a chase to make each light bump up and down at different intensities. If you have a board that can run two chases simultaneously, make two different sequences for the same channels, with different timings and intensities. Run the two chases together and it will create a random effect that looks exactly like the flickering light from a real fire. Keep it subtle . . .

Any control console that is designed to handle moving lights will be pre-programmed with the various DMX profiles from all the commonly available lighting instruments. As new instruments come out, their profiles are created and made available to all users of a console. If you are using a Martin MAC 250, you can pull down a menu on the lighting controller and select the Martin MAC 250 profile (or definition or library or template or personality, depending on which word the console manufacturer uses). From that point forward, whenever you want to change that instrument, the console will provide a fixture-specific interface that will let you grab a hold of that green filter and move it until you've got the Shreky look you crave. The console will translate your setting into a number that DMX, and the instrument in question, will understand. Some consoles go even further, translating DMX into real-world numbers, like listing the pan positions as 0 to 360 degrees.

HTP versus LTP

Considering the number of different ways that a channel can be addressed by a control console, including cues, presets, submasters, effects, and so on, it's not surprising that sometimes (often, in fact) a particular channel will be addressed simultaneously by two different controllers. In the sunset example I used before, you might have some beams of light streaming through the window that are programmed into the sunset as well as the interior room light.

When a control console is faced with two different levels for the same channel, it has to make a decision about what to send out. In essence, there is a competition happening between two different levels, and the control board has to pick a winner. It does this in one of two ways, and these two ways represent two different philosophies of lighting control.

Usually, when we are controlling the intensity to a light, we want the highest of the competing channel levels to be sent out. For that award show, we might have put the podium lights at a dim glow during a dance number. As the number is ending and the last of the cues in the dance sequence are fading out, the award presenter is heading toward the podium. Accordingly, we push the podium submaster up. Now the computer has to choose between the lower warm glow levels that were written into the dance cues and the brighter presenter levels that are written into the submaster. In this case, we definitely want the submaster levels to win, which is why our board is set to HTP, or "Higher Takes Precedence," which is almost always the right choice with competing intensity information. If we call up a cue or submaster or preset, we want to see those levels, regardless of what lower levels might be coming from some lower levels. If a control console is designed exclusively or primarily for lighting intensities, then HTP is the way to go.

Control consoles also control other things, however, including a lot of parameters for moving lights. Let's go back to that award show, where we have a set of moving lights that are creating a fan of green light beams during the musical number. As we shift focus back to the presenters, we want those moving lights to slide up onto the set and make a nice, pretty backdrop of purple patterns.

In addition to our submaster with the podium lights on it, we've also got a preset with the moving light positions and colors for the purple set wash.

The new position and color settings for the moving lights may be higher or lower than the ones during the dance number, but it doesn't matter. We want those lights to dump their old settings and move to the new positions and colors when we bring up the submaster and the preset.

In this case, HTP might be disastrous. The green light colors might be higher than the purple colors, which would prevent the color from changing. The rest of the parameters—pan, tilt, zoom, iris, etc.—might be higher or lower than the new positions, sending the lights into a patchwork of new placements.

The solution is a different mode, known as "Latest Takes Precedence" or LTP. In an LTP scenario, the console discards any old settings as soon as it gets new ones, even if the old ones are still part of a controller (fader, submaster, etc.) that is active.

If a lighting console is designed exclusively or primarily for moving lights, then LTP is the way to go.

A lot of control boards these days are hybrids, designed for both conventional lighting and moving lights. In this case, the operator can usually select which mode they want to use for which channels. If certain channels are designated as moving light controllers, the board will helpfully default to an LTP mode for those channels.

Tracking vs. Cue-Only

Things change. As soon as you create cues and record them in your console, you will need to edit them.

So let's say that you have just created a series of cues for your production of *Katie, Bar the Door*, the well-known log cabin drama. As the first act rolls along, the action shifts around the stage, and, being the good designer that you are, you have created cues that gently follows the action from the tattered sofa to the rustic table to the humble four-poster bed in this one-room cabin.

On the table sits a hurricane lantern, which is actually an electric lamp that provides the apparent source of light for the room. It's a lovely lamp, but too new looking so the prop master sprays it down with a little paint overnight. Great stuff, except now it's not bright enough anymore. No problem, you'll just turn it up in the cue. Actually, you've got twenty-two cues in the act, so you'll have to turn it up in all of them, one at a time. Bring the cue up, make the change, record it, repeat nineteen more times. Ak, what a waste of time . . .

Fortunately, you've got the tracking function turned on for your console. All you have to do is make the change in the first cue and then let the console do the rest. It will search forward through the rest of the cues and make the same change in every cue until it finds a cue where you have previously set a different level, where it will stop. If you have previously set the lamp to fade out at the end of the act, then the last cue will have a level of 0 so the computer will track the change forward through the act until it gets to that cue, where it will stop.

Of course, if you bring the same scene back up after the intermission, you will need to make the change in the first cue of that act as well, after which the computer will track that change forward until it sees a new level for the channel.

If you are working with a tracking console and you want to make a change to just one cue, without tracking the changes through subsequent cues, then you will put the console into "Cue Only" mode, which will only make the change in the current cue.

PC-Based Controllers

Since a lighting controller is essentially a personal computer with a lot of extra buttons, one might be tempted to ask, "Can I use a personal computer to control my lights?"

Yes, as a matter of fact, you can.

Of course, by using your PC to control the lights instead of a dedicated console, you give up all those convenient controls on the surface of the console, making operation and programming a bit more problematic, but you save the cost of a console, and it's easier to move around.

If you are using your PC to operate lights, remember to follow the standard set of rules for any situation where you are using a PC to operate some aspect of a show:

1. Run disk optimization and virus scan software before you open the show software.
2. Quit all unnecessary applications.
3. Disconnect the computer from network connections and turn off any wireless functions, such as Wi-Fi and Bluetooth.
4. Once you have gotten the computer working correctly in your theater, do not install any new software or update any software you are currently running.

To control theatrical lights, you need two things: lighting control software and a DMX interface.

For the software, there are numerous computer applications that will essentially turn your PC into a lighting control board. Just like the stand-alone consoles, these applications will output level information on 512 DMX channels. Like the consoles, the software comes in various versions and styles, depending on what you are controlling and how you want to control it. Some programs are designed for small, DJ-style lighting rigs, while others are designed to handle moving lights. There are versions for both Mac and PC.

If you are really dipping deep into digital theater, you might be tempted to run both your lighting system and your sound system off of the same computer. This is entirely possible, but let me fire a couple of warning shots. Modern computers have more than enough processing power to handle both lighting and audio programs, so no problem there. Professional system designers, however, shy away from this approach for two reasons. First, there will most likely be two different crews of people who are working on each system and the lighting designer may not want to move aside while the sound designer does his thing. Second, if your computer crashes, then you have lost everything. If you are locked in a frantic battle to get your lighting system back online, it's nice to know that at least the audio is working.

Off-line Editors

Most major control console manufacturers have software-only versions of their products. For example, High End Systems, makers of the sophisticated Wholehog control console, makes Hog 3PC, a PC-based software program that emulates their well-known console and ETC makes software versions of their entire line of consoles.

These software-only versions of stand-alone consoles are useful as **off-line editors**, a way for designers to preprogram their shows before they enter the theater. Some of them can also be used to run shows on their own or as backup consoles in case a problem emerges with the hardware controller.

Remote Focus Unit

It is often useful for an electrician to be able to control the lighting console from somewhere other than the booth. In this case, a **remote focus unit** (RFU) is highly useful. An RFU is a handheld controller that communicates with the main console and can perform rudimentary functions like bringing up individual channels or running cues. As smartphones have proliferated, many

manufacturers have created RFUs for the iPhone and BlackBerry phones, allowing them to control the consoles through Wi-Fi connections.

To make the smartphone applications work, your console must be on an
Ethernet network with a wireless access point. See the chapter 9 for more info
on using a smartphone to control a lighting network.

Rack-Mount Playback Consoles

For permanently installed lighting systems, like architectural and theme park
systems, a full-size console is only brought in for the initial installation and
programming part of the process. Once the show is finished, there is no need
to dedicate a large, expensive console to run it. Hence, many manufacturers
have created rack-mounted versions of their boards, designed to just sit there
and run the show, day after day. The Congo Light Server by ETC is a good
example. The shows can still be edited, of course, by hooking up a mouse,
keyboard, and monitor to the rack-mount console, but these machines are
really designed to run a show for a long period of time without changes.

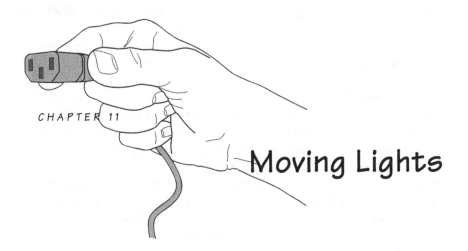

CHAPTER 11

Moving Lights

Okay let's say you're a rock star. Let's say that you are a really, really big rock star. Let's say that you are the band Genesis in 1981, with a number one album on the British pop charts and a huge tour coming up. You have a reputation for putting on huge, innovative concerts, so you are always looking for the next cool thing. After all, you are one of the bands that popularized the use of lasers in live concerts, so people have come to expect a lot of visual spectacle.

And then, one day, an American sound mixer and electrical engineer named Jim Bornhurst asks you to join him in a barn somewhere north of London. Nailed to the rafters is a large odd-looking light. Bornhurst turns it on and shows you how it can instantly change colors, which is unusual but not shocking. Lots of people are working on that. Then, however, Bornhurst hits another switch and the beam of light begins to *move*. It sweeps from side to side, up and down, throwing beams of light into every crevice in the darkened barn. You've seen a lot of cool lighting effects, but in 1981, this is the first time you've seen a light that could move automatically.

So what do you do?

You order a whole bunch of them, that's what. Genesis agreed to pay for the construction of the first fifty-five units for a concert in Barcelona, nine months later. Bornhurst worked for a Texas-based company called Showco, and you can imagine the mood in their shop when they found out they were committed to produce fifty-five totally innovative Vari*Lites,[1] including new systems for control, power, and data distribution, in nine months, for one of the biggest bands in the world. On the plane home, Bornhurst

---

[1] According to legend, the name was coined by Genesis manager Tony Smith.

upped the ante by telling his team that the current color-changing system wouldn't work and they would have to start designing from scratch. No stress!

Almost unbelievably, Showco came through and provided lights for one of the most famous concerts in entertainment technology history: the Genesis Abacab concert in Barcelona on September 25, 1981. On that night, the moving light was born and theater lighting would change forever.

The first Vari*Lites were shrouded in mystery. For many years, they could not be purchased, only rented, and they came with their own technicians. On tour, local stagehands were shooed away from the lights, and they were never opened in public. Because of their popularity, however, it wasn't long before other companies, among them High End Systems, Martin, and Clay Paky, released competing products. Together, they changed the visual image not only of rock and roll but of theater, industrials, fashion, award shows, and even architecture. Today there are dozens of different moving lights, and no large-scale event is complete without them.

Bornhurst did not invent any of the specific technologies in the Vari*Lite, any more than Henry Ford invented the internal combustion engine or the rubber tire. Like Ford, Bornhurst and his team took a string of recent innovations—like dichroic filters, stepper motors, and compact arc lamps—and engineered a practical, robust device that, quite simply, changed the look of live entertainment forever.

Many people refer to these lights as "intelligent lights," but that is a bit of a misnomer. The real intelligence still lies with the designer and the operator. The light can be programmed to move, change color, and do a lot of other tricks at the push of a button, so "automated light" is a better description, but folks in the trade call them "moving lights," so that's what we'll use. Many people just say "movers."

Even though moving lights originated in rock and roll, it didn't take long for them to invade the rest of the performing arts—not only because of the dynamic effect of moving light beams, but also because a single moving light could do the work of several different lights during the course of a show, allowing a designer to use one unit instead of many.

One obstacle to moving lights being accepted by the rest of the industry, however, was noise. The powerful lamps required cooling fans, which, along with the motors that moved the lights, were clearly audible during quiet shows. Design advances have led to quieter units that are suitable for theatrical drama, but they are still not silent, so you won't see them during a string quartet concert anytime soon.

Let's look at some of the features of the moving light.

The Lamp

In the beginning, all moving lights used a **high-intensity discharge** (or HID) lamp, also known as a **short-arc or metal halide lamp**. An HID lamp does not have a filament like a conventional fixture. Instead, it creates light by making electricity jump across a tiny gap inside a glass envelope filled with an exotic mixture of gases. It's like having a tiny arc welder inside a glass bulb. Depending on the manufacturer and technology, HID lamps may be called lots of different things, including **gas discharge lamps, HMI, MSD,** or **MSR**. Just for fun, some techs will mix the names together and call them metal discharge or mercury vapor lights.

For our purposes, we will call them HID, because, more often than not, that's what it says on the spec sheet. Furthermore, if you say "HID," then lighting techs and designers will know what you mean.

HID lamps are much more efficient than regular incandescent lamps, which translates into brighter light for the same amount of energy. An HID lamp turns about 25 percent of the electricity into light, which doesn't sound great until you consider that an incandescent lamp wastes 90 percent of its electricity on heat. A 2000-watt HID lamp will produce the same amount of light as two 55000-watt incandescent lamps and the lamp will be physically smaller than either of them.

The smaller-sized lamp means that the HID light source is closer to the holy grail of lighting instrument designers—a "point source" of light. If all the light emanates from a relatively small point, it becomes easier to focus that light into a hard-edged beam. These lamps also have a higher **color temperature** than standard incandescent or tungsten-halogen lamps, putting out a cool white light that is closer to real sunlight.

So, what's the catch? There are several.

Not surprisingly, the first one is cost. HID lamps are more expensive to manufacture, as they must stand up to very high pressures and temperatures (up to 1000 °F). They also require special circuitry, known as a **ballast**, to start up and maintain that arc of light. Most moving lights have the ballast built into the base of the unit, but some require an external box that sits next to the unit. Finally, they are impossible to dim. Some recent advances have produced dimmers that will take the intensity down part of the way, but HIDs always require a mechanical dimmer—a metal flap that closes down over the light—to make them go all the way to black. HID lamps also don't like to be turned off and turned on again, or restruck as the electricians say. Once an HID lamp is off, it wants to stay off until it cools completely, which can take up to twenty minutes. It is possible to "hot-restrike" some lamps, but both the lamp and the ballast have to be designed to do that.[2] Generally HR at the end of the lamp part number means hot restrike.

The ability to hot-restrike is occasionally useful, though, if only to recover from a mistake. I once did a low-tech effect for a children's dance show where the choreographer had all the kids walk in through the aisles of the theater. We were doing the show in a ballroom that had a mirror ball, so I bounced an HID follow spot off the mirror ball, while two hundred children floated down the aisle to a mysterious-sounding overture. All those drifting shafts of light looked great for the rehearsal, but, just before the show started, one of the parents became concerned about the hot spotlight so he turned it off "just to be safe." Unfortunately, the lamp could not be restruck before the show and the effect was lost. I was standing backstage when the children came through and a four-year-old little girl tugged on my sleeve. I looked down into her sorrowful enormous eyes as she asked, "But where was the magic light?"

'Bout to make me cry, child.

If our lamp had been able to hot-restrike, it would have saved us both some tears.

Not all moving lights have HID lamps. Some moving lights do come equipped with tungsten-halogen lamps for clients who want true dimming, an instant-on source, or just the warm color temperature that tungsten provides.

Finally, some smaller moving wash lights have LED light sources, which are nowhere near as bright as the HIDs (but can approach the tungsten-halogen) and cannot be focused into a sharp beam. They have a massive advantage when it comes to efficiency and lamp life, however. See the chapter 12 for more about the pros and cons of this technology.

Regardless of the type of lamp, make sure that you **check the voltage** before you buy or rent a unit. Many moving lights can only be run on 208 (or higher) volts. Of course you remember that standard power in the United States is 110 volts, so you can't plug these higher voltage instruments into your regular lighting circuits. If you use the higher voltages, you must have an electrician create a separate circuit to plug them in. This is not difficult or expensive, but it does require a professional electrician. Do *not* try to rewire your electrical system, no matter how many how-to websites you have read.

If you are using a 110-volt unit, you must **check the amperage** to make sure that it will not overload your circuits. Most standard lighting circuits can

---

[2] An electronic ballast can do it; a magnetic ballast cannot.

handle 20 amps, but make sure you know what you are plugging into and what else is on the same circuit.

If you are renting or buying moving lights, check the connector. If you are having special power points installed for your moving lights, go with the twist-lock style of connector, which is standard for use with moving lights and safest because the connector cannot come apart and arc if the cable is pulled. Twist-lock connectors also have a particular arrangement of keyed prongs so they cannot be plugged into the wrong voltage.

Finally, plugging a moving light into a standard lighting circuit may not be a good idea in any case, because that circuit is probably controlled by a dimmer. If the dimmer is accidentally dimmed below full power, the resulting clipped power wave could damage your moving light. The best solution for a moving light is to have your electrician create a dedicated circuit specifically for that unit; alternatively, use one of your regular lighting circuits, but swap out the dimmer module for a nondim module, which is designed to provide uninterrupted power. Regardless of where you plug it in, use only extra-hard-duty SO-type cable that you get from a theatrical retailer or electrical wholesaler. Do *not* use a household extension cord of any type. Actually, don't ever do that with *any* theatrical light. You're asking for a fire.

Pan and Tilt: Moving Yoke versus Moving Mirror

Pan means to move the light horizontally. **Tilt** means to move it up and down. The original Vari*Lite achieved these movements with two motors, one mounted in the base that spun the yoke in a circle and one mounted in the yoke to tilt the light up and down. This arrangement, not surprisingly, is called a **moving yoke** or a **moving head**. This scheme offers tremendous freedom of movement, allowing the beam to sweep 360 degrees horizontally[3] as well as tilt up to 300 degrees. It's an expensive way to go, however, requiring big motors and a complicated yoke mechanism. One way to build a less expensive unit is to leave the lamp where it is and just use a small mirror to direct the beam. This **moving mirror** instrument can move the beam a lot faster than the moving yoke: a 180-degree turn in half a second, as opposed to two seconds for the moving yoke. The trade-off is less range of motion, as the mirror cannot make a full circle or achieve the same amount of tilt. Typically, a moving mirror can pan about 170 degrees and tilt about 90 degrees. Some people, particularly in Europe, call these units **scanners**.

---

[3] All moving yoke lights can turn in a complete circle, but some can go even farther. The pan number listed in the specifications tells you how far the unit can turn before it has to stop and go back the other way. The Morpheus PanaBeam actually has a continuous spin mode that allows it to keep turning infinitely.

Stepper Motors

Whether a moving yoke or a moving mirror unit, a moving light depends on **stepper motors**, electric motors that can be precisely controlled. A stepper motor uses four electromagnets, mounted around a rotating shaft, that turn on and off in sequence, alternately attracting and repelling magnets that are attached to the shaft. As the magnets are attracted to each electromagnet in turn, the motor literally steps around each rotation. This stepping process allows a microprocessor to give precise, repeatable position information to the motor. Bottom line: The motor goes right where you tell it to and stays there. Standard brush motors, like the one in your windshield wiper, cannot move quickly or accurately enough to position a moving light. Stepper motors are also used to position templates, color filters, beam shapers, and anything else that moves in a moving light.

Many fixtures use two modes—rough and fine—for pan and tilt (for a total of four numbers). The operator will adjust the rough pan and tilt first to get the light in the right general area, then use the fine pan and tilt for a final adjustment. Using two numbers for each axis allows for a higher resolution and more precise placement.

The process isn't perfect, however, so moving lights must occasionally be "homed." A moving light has a home position that it uses as a reference point for all its movement. Generally, the technician will program all the lights to point to the same spot on the stage as their home position. This allows him to quickly check if the lights are correctly aligned simply by hitting the home button on the lighting controller. Any light that is not hitting that magic place on the stage is in need of some adjustment. By adjusting the pan and tilt of the unit, he can shift the position of the offending light until the beam hits the right spot again, reset the home position, and then put the light back into the show, confident that it will find all of its correct positions. Most fixtures will automatically go to their home position when they are powered on before the show.

Color Changing

The cheapest, easiest way to create colored light is to put a colored piece of plastic in front of it. In the theater, we do this every day. We call those little pieces of plastic gels because they used to be made from a gel-like substance derived from animal by-products trucked in from slaughterhouses. Too much information?

Anyway, the original animal gels produced great colors, but they didn't last long in front of hot lighting instruments, so they were eventually replaced by sheets of various kinds of plastics. Someone forgot to tell the guy who comes up with unofficial names for theatrical devices, however, so the term gel has hung in there for the same reason that we still "dial" the phone, even though no one uses rotary phones anymore. If you want to look good to a theatrical technician, call that piece of colored plastic a filter.

A plastic filter works pretty well when placed on the front of a lighting instrument, although it will eventually fade out, especially if the light is left on for long periods. If you need more than one color, you can attach a color changer to the light, the simplest of which is just a string of filters on a scroll. A motor rolls the scroll until it reaches to the color you want and presto—color.

When building the Vari*Lite, however, Showco needed a way of changing colors very quickly—preferably in a fraction of a second—and they wanted to be able to fade smoothly from one to another. A scrolling gel changer wouldn't change fast enough, wouldn't fade smoothly, and would probably fly off the spinning unit anyway. The solution was to use a color-mixing system with several glass filters placed *inside* the unit.

Even a plastic filter, however, cannot stand up to the inferno inside a lighting instrument. When placed next to a standard theatrical lamp, a plastic filter will shrivel like a senior prom wallflower when the captain of the football team asks her to dance. It will simply melt away. Fortunately, Bornhurst was an avid photographer and knew a lot about optics, so he turned to a new kind of glass called a **dichroic filter**.

A dichroic filter has the unique ability to allow certain frequencies of light to pass through while it reflects the rest. Previous to the Vari*Lite, dichroics were only used in high-tech scientific applications, but Bornhorst thought he would give them a try in rock and roll.

Dichroic Filters

A dichroic filter operates the same way as an oil slick on water. When light strikes the oil, some of that light is reflected directly off the top surface of the oil. Other frequencies, however, pass through the oil and bounce back off the bottom surface where the oil meets the water. Different frequencies of light produce different colors, which is why you see all those different colors on the surface of an oil slick.

Dichroic filters are made by laying down different layers of glass and various kinds of optical coatings in a superclean air-free environment. Depending on the type, thickness, and order of the coatings, optical engineers can "tune" a filter to allow certain frequencies through, while reflecting the rest. Plastic filters change a light's color by *absorbing* all the unwanted frequencies; dichroic filters do it by *reflecting* the unwanted frequencies. Because no light (and therefore no heat) is absorbed in the dichroic filter, the resulting beam of light is very clear and saturated, and the filter stays cooler. Plastic filters heat up because they absorb a lot of light (and therefore heat), which causes them to fade or, in extreme cases, shrivel up.

All this sharp color and heat resistance comes at a steep price, however. Dichroic filters are many times more expensive than plastic and are only cost-effective when the same filter will be in use for a long time. Therefore, you won't be seeing the end of plastic filters for conventional lighting anytime soon. If you can get through a run without burning through your plastic filters, or by changing them a few times, then dichroics don't make sense.

Despite their cost, there are some theatrical applications for dichroic filters outside of moving lights. These include long-term installations (particularly if the lights are on all day, like a museum or a theme park) or any application where high heat is a problem. For example, the *Waterworld* show at the Universal Studios Hollywood theme park uses them for lights that sit next to flame and pyrotechnic effects, where plastic filters would burn up.

Dichroics can be ordered through your theatrical supply company and are generally identified by the same filter numbers as normal plastic filters. Keep in mind that they are generally custom-made, so allow extra time to order.

After a lot of experimentation, Bornhurst and his colleagues came up with a color changing system in which three dichroic filters were "graduated"—that is, they faded from clear on one end to full-color on the other. By altering which part of each filter was in front of the light beam, the unit could mix the colors in varying amounts, producing an incredible range of sharp, supersaturated colors that could be changed in a fraction of a second. This type of mixing is known as **CYM color mixing**, because the three colors are cyan, yellow, and magenta.

Today, the various kinds of moving lights change colors in two different ways, but they both involve dichroic filters. Some units use the CYM system, which can give you any color in the rainbow, while other lower-budget units use a **color wheel**, loaded with preselected colors. In this case, you have to preselect your colors before you turn the unit on, and then you are stuck with what you have. Most lower-end units come with filters already installed in the color wheels, and some of those can't be changed. Check the specs before you buy!

Many units also offer **color correction**, which slides a filter in front of the light to match it to other kinds of sources, such as tungsten lights. This feature is used mostly in television and film.

Mechanical Effects

The features of moving lights differ depending on the style of light. Some units are **wash** or flood units, designed to give a soft-edged wash of color, similar to a Fresnel. Others are **spot** units, which act like ellipsoidal spotlights. There are also **beam** units, which give narrow beams of lights similar to aircraft landing lights (ACL), as well as moving **PARs**, which are–you guessed it–PAR cans on moving yokes. Depending on the style, the light may have various kinds of mechanical effects built in.

Both wash and spot units often have a **zoom** feature, which makes the beam larger and smaller. Spot units allow you to cut and shape the beam of light in other ways as well. They have **beam shapers**, which are lenses inside the light that shape the light and can rotate continuously, creating some cool effects. There are also dousers, which are flaps that close down over the entire light at once. Dousers can be used for a **strobe** effect, which is just what it sounds like: a quick flash of light. Strobe effects are rated by cycles per second: An 8 Hz strobe can flash eight times per second.

Some lights also have an iris, which allows you to close down the beam of light into a smaller circle.

Spot fixtures also have templates or gobos, which may be mounted in a wheel or in individual holders. Generally, the ones in the individual holders can be rotated, while the ones in the wheel cannot.

More expensive units will have other effects as well, including the prism, which creates weaving shafts of color, and the light cone, which is just what it sounds like: a way to make a cone of light with a dark center.

As I said before, HID lamps cannot be electrically dimmed, so moving lights also have a mechanical dimmer. This is a metal flap that slips into the light beam and decreases the intensity. Because the flap is farther away from the lamp, it does not create a hard edge shadow like the shutter. It just decreases the amount of light that gets out the front of the unit.

Control

All moving lights available on the market today use the DMX512 standard for control. This standard allows any DMX-compatible lighting controller (virtually all of them) to control a moving light. Here's how that works.

Every moving light has a list of things that can be controlled. That list includes all of the things that we talked about above: pan, tilt, color, templates, etc. Each one of these parameters requires one or more channels of DMX. For example, the Elation Design Beam 1200 uses DMX channel 1 to adjust panning. You can feed the unit any number from 0 to 255 on channel 1 and it will translate that number into a pan position. Sending 0 will turn the unit all the way counterclockwise while sending 255 will turn it all the way clockwise. The numbers from 0 to 255 correspond to 256 different pan positions. Like many lights, the Design Beam has both a rough adjustment and a fine adjustment; the fine one is on DMX channel 2. Using the fine adjustment gives you 256 positions *between* each one of the rough positions, making it possible to fine-tune the position of the light.

Bottom line, the Design Beam uses two DMX channels to send pan information from the lighting controller.

Every moving light has a DMX profile, which is a list showing which channels are used for what control function. This profile is unique to each style and brand of light. Here, for example, is the DMX profile for the Elation Design Beam 1200:

DMX channel	Function
1	Pan (rough)
2	Pan (fine)
3	Tilt (rough)
4	Pan (fine)
5	Color Wheel Position
6	Color Mixing - Cyan
7	Color Mixing - Magenta
8	Color Mixing - Yellow
9	Color Temperature
10	Gobo Wheel 1
11	Gobo Wheel 1, Indexing and Scrolling
12	Gobo Wheel 2
13	Rotating Effect
14	Focus
15	Shutter / Strobe
16	Dimmer
17	Frost
18	Color Mixing Speed
19	Pan / Tilt Speed
20	Color Macros
21	Lamp on/off

As you can see from this list, the Elation Design Beam uses twenty-one of the 512 DMX channels, but they don't have to be the first twenty-one channels. When you set up the unit, it will ask you for a **starting channel or address**. Whatever channel you enter will correspond to channel 1 on the list above. The Design Beam will then use that channel and the next twenty for its information. So, if you enter channel 150 as the starting channel, the unit will use channels 150 through 170 as its twenty-one channels.

You could, in theory, have more than one unit assigned to these same channels, but it would then receive all the same information, including position, color, effects, etc. This is rarely what you want, however, so each unit usually has its own set of channels.

Every unit on the market has its own profile, and it is a tedious business keeping track of it, so many lighting controllers (especially the ones that are specifically designed for moving lights) are preprogrammed with a **fixture library** containing the profiles of commonly available moving lights. When you start programming, you just select "Elation Design Beam 1200" from the fixture library, set a starting channel, and the lighting controller translates all these numbers into a simple on-screen interface where you can easily control the light. Because there are so many different things to control, moving lights are rarely controlled "live." A lighting designer will always program the looks ahead of time and then let the computerized controller play them back.

DMX cables are generally five-pin XLR but sometimes can be either three-pin or five-pin, and many moving lights have both kinds of plugs. I highly recommend using only five-pin DMX cable! That way, you can be sure that you are really using DMX cable and not microphone cable, which is less reliable.

Some moving lights have wireless DMX receivers, which means that you don't have to run control cables at all. This is a sweet thing, as long as your theater does not have any major sources of wireless interference.

Finally, some advanced moving lights will accept DMX over Ethernet and will have a place to plug in a network cable. Many electricians are hesitant to use Ethernet cables into the lights because they are not as robust as DMX cables, and I am inclined to agree. The theater is a rough place for equipment. Use the tough stuff.

A Less Expensive Solution: The City Theatrical AutoYoke

So you don't have ten thousand dollars for sexy new moving lights? You are not alone! Fortunately, the folks at City Theatrical have heard your call and designed the AutoYoke, a DMX-operated holder for a conventional theatrical lighting instrument. Just take your Strand SL or your ETC Source Four, bolt them into this motorized yoke unit, and presto, you can pan and tilt them just like the big boys. You still control the intensity of the unit with a standard dimmer, and you don't have the color, shutter, and template changing capabilities of a real moving light, but hey, it's still pretty sexy for something like a quarter of the cost. Actually, you can put a DMX-controlled color scroller on it, and get one step closer to a real moving light.

Renting or Buying a Moving Light

If you have decided to take the plunge and add moving lights to your show or your permanent stock, here is a general guide to making a decision. Whatever you decide, make sure you see the light in operation before you rent or buy. Visit your dealer and watch a demonstration, but don't stop there. Get the dealer to open up the unit so you can look inside to get answers to the questions below:

What is your budget?

Moving lights can cost as much as a small automobile, so the first thing to do is get a general idea of what you can spend and what is available. Call a lighting distributor and get some examples of retail prices at the upper end (Vari*Lite, High End), the lower end (Elation, American DJ), and in between.

What is your intended use?

If you are setting up a nightclub, you probably don't care as much about lamp noise or being able to swap out colors and gobos, for example. If you are using the lights for theatrical dramas, then those things are important. Determine what you will use the lights for most often, so you can talk to the dealer about what features will matter to you.

Is this a permanent installation or temporary?

If you are putting the lights up somewhere and leaving them, you won't care as much about portability or road cases.

Who will maintain the units?

With all their moving parts, moving lights can require a lot of maintenance and adjustment. Make sure that you know who will do this. If you have trained technicians on staff, you can look at the more complex units. If not, then you will want to look for a unit that is easier to maintain. Some units have modular designs that make it easier to swap out parts. Ask the dealer to open up the unit and let you look in. Ask them how hard it is to change lamps, color filters, and gobos. Ask about keeping all the mechanical parts properly aligned. If possible, talk to technicians who don't work for the manufacturer to get an unbiased opinion. If you are looking for the lowest maintenance, look at the LED units.

How will the lights be controlled?

Do you have an existing lighting controller that will be used to control these lights? Does it have enough channels available? Do you need to rent or purchase a dedicated controller for the lights? You will probably need to run DMX cables to the lights, so take some time to figure out where those cables will go. Check chapter 9 for more details about using this technology.

Where will the power come from?

As I said above, you need to pay attention to what voltage you have available and where you are going to plug in the unit. Make sure you know what kind of plug you want as well.

Is This the Future? The Truly "Digital" Light

For many years, designers have been shaping the beams that come out of lighting instruments with lenses, shutters, templates, and color filters. When moving lights appeared, they took all these things to the next step: Now the lenses could zoom automatically up and back, the shutters could slide in and out with remote control, the templates could spin and change, and the color palette became limitless. The designers added zooms, irises, and prisms and the options multiplied. Armed with moving light technology, lighting designers had an almost limitless ability to move and shape a beam of light.

And yet, they were unsatisfied. Despite the proliferation of moving lights that could not only light the show but write, direct, and star in it, a determined group of instrument designers kept pushing for something new and truly different.

It would be easy to write off this dissatisfaction as the normal complaints of early-adopting malcontents, or the desperate greed of lighting salesmen always pushing that new-instrument smell, or the creative hunger that dogs innovative minds, causing them to push the technological envelope, expand human endeavor, and someday, oh yes, someday finally invent that espresso-machine-in-a-thermos-bottle that I've always wanted.

Or, you could say there was actually something missing.

The moving light is, at a fundamental level, a souped-up version of a standard theatrical lighting fixture. Everything about it is simply a really cool version of the conventional lighting instrument. Instead of having a single-color filter slapped on the front, it has a color mixing system that can produce any color in the spectrum. Instead of having four metal shutters that an electrician manually shoves in front of the light, it has remote-controlled shutters mounted in a rotating disk that can slide in and out continuously. Instead of having a slot that can only hold a single template, it has a rotating wheel of templates, each of which can be spun individually. The list goes on. The important point, though is that a moving light is built around all the same forms and philosophies as a conventional light. Start with a beam of white light, then shape with shutters, templates, lenses, and color filters. The moving light is just faster, brighter, more flexible, and way sexier.

But what if you didn't have to change each one of these things—color, shape, filter—individually? What if you could just sit down and draw out the shape and color of the light beam that you wanted on a computer screen and then have the light project that image? And, of course, change it over time? In other words, instead of having to manipulate a beam of light with a bunch of complicated mechanical devices, why not just have the beam of light you want in the first place?

This is the fundamental idea of a digital light, and it had its first moment in the dark at the annual LDI[4] convention in Las Vegas in 1989.

The major leap of innovation was to take out the standard theatrical lamp and install a video projector in its place. That way, the beam could be anything that you could get on a video screen: a still image, a moving pattern, a computer effect, the *Millennium Falcon* going into hyperspace, *anything*. You could make the light beam into anything you could imagine.

The first digital lighting instrument to step onstage at LDI was called the Icon M, and it created quite a stir among lighting designers who saw it as a way to dispense with physical templates and color mixing. No need to load up instruments with gobos and dichroics, just dial up what you need on a computer screen! Unfortunately, the Icon M was not quite as bright as the world wanted, so it faded away, pun intended. A few years later, armed with a brighter projection system, High End Systems brought out their DL lighting instrument, which actually had its own video server attached. Now, you can create an unlimited library of still and/or moving images and project them out of a moving light. Of course, it wasn't a completely unfamiliar animal. The DL panned and tilted like a moving light, included a library of theatrical templates, and was equipped with some of the physical effects that lighting designers were familiar with, including zoom, focus, and shutters. Under the hood, though, it was a fundamentally different philosophy for creating a beam of light, one based on video projection rather than on a souped-up ellipsoidal.

The DL even contained a video camera, so not only could it project video images; it could collect them (including infrared images), reprocess them, and send them out to other video projectors or servers. In later generations, they actually built the server right into the light, so video images no longer needed to be sent to the unit over RBG cables from a server sitting in the control booth. Once the show starts, the only connection the DL needs (besides power) is DMX, so the lighting controller can run the physical effects and

---

[4] Now known as LDI/Live Design, this is an annual convention for people in theatrical technology.

pull up images from the onboard library. Typically, however, the DL instruments are on an Ethernet network, to allow for image uploading, software upgrades, and remote configuration of the units. This also allows you to use multiple projectors to create a single image, using edge blending and keystone correction.

Over the years, High End has continued to develop the DL series, and as of this writing, it has not been challenged at the top of the moving digital lighting world. You might be hard-pressed, however, to find any one production that is using anywhere near all of its features. Shortly put, this thing does *everything*.

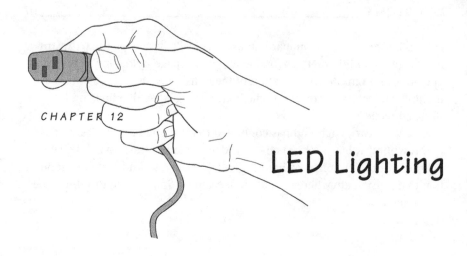

CHAPTER 12

LED Lighting

LEDs are magic.

I'm sorry, but that's the truth. There's no other logical explanation for how an electronic circuit containing neither filament nor fuel nor phosphorescent gas nor any other visible means of creating light can actually create light using very little electricity and creating very little heat.

They're magic, I tell you.

If you really want to, you can look up "How LEDs Work" online and find some excellent, in-depth explanations about how electrons move from one substrate to another, spinning up to a higher orbit and releasing energy as a result, but really . . . why bother? Just accept that LEDs are magic and everyone will be happier. Trust me.

You can trust me on something else as well: LEDs are the wave of the future. There will certainly be more than one solution to creating light in the twenty-first century, but trust me, the LED is going to be a major part of your life for a long time to come. They have already taken over traffic lights, automobile taillights, bus destination displays, and billboards, and they are poised to take over the theater.

Here are the basics:

A light-emitting diode (LED) is an electronic circuit that produces light. It does not have a filament, like a standard lightbulb, nor does it have a glowing gas, like a fluorescent bulb. All the light is produced electronically.

LED circuits do not run directly off of 120-volt power. They must have a separate power source. Sometimes, this power source is built into the unit; other times it is a separate box that hangs next to the instrument.

LEDs come in a variety of colors. The different colors are produced by different types of electronic circuits. For that reason, different colors may have different prices. Often, an LED lamp will have red, blue, and green diodes built into the same lamp, so that the colors can mix and produce a wide spectrum of colors. One LED diode, however, can only make one color.

LED applications come in two groups, often called direct and indirect. (Some manufacturers call them active and passive.) In the direct category, we find LED units that are designed to replace standard theatrical lighting instruments. They are mounted on lighting beams, booms, electrics, and light stands, just like standard instruments, and their job is to throw light on something else.

The LED units in the indirect category are designed to be looked at. These units are built into scenery or architecture or parade floats as a visual element. They are often intended to act as a sort of video screen.

Let's begin with the direct applications.

Direct LEDs

Many familiar types of theatrical instruments, like ellipsoidals, PAR cans, and even moving lights, now come in LED versions. For reasons we'll get into in a moment, most LED fixtures are wash-style fixtures, which produce a blast of unfocused, wide-angle light. Fixture design is slowly catching up, however, and you can expect to see more focusable LEDs in the future.

Direct LED lighting instruments are truly a good-news/bad-news technology so that's how we are going to approach learning about them.

First, the good news:

LEDs use a lot less power than conventional lamps

There is a lot of variation between brands, types, and applications; but most LEDs put out between 50 and100 lumens per watt of power, whereas incandescents put out around 14 to 17 lumens per watt. As it turns out, heating up a filament wastes a lot of power by turning it into heat. LEDs don't have to heat anything up, so a much larger percentage of the power gets turned into visible light. Hence, they don't use as much power and they don't get as hot.

Nothing is perfect, however, so LEDs do put out a little heat, but it is nowhere near what an incandescent lamp throws off. Anyone who has ever tried to focus a hot ellipsoidal knows that theatrical lights make excellent space heaters. An incandescent light has to heat up a filament to make it glow, and that heat gets transmitted to the glass bulb surrounding the filament, then to the metal housing, then to the cloth drape that is resting against the electric. Next thing you know, you've got a hole burnt through your drape.

Because of their cooler operating temperature, LED lamps can be put in smaller housings, don't need cooling lamps, and will not damage sensitive electronics. Furthermore, because they don't rely on a heated filament, they don't have to wait for it to cool down. Experienced actors know that they must hold their position for a few seconds after a blackout while the filaments cool and the stage goes absolutely, completely black. This is not true with LED lights. A blackout happens instantly.

They can create lots of different colors

LEDs themselves are available in an ever-increasing range of colors, but theatrical LEDs often have a combination of red, blue, and green diodes grouped together to form a single light, allowing you to create a wide range of colors by adjusting the intensity of each color. You can also get instruments with just white LEDs, which can then be colored in the conventional way, by plastic or dichroic filters.

They don't need external dimmers

LED units come with their own internal dimmers, which are sometimes built into the unit itself and sometimes built into an external power supply. For units with multicolored LEDs, there is a dimmer for each color. By adjusting these dimmers, you control both intensity and color.

Many of them can be controlled by DMX

Most LED units have a DMX plug and can be addressed by a standard DMX-compatible dimmer board. As with any other DMX device, you will need to enter a starting address for the unit so it knows which DMX channels to follow. The number of DMX addresses required depends on the number of different LED colors and what additional features the unit has. The simplest one-color unit will have only one address that will determine its intensity. A simple red-green-blue unit will have three addresses, one for each color. A more complex unit might have additional features, like **zoom**, **strobe**, or other preprogrammed sequences, each of which requires more DMX addresses.

Some LEDs can also be controlled in other ways, like with an audio input that allows them to flash in time with a music signal. For this reason, LEDs have caught on quickly with DJs, who also like them because they are easy to carry and don't use a lot of power.

If the LED instrument has an external power supply, then the DMX cable goes to the power supply, not the instrument itself.

They last *a Lot* longer.

An average tungsten or HID lamp lasts about 1,000 to 2,000 hours, less if it is bumped around, turned on and off quickly, or otherwise abused. A sudden shake can break a filament and kill the lamp. An LED lamp can last up to 100,000 hours, and due to its durable, solid-state construction, it is a lot harder to kill. With an average amount of use in a theatrical environment, an LED lighting instrument might never need its lamp changed. Ever.

Combined with the power efficiency mentioned above, this makes LED lamps a whole lot greener, both because they use less power and because there won't be all those incandescent lamps ending up in a landfill.

And now, because life is fair, here's the bad news about LEDs.

They are more expensive than standard lamps

Technology is always moving forward, and as a product becomes more popular, the price always drops, but you can still expect an LED lamp to set you back several times more than a conventional lamp. This really isn't a fair comparison, however, because you won't need a dimmer for it, and as mentioned above, it is going to last a lot longer. Nevertheless, it will cost you more upfront, and you will have to patiently explain to the pencil pushers that the real savings will come over time.

They do not focus as well as standard lamps

In a standard lighting instrument, the light is coming from one spot, either a filament or an electrical arc jumping between two electrodes. In either case, it isn't difficult to design a set of reflectors and lenses that take this relatively small point of light and focus it into a single, sharply focused beam that looks good with a gobo in front of it.

With LEDs, the light is coming from a lot of different bulbs that are spread out over a wide area. This makes it difficult to design a set of optics that gathers all those little beams of light into one big one. For that reason, LEDs have been most successful in wide, unfocused lights like PARs, strip lights, or other wash-type units. One of the more popular LEDs is called a ColorBlast™ (by Color Kinetics), and it is just what it sounds like: a big blast of color. Furthermore, without reflectors and lenses, the beam of light appears to fall off more quickly than, say, a Fresnel. It's just harder to get all those stray light beams to go where you want them to go.

There has been progress, however, and a few companies like Elation and Martin have put out units with beams that approach the sharp focus on an ellipsoidal. You can be sure that, with all the advantages of LEDs, this is an area that will continue to see innovation.

They are not as bright

The difficulty in focusing LEDs also makes the beam appear to be less bright. An instrument designer can pack a light with as many LED bulbs as he wants, but, without a way to focus all those lamps in the right direction, there is a practical limit to how a beam he can get. Therefore, LED units tend to put out less light. This generally means that they are most useful in situation where the throws are shorter.

They don't do all colors well

The red-green-blue combination that I talked about can't really create all colors equally. Unfortunately, one of the colors that it doesn't do well is pure white. Fortunately, if you are really concerned with getting precise colors, you can get pure white LEDs and put regular plastic or dichroic filters in front of them. More instrument designers are following this philosophy to create LED units that can compete with the bright, brilliantly colored moving lights used in concerts. Just this year, Phillips came out with a 50-watt homogenized LED source that produced all colors from a single lamp. It was built into a theatrical lamp by Elation, a very active theatrical LED company, and it appears to be working well.

Indirect LEDs

If you have ever seen one of those electronic billboards that play video and distract you from your driving, then you have seen indirect LEDs in action. As we are going to discuss in the video chapter, a video image is made up of a grid of small lights, known as picture elements or **pixels**. In the case of an LED display, each pixel is composed of one red, one blue, and one green LED diode, giving that pixel the ability to create a wide range of colors. The computer that is driving the screen sends intensity commands to those three diodes, altering their brightness and changing the overall color of the pixel. As the video image is changing quickly, the computer is constantly updating the pixels, which creates the image that we see.

LED screens have taken over billboards because they do not wash out in the sunlight, unlike previously technologies, and they can be built quite large. The LED-coated roof over the Fremont Street Experience in Las Vegas is over 1,500 feet long. In fact, theoretically, an LED display has no maximum size, as long as you have a computer powerful enough to send information to all those pixels.

LED screens have taken over a lot of video displays on stage because they are bright and much cheaper, inch for inch, than LCD or other monitor technologies, all of which can only be built up to certain sizes.

It's also possible to create LED screens in odd shapes and sizes, because the screens are built up from individual modules. Depending on the manufacturer, these modules range from one square foot to one square meter in size, in a 4:3 aspect ratio (same as your standard television screen), a wide-screen 16:9 aspect, or a 1:1 square. These modules are stacked on top of one another, locked together, and connected to a controller that takes a video input and sends the proper pieces of the image to the proper modules. The modules themselves can be arranged however you like, in a standard television shape or any other bizarro shape you can come up with. All you do is tell the software in the controller how you have the modules arranged and it does the rest.

Besides their overall size, LED panels are designated by **pixel pitch,** which is the distance from the center of one pixel to the center of the next. Smaller pitch increases the resolution, making the screen more viewable up close, with better-looking pictures and graphics. It also makes the screen more expensive. Larger pitch sizes are used for larger displays that will be viewed from farther away, where your eyes can mix the pixels together better and there is no sense spending the money on more pixels or the power to drive them.

Indoor screens that will be viewed up close have a pitch between 6 and 10 mm. For outdoor displays and billboards, the pitch is around 16 to 25 mm. What you use onstage depends on what kind of a look you want and what kind of a budget you have. Consider the distance to the viewer and also what kind of images you want to display.

Of course, you don't have to use LED screens just as big television monitors. The new Broadway production of *Spider-Man* uses small LED screens as lighted windows in the set. Because they are LEDs and not just light boxes, the designer can delicately change their color as well as create all sorts of images in them, including the shadows of distant people.

Driving the LED Screens

LED panels are usually used to display some sort of video, but you can't just take a video signal and plug it straight into the module. The module won't have any idea what to do with it. The modules themselves have no brains to understand a video signal. What the module wants is a list of intensities for each LED diode it has. Nothing else matters. "How bright do you want that diode?" That's it.

Furthermore, in most cases, you will be controlling more than one module, so you need a device that figures out which part of the image should be sent to which module.

What you need is a device that takes in a video image and translates it into giant strings of intensities. You need something that drives the LED screens.

The process of displaying video or still images on an LED screen depends on a technology called **pixel mapping.**

An LED screen is composed of a grid of pixels. When a video image is being sent to an LED, the various bits of that image need to be told which LED diode to go to. The device that is sending the image has to break that image down into parts and then decide which parts of that image will be represented by which pixel. In this way, the image is mapped onto the pixels of the LED.

The pixel-mapping process is carried out by an LED image processor or a video server. An image processor takes in a video image and, in real time, breaks the image down into pieces, creating a pixel map. It then translates those pixels into intensity information that LEDs can understand and sends that info out to the modules. A video server does the same thing, but it does it with images that it already has stored on a hard drive. As it pulls the images off the hard drive, a media server can also combine, mix, and change those images. Sometimes it's a fuzzy line between an image processor and a media server, because high-end image processors can perform some mixing functions and high-end servers can take in a real-time video image.

We'll go much deeper into media servers in part 3.

You can start to get really creative when you realize that pixel mapping doesn't just work with LEDs. All those points of light can be anything, including conventional lighting instruments. You can hang a grid of anything, from PAR cans to LED rope lights, just as long as each one is individually controlled by a DMX-capable dimmer. The pixel mapping software will translate the image into a stream of DMX intensities that can be used to control your grid of lights.

Once you have a grid of 3 × 3 or more, you can start mapping pixels. You could hang nine PAR cans in a grid, map your image to the nine DMX addresses for the dimmers and then start feeding in video images. Of course, the resolution (3 × 3) is nowhere near enough to actually make out an image, but it might give you some interesting effects. If you have moving lights available, you can hang them in a matrix and feed those DMX numbers into the color changing system in the lights. Pixel mapping works with any size grid, from 3 × 3 on up. Several companies now make LED drops, which have LEDs embedded into a fabric drape that can be folded, draped, and manipulated like a curtain. Map those LEDs in your software and you can play a video image on a curtain. Your matrix doesn't even have to be square. You can take strings of LEDs and wrap them around any shape, just as long as you use pixel-mapping software to address each one.

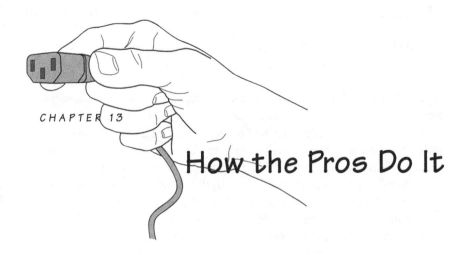

CHAPTER 13

How the Pros Do It

Are You a Good Switch or a Bad Switch? Lighting *Wicked* on Broadway

When *Wicked* brought Elphaba and Glinda, the dueling witches of Oz, to Broadway, it didn't use a lighting control console; it used *three* of them. Like most high-end musical shows, it is illuminated by an entire lighting catalog of devices including conventional lights, moving lights, projectors, color scrollers, follow spots, AutoYokes, and strobes, as well as LEDs in a custom-manufactured Emerald City Green. Besides the lights, the lighting consoles have to control dry ice and smoke machines as well as a simultaneous translation system.

For the purposes of control, these devices break down into three groups: video projection, moving lights, and everything else.

Let's start with everything else.

The conventional instruments are controlled by an ETC Obsession 1500. Of course, the Obsession doesn't control the conventional instruments themselves—it controls the eight 96-dimmer racks that, in turn, power the hundreds of conventional instruments hung on nine electric pipes over the stage, five thirty-foot-tall ladders in the wings, and a forest of front-of-house positions. The Obsession puts out three universes of DMX addresses, which covers the eight 96-dimmer racks as well as the color scrollers, strobes, and AutoYokes.

The Obsession also controls a number of nondimming devices. Many of the conventional lights have color scrollers, which receive their color selections over the DMX network. Even the follow spots have DMX-controlled color scrollers, although their dimmers are controlled manually by the human follow spot operator. There are other types of effects that also require DMX, including gobo rotators and AutoYokes.

The Obsession also controls thirty-two DMX addresses of LEDs. When *Wicked* first opened, it did not have any LEDs, emerald or otherwise. The touring company, however, was equipped with several panels of custom green LEDs that light up when Elphaba, the green meany title character, arrives at the Emerald City. Seems that everybody liked them so much that they were eventually added to the Broadway set. Unfortunately, the hanging panels where they are installed have to track on- and offstage during set changes, so the show installed a City Theatrical wireless DMX system, removing the need to run a DMX cable to the panels. Of course, there are still power cables running to the units, but putting the DMX on a wireless system meant one less cable in the way of the rolling scenery. Considering how much stuff is moving around backstage during a production of *Wicked*, it was apparently worth it.

Besides all the lighting gear, the Obsession uses DMX to control smoke and dry ice fog machines, both on and under the stage, as well as the Show Trans simultaneous translation system that broadcasts a translated version of the show to headphones in the audience. The translated lines must sync up with the show, so they are cued by the lighting console.

As if that wasn't enough, the Obsession also acts as the master lighting control board, putting out MIDI signals to the other two. These signals aren't too complex—just a Go and a cue number. It can also say Stop.

The moving lights are controlled by a High End Systems Wholehog 3. As I said earlier, a moving light console is philosophically different from a conventional console, requiring a different style of interface, including fixture personalities, LTP functions, and preprogrammed looks, so many shows have different controllers for conventional lights and movers. The Hog was one of the most popular moving light controllers when *Wicked* opened in 2003, but it has now been challenged by the appearance of the GrandMA control console. More about that in a minute as well.

For the sixty-five (now seventy-eight) moving light fixtures, *Wicked* went with Vari*Lite. Generally, a large show like this will not mix manufacturers when it comes to moving lights. Movers require a lot of complex maintenance by trained technicians, so it makes sense to settle on a single brand so you can keep your people supplied with tools and training. Of course, everyone has their favorites, but Brendan Quigley, *Wicked*'s head electrician, who has been with *Wicked* since Glinda was good, is an unabashed Vari*Lite fan. "Easy to maintain," is all he needs to say.

Wicked uses the VL2000 and VL3000 series of fixtures, and Brendan is proud to say that when the show opened, his fifteen VL3000s had serial numbers 1 through 15, meaning they were the first fifteen units ever made.

The Hog puts out four universes of DMX to control the moving lights. If you're keeping count, that's seven universes of DMX so far, with up to 3,584 addresses.

Of course, you could run seven huge loops of DMX around the theater to plug everything in, but considering the number of fixtures, the distances involved, and the need for quick repairs, it would be better to have a more logical system of organization—one that could divide up the universes into logical chunks and send them out into the theater in a sensibly organized bundle of cables.

Enter the opto-splitters.

Remember that I said DMX could not be run through a two-fer like electrical cable? In order to preserve the accuracy of the data, the DMX cables from the two lighting controllers are brought into a rack of sixteen opto-splitters, which carve up the seven universes into smaller slices. Coming out of the opto-splitters are reams of five-pin DMX cables, each of which runs to an individual position in the theater, like Electric #2, Stage Right LED, FOH VL3000, etc. You've still got DMX cable running everywhere, but now it can be more organized, making it easier to troubleshoot.

And speaking of trouble, a word about backup.

Losing either the Obsession or the Hog during a show would be catastrophic, but let's face it, all machines break sooner or later. For a show of this scale, that's an unacceptable risk. For this reason, there are actually *two* Wholehog consoles running the moving light program at *Wicked*. Only one of them is physically connected to the DMX cables at any one time, however. In the control booth, there is a switch that determines whether the regular board or the backup board is connected to the DMX networks. Both boards are connected by MIDI to the master board, the Obsession, so that both of them are actually running the show program all the time, even though only one of them is actually talking to the lights. If the main Wholehog experiences a failure, Brendan can reach up, flip the switch, and the backup Wholehog seamlessly takes over.

The Obsession actually has a redundant processor built into it, so if a problem occurs with the main processor, Brendan can turn a key switch on the front panel and the backup processor takes over.

Video projection is lorded over by yet another Wholehog 3 console, which produces yet another DMX universe that transmits information to a Catalyst video server connected to Mac Pro computers. Two Barco RLM R6+ projectors produce the images, which are projected onto various drops. When the show first opened, the Catalyst server was on version 1 and the Macs were state-of-the-art G4s. After seven years and 2,800 performances, the systems were working fine, but they were quite out-of-date. At this point, the show was faced with a quandary. Upgrade or not?

This can be a tough conversation to have with a producer. The original Catalyst and Mac G4 combination are working fine, so why mess with them? The unavoidable answer is, because someday, they will fail. All machines, from cars to computers to lawn mowers, will someday fail, and when they do, you need trained technicians, backup gear, and spare parts. That '64 Buick is a cool ride, but if you can't get a new distributor cap when the original one cracks, that chunk of American muscle is just so much eye candy. The older the machine, the harder it is to get it fixed.

The same is true of electronic equipment, except that the obsolescence cycle is lot shorter. A seven-year-old computer is positively ancient, and chances are good that when it fails, you won't be able to find a replacement. Leaving a multimillion-dollar show in the garage is not an option.

And that's why *Wicked* bit the emerald bullet and upgraded all their servers, computers, and projectors in 2009. Of course, that upgrade process involved days of replugging, replacing, and reprogramming, all of which had to be done without shutting down the show for a single performance, which is bit like swapping the tires on that Buick without pulling over. That's why you hire good people, like Brendan.

"Every afternoon, we would unplug the current system, plug in the new system, and then program and test all afternoon. When we were done, we would put it all back for the regular show." Brendan also reminded me that it wasn't just a matter of finding time for the techs. "There are dozens of other things that have to happen on the stage every day, just to keep the show functioning. You may want to program your servers, but the show is rehearsing a new Glinda that day. The whole process has to be coordinated from the top." Fortunately, the changeover went without a hitch, and the show is now running on state-of-the-art hardware and software again.

All three control consoles on *Wicked* sit in the follow spot booth, where they are connected by MIDI, allowing Brendan to run all three consoles from the front panel of the Obsession. When the show was being originally programmed and rehearsed, there was actually an operator in front of each console, but once the program was locked up, the show went down to a single console operator.

Besides Brendan, nine other electricians operate the show, including five follow spot operators, two deck electricians backstage, a moving lights technician, and the house electrician, who controls, not surprisingly, the house lights.

All those control consoles take up quite a bit of space, so when it came time to put the show on the road, the staff went in search of a more efficient solution. They found it in the GrandMA, manufactured by MA Lighting. The GrandMA (pronounced "Grand-M-A," not "grandma") was designed to have a split personality, capable of controlling conventional lights, movers, and projection systems. It's the all-in-one board, and it has become quite popular for these massive shows. Both touring companies of *Wicked* have boiled the three show programs down to a single program, run by a single GrandMA, which takes up a lot less space.

As of this writing, the Broadway show still has three control consoles, but Brendan, ever mindful of the obsolescence factor, has his eye on moving the New York show over to a single GrandMA soon. Even after seven years, there is still no rest for the *Wicked*.

Part 3: Video

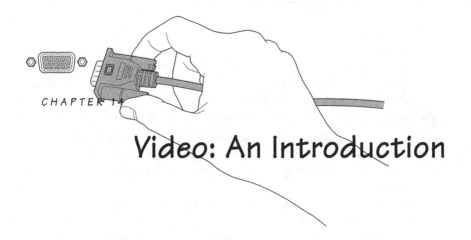

CHAPTER 14

Video: An Introduction

About halfway through the first act of *Young Frankenstein*, the Broadway adaptation of the classic Mel Brooks film, the hapless Young Dr. Frankenstein lands in the back of a hay wagon with his buxom assistant, Hilda. As the horses start clip-clopping their way up the road, the shadowy rows of trees on either side of the road begin to move, emerging from the darkness ahead, growing tall as they slide past the wagon, then disappearing in its wake. It looks for all the world as if we are following along behind the wagon as it trundles through the dark and mysterious woods of Transylvania, toward the distant castle.

It was a skillful effect, one that seems to put the flesh-and-blood actors smack in the middle of a film, and it got applause every night.

The mechanics of the effect were fairly simple—basically, a video projector, mounted on the front of the balcony, projected an image of passing trees on a drop behind the prop wagon. Add a couple of bobbing horse heads upstage and the illusion is complete. Of course, these types of effects, while they may be "simple," are never, ever easy, and projection designer Marc Brickman's team spent months getting this one right.

I bring this effect up because it spotlights the increasing audience expectation for the inclusion of media in live performance. As we grow more comfortable with the storytelling framework of film and television, we expect the action to change quickly between locations, even when the locations are right in front of us on the stage. As we grow used to film and television visuals, we expect a more immersive environment on stage. We have become accustomed to a performance that completely fills our visual field and even surrounds us. As theater producers try to up the visual ante of stage productions, they rely more and more on projected effects, which can be produced (and changed) more quickly and less expensively than elaborate physical scenery. Our brains have become accustomed to complex, multilayered input and constant motion.

The theater pundits call this phenomenon "convergence," the expanding mash-up of live action and media that is redefining live entertainment, from the premium level of Broadway, Cirque du Soleil, and the Blue Man Group right down to high schools and community theater. Others have become concerned about the visual desensitization and sensual overload that is the inevitable byproduct of the visual arms race in modern entertainment, as all parties seek a bigger, newer, more visceral spectacle that will capture our eyes and open our wallets.

Love it or hate it, though, video is here to stay in live theater, so, if you haven't before, it's time for you to learn the basics of video technology, even if you only want to use a video camera to document your show.

As with all of the introductory chapters, there is a test to see if you need to read it. If the following sentence makes sense to you, skip the intro and dive into video projection.

"We will be shooting our content in HD to get the 16:9 aspect ratio, but our projector does not have an HDMI input, so make sure the server can output analog component video."

Just technobabble to you? Great! Read on, and all will become clear.

How Video Is Made

A video image is "drawn" on a TV screen by passing an electrical signal across thousands of tiny points lined up in a grid. In the olden days, the signal was provided by an electron gun mounted at the back of your television, firing electrons at rows of luminescent dots on the back of the television screen. The more electrons that were fired at the dots, the brighter they glowed. Each of these tiny cells is called a picture element or a **pixel**. Pixels are arranged in rows known as **scan lines**. If you lean in close to an old-style, cathode-ray television screen, you can clearly see the individual dots, glowing with the energy being fired from the electron gun in the back of the set. Turns out that your mother was right; it's really not a good idea to sit too close to a CRT screen.

Nowadays, with the advent of flat-panel screens, there is no longer a gun shooting electrons at the back of the screen. Instead, those pixels are energized by an electrical current, fed to them by a grid of tiny wires. The names haven't changed, however. We still call them pixels and scan lines, although it's no longer hazardous to put your face right up to the television screen.

When the electron gun was firing at your CRT, it scanned the entire screen, or frame, thirty times each second, creating a **frame rate** of thirty frames per second, or 30 fps.[1] With flat-panel screens, that hasn't changed. The picture on the screen is still renewed thirty times per second. At that speed, your eye doesn't see the individual images; it blends the images together into a continuous, moving stream. Presto, you are watching TV.

The Tyranny of Format

As you might expect, this process of drawing a frame of video is a lot more complex than the simple explanation above, and more importantly, there are a lot of variables. How many scan lines are there? How many pixels in each line? How often will we redraw the screen? And on and on. . .

Unfortunately, if any of these variables (and dozens more that I haven't mentioned) are different between two video signals, or between a video signal and a display device, then they are incompatible with one another. What happens, for example, if the frame rate of an incoming video signal is not the same as the frame rate of the television on which it is displayed? Imagine two musicians trying to play a song simultaneously, but at two different tempos. Chaos.

For this reason, video has formats: lists of standards that allow video signals to agree with each other and with the display, storage, and processing devices through which they are going.

The bad news is, there are a lot of formats. Over the years, creative, intelligent people have found lots of different ways to use and improve video signals, creating ever-expanding lists of formats, dividing video signals, and multiplying their differences. Today, video exists in hundreds of formats, many of which don't live together well, or at all. And unfortunately, if we want to use video, we have to understand and follow these formats.

Let's look at some of the ways that formats are defined.

Aspect Ratio

Aspect ratio is the answer to the question: What shape is the picture?

The aspect ratio is the ratio of the height of the image to its width. A square image would have an aspect ratio of 1:1, or one to one. A rectangle that was twice as wide as it was tall would have an aspect ratio of 1:2, or one to two. This number is expressed as a ratio, rather than as a specific measurement, so that it can be used for any size of screen. A screen with an aspect ratio of 1:2 could be one inch by two inches or it could be forty-two inches by eighty-four inches. Same aspect ratio.

_____

[1] In the USA, that is. If you are elsewhere in the world, you may be using the PAL standard, which has a frame rate of 25 fps as we will see shortly.

Back when silent films were first being made, there was very little agreement on the size of the image. Blank film stock was just a continuous stream of gelatin and each camera printed images on it slightly differently. More variations were introduced when the film was printed. When sound came in, the labs had to find a place to put the optical stripe that had the audio information, so the image got moved around even more. Each film distributor had their own standards for the size and shape of the image, causing confusion in the movie houses.

In 1932, the Academy of Motion Pictures Arts and Sciences (yes, the Oscar people) decreed that all studio films should have an aspect ratio of 1:1.375, which became known as the Academy format. In other words, if you were projecting a film image that was a foot tall, the image would be 1.375 feet wide. All studio films shot from 1932 to 1952 were shot in the Academy format, which is generally abbreviated to 1:137.

When talking about formats, it is normal to drop the one at the beginning, as it is assumed. Therefore, when people talk about the Academy format, for example, they call it "one three seven."

When television first appeared, it was natural to adopt the familiar rectangle of the Academy format, although television ended up with a slightly different shape: 1.33.[2] Video people commonly refer to this format as 4:3 or "four three," which is basically correct, give or take a few decimal places. If your screen is four feet wide, it is three feet tall.

Concerned about the incursion of television on their entertainment market, the film studios left the Academy format behind in the fifties and switched to wider-screen formats like 1.66, 1.85, and even 2.40. Video, however, stuck with 4:3 for decades, until the advent of high-definition television which has a wider filmlike aspect ratio of 16:9.

If you are dealing with video, then, you will generally be using one of these two ratios: the older 4:3, or the newer, wider 16:9.

Resolution

Resolution refers to the number of pixels in a video image. This number is determined by the number of scan lines and the number of pixels on each line. More pixels means, in theory, a better image with more detail.

For half a century, the resolution of your television screen did not change. Back in 1953, the National Television System Committee (NTSC) decreed that a television screen should have 525 scan lines, with 486 of them used for the picture (the rest were taken up with various kinds of

---

[2] Because of this difference, the Academy format is often incorrectly listed as 1.33.

data). Due to the limitations of a television screen, about 440 of those lines were actually visible on the screen. The screen was 486 pixels wide, so the resolution was 486 × 440 for a total of around 210,000 pixels in each frame. That's what they set up in 1953 and that's the way it stayed for more than half a century.

Then, in the late twentieth century, a new wave swept the world of video: high definition.

One of the reasons that high definition looked so much better than standard definition was the higher resolution. There are two major HD formats in common usage: 1280 × 720 and 1920 × 1080. Both of them are well above the 486 × 440 that we all lived with for half a century.

One of the major points of confusion in video is the difference between a television screen and a computer screen. One of the major differences between the two is resolution.

The first widely adopted standard for computer screens was called VGA, and it was 640 pixels wide and 480 lines tall. Consequently, right from the beginning, computer screens had a higher resolution than television. And the gap has only gotten wider: The Mac PowerBook that I am using to write this chapter has a display that is 1440 × 900 for almost 1.3 million pixels, six times as many as my analog television. Computers needed this extra resolution from the beginning because they display so much text, which requires high resolution to be easily legible.

Frame Rate

Sometimes called the **refresh rate**, the **frame rate** refers to the number of times that the image is redrawn every second, expressed as frames per second or fps.

I hate to keep giving you ancient history, but it is occasionally useful to understand why things are the way they are (and to remember them). Frame rate is a good example.

As you know from reading the lighting chapter, our electrical power is alternating current, meaning that the electrical current is constantly reversing direction. It reverses sixty times per second, or 60 Hz, which is referred to as the power frequency. Early television engineers discovered that when the frame rate for the video was different from the power frequency, the video image would tend to "roll" or become distorted. The easy solution was to make the frame rate the same as the power frequency, or actually, exactly half the frequency. Later on, circuitry was invented that prevented this problem, but by then it was too late: The video frame rate in the United States was set at 30 fps.

In Europe, they have a different power frequency—50Hz. Consequently, the frame rate there was set at 25fps, half of their power frequency, which immediately made European video incompatible with Americans.

When color came into the picture, those clever engineers discovered that, for complex technical reasons, the picture was actually a bit more stable if the frame was ever so slightly less than sixty, so it actually became 59.94Hz, which is just annoying.

Scanning System

When the video standards were first being written, they had to take into account the reality of the equipment that was available at the time. One of the realities was bandwidth—that is, the amount of video information that could be pushed down a video cable at one time.

The engineers creating the first video signals really wanted to draw or "scan" a new frame sixty times per second, which was both equal to the power frequency and fast enough to create a sharp, detailed picture. Hence, they really wanted to set the frame rate at 60fps. The problem was they couldn't get that much video information down the pipe at that speed, so they compromised. Every sixtieth of a second, they drew half of one video frame, which meant they only had to push half as much information down the cable. These half frames are known as **fields**. Two fields make up one frame, which made the frame rate 30 fps. The fields are not the top and bottom of the frame, however; they are each composed of every other line in the frame. The first field of each frame is composed of all the odd-numbered lines (1, 3, 5, etc.) in the frame, while the second half has all the even-numbered lines (2, 4, 6, etc.). So the electron gun would start at the top of the frame, scan all the odd-numbered lines, then return to the top and scan all the even-numbered lines. This technique of scanning every other line in each frame is known as **interlacing**. Because the fields are interlaced with each other, the eye is tricked into thinking that the frame rate is actually faster than it is. Not only that, but interlacing the fields, rather than just making one big pass from top to bottom every thirtieth of a second, tends to smooth out motion in the image, because the eye is getting new information every sixtieth of a second. You can see the difference if you go to a movie theater where actual film is being screened (as opposed to digital projection). Film has a frame rate that is even slower than video—24 fps. When a film camera pans quickly, you can see the blurriness in the image, caused by the slower noninterlaced frame rate. In fact, one way to make a video image look more like film is to introduce this motion blur into the video image.

Interlacing worked just fine for decades, but once higher-resolution video and higher bandwidth became available, engineers began to debate whether interlacing was still necessary. Some formats have ditched it in favor of **progressive** scanning, which scans all the lines in order from top to bottom, while others stick to interlacing, both to reduce the amount of data in the pipe and to retain smoother movement. If you want to start an argument in an engineer bar, stand up and yell, "Interlacing is still better than progressive scan!" You will be rewarded with a satisfying technogeek brain brawl as very smart people hotly debate this ongoing issue.

Standard

With all these different possibilities out there—different aspect ratios, different resolutions, different frame rates, and so on—there needed to be some agreement on standards before television could be brought out for general usage.

Enter the National Television Systems Committee, known as the **NTSC.** In 1953, this group of brainiacs decided on a set of standards that defined all these things for color television in the United States. Among other things, the NTSC determined that all broadcast signals in the US should have the following:

525 scan lines
30 frames per second (actually 29.97 fps)
Interlaced video
1.33 aspect ratio

Unfortunately, there were other standards organizations in the world, and for various reasons, they decided on slightly different standards.

In Europe, the brainiacs created a standard known as Phase Alternate Line, or **PAL.** The engineers behind PAL agreed with NTSC on some things, like the aspect ratio and interlacing the video, but they disagreed on the number of lines and the frame rate, making the two standards incompatible with each other. This is why the DVD that you bought in Germany looks screwy on your home television, if you can get it to play at all.

Of course, as previously stated, Europe has a different power frequency, so some of the differences in standards make sense.

What doesn't make sense is why France decided to come up with their very own standard and ignore the rest of Europe. The Sequential Couleur Avec Memoire (**SECAM**) was basically a political move intended to protect the French manufacturers of video equipment, but SECAM was also adopted in the USSR and some Eastern bloc countries. It's not hard to imagine why the folks behind the iron curtain saw a benefit in making their systems incompatible with Western TV signals. I guess they weren't worried about the French.

In any case, you only have to worry about the standard if you are sending or receiving video content from a foreign country. There are many excellent online lists that will tell you the video standard for the country you are dealing with.

Google me

Worldwide Video Standards

NTSC and PAL are less of a problem for video inside your computer, which can play either one. In fact, your computer can play any frame rate and resolution you want. The standards are still relevant, however, if you are importing video into a video-editing program. If you want to combine two chunks of video, they have to be the same standard. Fortunately, any video-editing program worth a byte can do that for you.

Composite vs. S-Video vs. Component

A video signal is actually composed of a bunch of different signals. Each pixel needs two pieces of information: brightness (or luminance) and color (or chrominance). The color information is broken down into three streams: red, blue, and green. Furthermore the whole signal needs **sync** information to tell it both when to move to the next pixel and when to move to the next line.

When you are carrying a video signal from one device to another, say from a DVD to a video screen, you have two choices: You can send all this information down the same cable, or you can split it up into separate cables. As we talked about previously, bandwidth is always an issue with any cable, so trying to send all these signals down the same line means that you can't send as much information (or some of it might be lost). That's why higher-quality video signals are sent down multiple cables.

Video that is combined onto a signal cable is called **composite** video, because it is all mixed together. One video cable carries all three colors, plus brightness and sync. With all this information going down the same pipe, there is definitely a limit on the quality of the image.

Some video systems use two wires, one for luminance and one for chrominance, both of which are wrapped up together into one cable. This is known as **S-Video**, and it was popular among consumer video applications for quite

a while. Even today, you will still find lots of S-Video plugs as the standard "Video Out" plug on laptop computers. In higher-end applications, however,

S-Video has been replaced by digital video standards (more about that in the next chapter) and **component** video.

A video signal where each color has its own wire is called **component** video. The most common form of component video has three cables, one each for red, blue, and green video, the so-called **RGB** cable. The sync information is carried along with the green video stream. There are also higher-end component video cables that have four or five cables, so every piece of the signal has its own piece of wire, but these are only in the pro world. In the consumer or "prosumer" world, component cable has three cables and is called RGB.

Standard Definition vs. High Definition

Both composite and component video cables are designed to carry standard definition video, the kind of video that has been around since the NTSC standardized it in 1953.

Times change, however, and as equipment improved, it became capable of handling more data. The audience's eyes also developed, helped along by advances in film technology. Finally, the broadcasters, always looking for a way to keep people watching television, got together with the government and created a new standard, now known as high definition. This time, the Americans got along with the rest of the world, and a new international standard was adopted in the late 1990s.[3]

High-definition formats are defined by three things:

Resolution

HD comes in two different resolutions, known in video circles as 1080 or 720, based on the number of scan lines that they have. Remember that standard NTSC had 480 lines, so you can see the huge difference in an HD signal. All HD formats have an aspect ratio of 16:9, so the layout of the pixels looks like this:

a. 720 format: 1280 × 720 (921,600 pixels)
b. 1080 format: 1920 × 1080 (2,073,600 pixels)

---

[3] Well, almost. Both Brazil and China adopted slightly different standards. However, as these signals are now digital, meaning that they are composed entirely of numbers, it is not too challenging to alter the offending signals to match everyone else's.

If you compare those pixel counts with the measly 153,600 pixels that we get from standard NTSC, you can see that we have a *lot* more to play with in HD. This is why it looks so good.

Scanning System

The 720 resolution is always scanned progressively, with the entire screen being drawn in one pass, while 1080 can be either progressive or interlaced.

Frame Rate

As with standard-definition video, there are two heavily used frame rates, 50fps and 60fps, mostly depending on what country you are in. Note that for interlaced formats, these two rates will be listed as 25fps and 30 fps, since it takes two passes to draw the entire screen, effectively cutting the frame rate in half.

Taking these above into account, you should now have no trouble reading formats like these:

1080i30 (1920 × 1080 pixels, interlaced, thirty frames per second)
720p50 (1280 × 720 pixels, progressive scan, fifty frames per second)

On occasion, the frame rate will be left off entirely (particularly when a manufacturer is trying to sell something), and you will see a product labeled simply 1080i or 720p. In this case, you can safely assume that the frame rate is 60 or 50 (30 or 25 for interlaced) depending on whether you are in the United States or not.

There are other more exotic resolutions, which you might find if you work in special venues, most notably 24p, which the pros really like because it has the same frame rate as film: twenty-four frames per second. The 24p format, therefore, can easily be printed to film or vice versa.

A Word About Cables

Standard-definition video travels on two kinds of cable: RCA, in the consumer world, and BNC, in the pro world. Component video requires a single cable, while component requires three on consumer gear and three to five on pro gear.

High-definition video can be sent over component video cable, but it will suffer some loss of quality. To do it right, use DVI-D or HDMI cables. Note that DVI-D will require separate cables for the audio, while HDMI carries the audio signal along with it.

A Note About DVDs

Around the end of the twentieth century, we all threw out our VHS tapes and made the switch to DVDs. Why did we do that? Two reasons. First, the DVD format has a higher resolution than VHS did, but that is mostly because VHS resolution was truly awful. It was only 480 × 320 which meant that you immediately threw away a third of your resolution when you committed a NTSC signal to a VHS tape. Secondly, by recording the video content digitally, the DVD kept it in a form that didn't degrade. A VHS tape degraded every time you played it, and it wasn't long before the image disappeared completely. DVDs don't last forever, but if cared for properly, they can be played hundreds of times with no visible loss of quality.

Lots of people think that the DVD format is high definition. It isn't. A DVD cannot reproduce any more scan lines than standard NTSC or PAL. It does have one advantage over those two formats, however. It can have either a 4:3 or 16:9 aspect ratio. That's why you will often see commercially produced DVDs that are wide-screen on one side (16:9) and standard on the other (4:3).

Remember, though, DVDs are digital, but not HD. That's why everybody is so hot and bothered about the Blu-ray format. It is digital, like a DVD, but it is also high definition.

One More Thing

I have saved my most important comment about high definition for the end, and I'm going to put it in bold type. **In order to have a high-definition image the entire system must be high definition.** If your source material is not HD, then there is no benefit displaying it on an HD screen. Likewise, if you have HD source material, but not an HD monitor, then you are wasting the benefit. Even the cables matter. If you are playing HD content onto an HD monitor, but sending the content through standard cables, it might as well be standard definition.

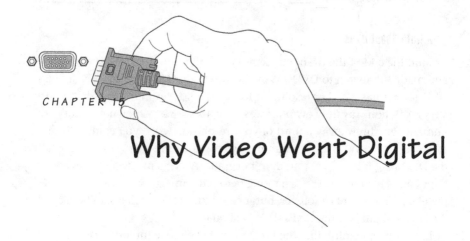

CHAPTER 15

Why Video Went Digital

Video went digital for the same reason that audio did: image quality.

Like analog audio, analog video is subject to signal loss and degradation every time it is transmitted from one device to another. Electrical interference, long cables, inconsistent storage materials—all these can reduce the quality of a video image, especially when the same information is copied, retransmitted, or stored for long periods. Analog signals simply wear away over time.

Digital signals, however, are composed of strings of numbers (1s and 0s) that can be accurately transmitted, copied, and stored with no loss in quality. Changing a video image over to digital numbers also greatly reduces the bandwidth required to broadcast it, which is currently making it possible for our nationwide video transmission system to switch to digital without using up any more space in the always-crowded transmission frequencies.

In the world of audio, the process of going from the analog realm into the digital one is called sampling. In video, we talk about **image capturing**, the way that a digital device scans a visual image and redefines it as a string of 1s and 0s.

A digital camera captures the image using a sensor known as a **charge-coupled device**, or CCD, which is basically a computer chip that is sensitive to light. Less-expensive cameras have one CCD, while the pricey ones have three—one each for red, blue, and green. The CCD is covered with a grid of light-sensitive pixels, each of which reacts to a tiny piece of the image focused on the CCD by the camera lens. When the light hits the pixel, the pixel puts out a number corresponding to the brightness of the light. Like audio, the pixel has a certain number of bits that it uses to describe that light level. The more bits it has, the more precise it can be.

On a single CCD camera, each pixel is covered with a color filter so that it only "sees" red, blue, or green light. Out of every four pixels, one is devoted to red and one to blue, while two are devoted to green (the human eye is less sensitive to green, so twice as many pixels are devoted to it). On a three-CCD system, a prism divides the light into red, green, and blue and focuses each color on its own CCD. The output of the three chips is added together to come up with the average color of each pixel. This creates higher resolution and a sharper picture.

The CCD image capture process produces a stream of numbers, which is used to create a visual image, known as a **frame**. These frames are displayed at a constant rate to create a moving image. Like analog video, the rate at which these frames are played back is known as, wait for it . . . the **frame rate**. Digital video uses the same frame rates as analog: 25fps for the European standard, 30fps for the American standard, and 29.97fps for the drop frame American standard.

Digital video is described just like analog in many other ways as well. For example, we talk about the **frame size**, which is a measurement of the width and height of the image in pixels. Because of the legacy of analog video, these frame sizes almost always have an aspect ratio of 4:3 or 16:9. For example, one of the most common digital frame sizes is 640 × 480 which corresponds to an aspect ratio of 4:3.

Like digital audio, digital video also uses bits to describe the brightness of that light hitting the pixel, and the more bits you've got to work with, the better. In audio, we called it the bit depth; in video, it is known as the **color depth**, because it is how the pixel describes its own color. Interestingly, 24 bits seems to be the high-end of color depth, just as it was in bit depth.

When you combine frame size, color depth, and frame rate, you begin to see how much data is really required to transmit digital video, known as the **bit rate**.

Bit rate is measured in bits per second, abbreviated as bit/s or bps. Note that these are *bits* per second, not *bytes* per second.[1] A thousand bits per second is one Kbit/s while a million is one Mbit/s.

Let's take the 640 × 480 example above run the numbers.

A 640 × 480 pixel image has 307,200 pixels, each of which has 24 bits of information. That's 7,372,800 bits of data per frame. Run those frames at 30 fps and you get a bit rate of, whoa, Nelly:

---

[1] If you recall from the digital audio chapter, a bit is a single piece of data, a 1 or a 0 while a byte is actually 8 bits. Bytes are used to measure sizes of physical objects like disk drives and computer memories, while bits are used to measure data rates.

221 Mbits per second.

How much is that?

Well, think back for a moment to the audio chapter, where we figured out that one minute of uncompressed stereo audio ran about 10 MB. A standard CD, playing that audio file, puts out about 1.4 Mbit/s. Now here we are with uncompressed digital video putting out over 150 times more information.

And 640 × 480 is actually not a very big video image. Full-blown HD is 1920 × 1080, which can produce a bit rate up to 2.9 gigabits per second, over two thousand times as much data as the audio file.

The bottom line is, you don't have to get very far into digital video before you see that the key to the entire thing is going to be . . .

Compression

As soon as video started going digital, there was a problem, and the problem was where to put it all. Video was just too darn big.

Uncompressed video, the kind we were talking about above, isn't really useful for any practical application. It takes a major amount of computer processing to deal with 221 million bits of information every second. From the beginning, then, the challenge with video was to squeeze it into a much smaller amount of space, to compress it, and to get that bit rate down to something that a reasonably cheap processor could handle. This was necessary to conserve storage space on hard drives, distribute the content on disks, and broadcast it on television and the Internet. For all these things, small was beautiful.

It was beautiful, at least, unless it was ugly. There are easy ways to make a video file smaller, of course, but a lot of them looked horrible on the screen. For example, instead of using thirty frames per second, you can create video that plays more slowly, like fifteen frames per second. All of a sudden, your file is half as big, but it's also jerky and hard to watch.

The science, nay, the *art* of **compression**, then, is concerned with this simple question: How can we make the file smaller without reducing the apparent quality of the images?

Before getting into compression, though, let me tell you why you should care about this complex and rather esoteric subject.

If you slip a DVD into a player and push play, you are using compression. The video images on the DVD have been prepared for distribution using a process known as MPEG-2 compression. For you as a user, this process is "transparent." You don't see it and you don't have to.

If you are going to create video, however, you will need to decide whether you are going to use MPEG-2 compression or one of its brethren—MPEG-1 or

MPEG-4—or another format, like H.264. If you get content from someone else and the image is full of big, blocky chunks, you will need to understand why the compression isn't working right. If you want to create a DVD, put a video in an e-mail upload to YouTube, or put your acting reel on your iPhone, you will need to understand compression, at least to a point.

Like audio, though you need to understand **what** compression does, but not **how** it does it. Very few people without PhDs in electrical engineering understand how compression does what it does. Arthur C. Clarke's famous admonition that "any sufficiently advanced technology is indistinguishable from magic" most certainly applies here. Video compression works with mystical mathematical formulas known as algorithms, which come with names like Fourier-related transform and Chebyshev polynomial. If esoteric mathematics is your thing, knock yourself out on Mathepedia, but for the rest of us, here is what you really need to know about video compression.

Codec

A codec is a computer program that compresses and **de**compresses video (often called **co**ding and **dec**oding). Each codec is designed to compress and decompress a particular compression format. Think of it as a translator. If you want to translate a book into Latvian, you need someone who speaks Latvian. If you want to compress a video file into the MPEG-2 format (more about that it in a minute), you need a program that speaks MPEG-2. That's an MPEG-2 compressor.

Of course, at the other end, you need someone who can take the MPEG-2 file and translate it back into something that you can watch. That is the de-compressing part.

Codecs usually contain both the compressing and the decompressing parts though, so hence the name.

The Motion Picture Experts Group

You will never see the names of the people who make up this international group of experts, but if you use a computer, they affect your life every day.

Back in the 1986, a group of people known as the Joint Photographic Experts Group got together to figure out a format for digital photos and other images. The JPEG, as it became known, created an extremely successful format that swept the world and allowed everyone to compress images down to sizes that could be stored on computers, distributed on digital media, and sent over this newfangled bunch of pipes that the kids were calling the Internet. The format has been through some changes over the years, but, if you use the Internet, you are constantly looking at JPEG images.

In order to pull off the same feat for video, the Motion Picture Experts Group convened in 1988. More than twenty years later, the set of standards that they created for video compression are ruling our lives. As of this writing, there are three major MPEG video standards that you will run into in everyday usage:

MPEG-1

The first major standard that the MPEG created is still around and may be the most compatible of all video compression standards. If you are putting files on the Internet and want to maximize compatibility, you might want to use this original format, even though it has since been surpassed in quality.

MPEG-2

This format was chosen for DVDs, digital television broadcast, digital satellite and Blu-ray disks, so it's going to be around for a while. Unlike MPEG-1, it supports high-definition and interlaced images. If you are outputting video to a DVD, you will be using this format. MPEG-2 reduces the size of an uncompressed file by fifteen to thirty times. MPEG-2 is also used as a professional distribution format, that is, as a format the pros use to pass files amongst themselves.

MPEG-4

After the short-lived MPEG-3 was declared redundant and abandoned, the MPEG-4 format became the most advanced one yet. Blessed with more efficient compression and higher quality, it also contains support for proprietary standards for managing and protecting content, like the controversial digital rights management that was used in the original Apple iTunes Store. DRM was later abandoned after a storm of user complaint. This is a fairly common format for Internet files, giving you a higher level of quality than MPEG-1.

MPEG compression is by no means the only form of video compression out there—just the most common. Here are a few others that have gained attention recently:

DV

Actually, DV isn't just compression; it's a format for recording and playing back digital video invented by a consortium of companies back in 1995. It allowed for the creation of a new generation of video cameras as well as relatively inexpensive nonlinear editing software, which allowed just about anybody to shoot and edit broadcast quality video. It was a huge boon to independent filmmakers, small newsgathering organizations, and anyone else who was looking for an inexpensive way to get good-looking video.

Besides a compression scheme, DV also included specs for physical tapes, magnetization, recording methods, and so on. Lately, though, almost all video cameras are turning away from tape-based recording to file-based recording. Rather than running a physical tape over a physical head, which would imprint the ones and zeros on the tape by magnetizing tiny metal particles in the tape, newer cameras create a computer file on some kind of internal memory device. Optical hard drives are used in the pro cameras, while the consumer and prosumer market use solid-state memory cards like the SD and CF cards.

DV, then, is no longer really a format for creating tapes, but a format of computer file. As such, what DV really brings to the table is an efficient compression scheme. If you shoot footage with a camcorder, the file that is created on the memory card is most likely some variant of DV.

H.264

Following onto the MPEG standards, another group called the Video Coding Experts Group (VCEG) got together with the MPEG people to push the quality of compression even higher. They created a series of standards, culminating in H.264, which succeeded at increasing image quality while reducing bit rates. H.264 doesn't exist by itself; it is a variant of the MPEG format, so you will commonly see file formats like H.264/MPEG-4. As of this writing, H.264 is used for YouTube, the iTunes Store, and digital satellite services, among other things. If you are encoding a video for the Internet, you might choose this format.

So, what do these formats actually mean? Each format is a way of compressing a video file, always trying to keep file size low and quality high. They all have different ways of achieving that by using the aforementioned "magic," but they all have a few things in common, like . . .

Lossy Compression

All video compression is **lossy**. What this means is that the codec is actually throwing away information that it deems unnecessary, like your mom throwing out old clothes that don't fit you anymore. The opposite of lossy compression is **lossless compression**, where the computer reduces the file size without throwing away any information. Lossless compression works well in audio, but not in video, where it doesn't really produce significant savings in file size. (Apparently it's easier to fool your ears than your eyes.) Therefore, virtually all video compression is lossy. What this means is that video compression is a one-way street: Once you compress a video file, you will never get it back to its original quality. For this reason, it's a good idea to save your original uncompressed files, just in case. Furthermore, once you have compressed a file, it's a bad idea to compress it again, so, if you are compressing a file, try to start with an uncompressed original.

There are two strategies to lossy compression:

Interframe Compression

In this case, the encoder compares two successive frames to see how much has changed between them. In the case of a completely still image, nothing will have changed. In the case of a sequence with lots of movement, like an explosion, car chase, willow tree blowing in the wind, etc., quite a bit will have changed. The encoder scans the two images, looking for blocks of pixels that do not change or only change slightly. Then, it removes those pixels from the second image and substitutes a command to repeat the previous pixels from the previous frame. If the two images are part of a sequence showing someone talking, then the pixels showing the background areas are most likely not changing from one frame to the next, so they can be copied from the previous frame. Even if the pixels have moved or changed intensity, the encoder can still get rid of them in the second frame, substituting a longer command that says, essentially, "Copy those pixels and change them like this." It's a longer command, but it still requires less data than redrawing all those pixels from scratch.

It is worth noting that the amount of compression that can be achieved by this process varies greatly depending on the content of the video. Scenes with lots of camera movement and action will not compress as much as a "talking head" with a consistent background.

Using this kind of compression can make editing difficult, as each frame may not have a complete image. If you cut up a piece of video, you may end up with a starting frame that is supposed to copy pixels from a previous frame that isn't there anymore. This is why certain video formats that use a lot of interframe compression, like MPEG-2, do not edit well. These formats are only used for distribution. If you want to edit these formats, you will want to convert the video back to a format that does not use interframe compression, like DV.

The more compression you are using, the more likely it is that the encoder will stumble and create artifacts—little blocky bits that appear on the screen because the encoder couldn't keep up with the video stream. In poorly compressed video, you will see these little blocks during very active scenes or immediately after a cut, when the frame of video completely changes. One of the ways to reduce artifacts is to create **key frames**, which are frames that contain all the pixels, with no commands to repeat previous frames. When you are saving, converting, or encoding video, you may be asked how often you want key frames. The more often you have key frames, the less chance that you will have artifacts. However, more key frames means less compression and thus a larger file. It's all about trade-offs.

Lastly, when you are setting up encoding specifications, the computer might ask if you want one-pass or two-pass compression. With one-pass, the encoder only goes through the file one time, figuring out the encoding as it goes, frame by frame. In two-pass compression, the encoder scans through the entire file first, looking for the best places to remove data. Once it has things figured out, the encoder goes back and scans the file again, compressing all the data. Because it has had a look at the big picture first, however, the encoder can make better decisions about how and where to remove data. Two-pass compression is generally better quality. The trade-off here is time: It takes longer to go through the file more than once so the encoding process is slower. If you have the time, though, two-pass (or multipass) is a better way to go.

Intraframe Compression

This is compression that happens within a single frame of video. The encoder scans each frame, one at a time, and decides if there is information in each frame that can be tossed. This type of compression depends on algorithms that exploit limitations of the human eye. For example, the human eye is better at distinguishing differences in brightness than differences in color, so the encoder will throw away some of the color information that will not be noticed by the eye. This is the same process that is used in JPEG compression, the kind that is used to compress still images. In fact, one kind of compression, known as Moving JPEG, is exactly the same as JPEG.

Writing algorithms that mimic the abilities of the human eye is where the real alchemy comes into compression. As a user, you can set the amount of compression that the encoder applies to the video by setting the **bit rate** (see below), but after that, it's really up to the magicians.

Bit Rate

At times, digital video may be read off of a hard drive, downloaded from the Internet, sent over a cable to other devices, and decoded by a computer or media player. The ease with which these things happen depends partly on the amount of data that is being pushed through the circuits every second, a measurement known as the **bit rate**, sometimes written as bitrate. We talked a bit about bit rate above, as a way of understanding file size, but when you are dealing with compression, bit rate becomes very important.

When a file is being encoded, the user can usually choose a bit rate, and like everything else, it's a trade-off. Higher bit rates create bigger files and require more computer power to decode, but they look better because the encoder has kept more of the original data. Lower bit rates are the opposite: smaller, faster, lower quality.

In order to get a feel for these numbers, let's look at some examples of bit rates:

128–384 Kbit/s – Business videoconferencing
3.5 Mbit/s – Standard definition quality
9.2 Mbit/s –DVD quality (maximum recommended)
8 to 15 Mbit/s – HDTV quality
40 Mbit/s – Blu-ray quality (maximum recommended)
2.9 Gbit/s – Uncompressed HD video (1920 × 1080)

When choosing a bit rate for encoding a video file, you might also be offered the option of a **variable bit rate**, or **VBR**. This is almost always a good thing. A variable bit rate means that the encoder will decide the bit rate "on the fly" while encoding, and it can change, depending on the content. Portions of the file that would benefit from a higher bit rate will get it, while other portions that are not so demanding will get a lower one. This helps keep the file size down while keeping quality high.

So what's the right bit rate to use? Well, it depends on what you are using the file for. If you are preparing video for a video server, then the server specs will tell you what it can handle. The best approach is to take advantage of the presets that are included in your video-editing program. There may be settings for things like "iPhone" or "DVD" or "streaming video." Use VBR whenever possible.

Uncompressed Digital Video

With all this talk about compression, you might think that all digital video is compressed, which is not true.

Video is compressed in order to send it over a limited bandwidth network, like an Internet connection, or to store it in a limited space, like a DVD or a consumer hard drive.

When video is handled by professional cameras, editing suites, and live broadcast gear, however, it is high quality and uncompressed, which usually means it is handled by an **SDI** interface. The serial digital interface is how television stations pass around video content within their facilities. If you are setting up a high-quality video-editing station in your facility, you will want to invest in computer cards and cables to handle the uncompressed SDI format.

In the consumer world, the cables that handle uncompressed high-quality video are called **HDMI**, or high-definition multimedia interface. If you are getting HD video signals from your cable provider, then you should be using HDMI cables to get the signal to your video screen. Otherwise, you are giving up some of the image quality by sending it through lower-quality cables, like composite, S-video, or even RBG (although you won't lose much with RGB).

Media Container Files

One of the issues about media files is that they typically can only handle one kind of media, like pictures or audio. In order for more than one kind of data to live together, play together, and be stored together, they have to be placed into a media container file. Media container files are metafiles—files that contain other files.

This can get a little complicated, partly because some kinds of container files are referred to with the same names as the files they contain.

We have already talked about one set of container files, although we didn't identify them as such. The AIFF and WAV formats are actually media container files that contain chunks of audio, as well as additional information that helps play the files back correctly. In this case, AIFF and WAV are exclusively associated with audio, so we don't really have to bother about the distinction between media containers and the media they contain. This isn't always true, however, especially with video.

A video media container commonly contains one or more video files, as well as one or more audio files. They might also contain subtitles, chapter information, or other meta-information.

Two of the most common computer media container formats are AVI (primarily used on Windows machines) and Quicktime (primarily used on Apple machines). Both of these containers can contain multiple formats of media. AVI can contain almost any kind of compression scheme, including Motion JPEG, RealVideo, and MPEG-4. AVI files always have the extension ".avi."

Quicktime, invented by Apple to handle video on the Mac computer, has spread widely and become a go-to format for lots of different devices. A Quicktime container, which always has a filename ending in ".mov" can contain a zillion different formats of video and audio.

Both AVI and Quicktime are sometimes used by video cameras to hold the media files generated by the camera. Don't be surprised if you slip the SD card from your camera into your computer and see a lot of .mov files.

When you are creating files from a video-editing program, you will be faced with a huge variety of choices, but the first one will generally be which media container format you want to use. After that, you get to choose which compression scheme you want to use.

Besides Quicktime and AVI, a few other common container formats are the following:

MP4

The container specifically designed to carry MPEG-2 and MPEG-4 files, especially with the H.264 compression scheme, and the audio files that go with them. Files will have the ".mp4" extension on the filename, unless they are audio only, in which case they sometimes end in "M4a."

RealVideo

The RealVideo format is used for real-time media streaming. When you click on a video link on the Internet, there are two ways of delivering you the video: downloading or streaming. If it is downloaded to you, the entire file is sent to your computer, which then starts up a program to play the file. (In some cases, you can start playing the file as it is downloading.) The important thing is, the file is completely sent to you. When the download is complete, you have a file on your computer.

Media streaming, on the other hand, means that a file is played for you from a remote computer without actually downloading the file onto your computer. It's like having someone read a letter to you over the phone instead of actually sending it to you. When you shut off the media stream, the only thing you have left on your computer is a tiny file that references the streamed file.

If you are encoding a file, the RealMedia format is only useful to you if you have a RealMedia server computer that will broadcast the file out to the world, something that a casual user would not have.

Chances are good, however, that you will watch a RealVideo stream on the Internet at some point. Many news services use this format.

MPEG Program Streams

This is the container file that contains MPEG files. Among other things, this is the format that contains the files that make up a DVD. More about DVDs in the next chapter.

Flash Video

One of the most common ways that video is embedded in websites is Flash Video, a media container invented by Macromedia to serve their Flash Video player. Flash Video container files exists in two forms: the older ".flv" and the newer ".f4v, which works specifically with MPEG-4 files. If you are creating Flash-based content for the Internet, this is the way to go.

Let's Get Started Already

So, why do you need to know any of this, and why does it matter?
Video is a system, and it has four parts:

1. Content
2. Storage
3. Display
4. Control

Every video system, from Mrs. Brungardt's second-grade class up to the
Cirque du Soleil, has those four parts. All of the information that I spewed out
above—resolution, aspect ratios, compression, etc.—is relevant for every part
of that system. Take aspect ratio, for example. If you know that your final
display mechanism (monitor, projector, LED wall, etc.) is 4:3, then that tells
you that you need to start by creating content that is also 4:3. And knowing
that you are creating 4:3 content will help you make decisions about what
kind of images you collect to put into that content. The same is true for your
more technical data, like scanning system and standard. Whatever specifications you settle on (or discover, or get stuck with), they will run throughout
the entire system, from the first piece of video you edit to the last bit of light
that hits your projection screen.

Now that you have a basic set of tools to work with, let's dig into the four
parts of the system. First up, content.

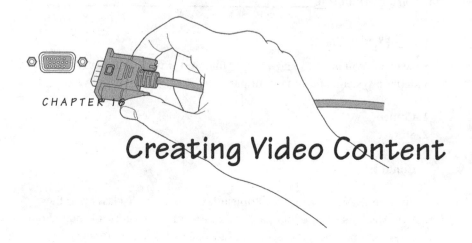

CHAPTER 10

Creating Video Content

So, you're considering using video as part of your production. Before you get all technical, you should consider the video first and foremost as a design element. Therefore, your first job is . . .

Decide What Kind of Images You Want, and Why You Want Them

What is the image? This is not a technical question. What are you trying to say with these images, and why do you want to say it with a projection? After all, the worst reason to use projection in a show is, "Because we have a projector!"

Step 1 is to embark on a creative process that helps you discover what kind of imagery you want to present to the audience.

Projected images will always have a different quality than solid, three-dimensional scenery. No matter what you do to them, they will always be composed of light alone, a fact that will always give them an ethereal quality, a sense that they are not of this world. Projected images always have a bit of magic in them, a bit of fairy dust.

Projected images also have a tendency to decrease the scale of the actor. In order to be worth the trouble, projected images tend to be large, and they create an aesthetic scale that can loom over and even overwhelm the actor. If your image is moving, fuggedaboutit. The audience will get back to your live people when the video is standing still again. Several times in my career, I have done shows where an actor is "conversing" with a projected image, and frankly, folks, it never works. The video image is usually larger, for one thing, and, don't ask me why, it's always more compelling to watch than the actor. Any parent who has ever stood in the living room trying to get their children's attention while they are watching television knows what I am talking about.

Audiences are not stupid either. Consciously or subconsciously, they know that the video image is not live, and it is hard to sell the idea that the performer is actually having a real conversation with it, even if the image is actually being generated in real time. Live is live, video is video, and when they try to talk to each other, it just feels . . . strange.

This doesn't mean that video imagery can't be used effectively onstage. It most certainly can. You just have to recognize that the look and feel of video is unique. It is not a live performer, and it is not static scenery. It is a third thing, something both mechanical and alive, and it can be strong competition for things that are mechanical, like scenery, or alive, like people. Above all, video is its own thing.

Moving video can offer a fascinating way to open up the boundaries of the stage, as it does in the Blue Man Group show in Las Vegas, when an audience member is taken offstage, followed by cameras. As the audience watches, the hapless audience member is wrapped up in a canvas bag, splattered with paint, and used as a human paintbrush backstage. In this case, it gives the audience a chance to leave the confines of the theater, take a look at a totally different performance area, and have a voyeuristic experience, which is rewarded when the audience member and the newly created painting are brought back to the stage.[1]

Video can offer a cinematic way to move the audience from place to place, as it did in the London (and later Broadway) production of Andrew Lloyd Webber's *The Lady in White*, designed by William Dudley, where the entire show was performed in front of a giant white wall, on which the sets were projected. As each scene ended, the actors would exit, and the "camera" would swoop up from the location, fly across the countryside, and settle in a new place. Once the image was stable, the actors would reenter and play the next scene. Using video allowed the designers to dynamically link the locations together in ways that would be impossible with ordinary scenery.[2]

Video can add an element of the fantastic to a scene, as in the Cirque du Soleil's *Ka*, also in Las Vegas, where a character falls off a scenic ship and "drowns." After a brief blackout, the performer is lowered from above the stage, slowly turning like a body slipping deeper into the ocean, as a projector paints a stream of bubbles escaping from his mouth as he sinks to the ocean floor.[3]

---

[1] This sequence also allows the show to use some prerecorded footage to avoid having to put the hapless guest in physical jeopardy.

[2] It should be noted that the original production was dogged by fuzzy images and uneven synchronization with the moving walls, which may or may not have contributed to the show being one of ALW's shortest runs.

[3] This particular effect, designed by interactive projection artist Holger Förterer, was also technically interesting because the bubbles were created live, aided by a sophisticated camera system that

First and foremost, then, start with your story. Go back to the campfire, lean over low, and say, "Once upon a time. . ." If the visual image that comes to you when you are thinking about the story at that level is a projection, then you are in the right place.

Any kind of visual image—anything at all—can become a projection, so before you begin to burden yourself with any technology, take the time to stop, look, collect images, experiment, think, ponder, sleep, and repeat until you are clear on the visual images you are after.

Know Your Output Device

Once you are clear on the images, the next step is to think about how and where they are going to appear on the stage. This is when you will want to look at the model, walk around in the theater, consult with the designer, and decide where the images are going to be projected. You need to know the size and shape of the projection surface.

You also need to know the general specifications of your storage and display devices. Once you've read the next two chapters on storage and display, you'll know more about this; but when you jump into the process, this is the point where you want to find out the capabilities of your devices, so you can have them in your pocket throughout the creation process. In particular, you need to know what your devices can do in the following areas:

Aspect ratio (4:3, 16:9, etc)
Resolution (64 × 480, 1920 × 1080, etc.)
Scanning system (progressive or interlaced)
Standard (NTSC or PAL)
Media container format (AVI, Quicktime, etc.)
High definition (yes or no)

Decide on a Video-Editing Program

Video-editing software is commonly available at all price ranges. Both Mac and Windows computers come with a simple video-editing program preinstalled (iMovie and Windows Movie Maker respectively), and they are surprisingly flexible. The industry standard programs for prosumer use are Final Cut Pro and Adobe Premiere, both of which are fast encroaching on the previous industry-standard Avid editing system. The prosumer world also uses Adobe After Effects and Boris Continuum effects programs, among

---

tracked the performer's position in space and perfectly positioned the bubbles coming from his mouth, regardless of how fast or slow he was lowered.

others, for video special effects. You don't need to start with an expensive program, though. There are also lots of shareware programs for editing as well as creating effects.

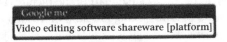

Set Up the File Correctly

Once you have decided on a video program and you know the specs from the list in item #3, you can set up your video file. Of course, you can change these specs later if need be, but it saves a lot of time and trouble to get them right from the beginning.

If Necessary, Create a Mask

Depending on your projection surface, you may not have a perfectly rectangular image. You might have bits of scenery that are protruding into your image, or a curved projection surface, or, if your video server is set up with more than one output channel, you might have more than one screen. For all of these situations, you may want to start by creating a mask in your video program, so that you are seeing what the audience will see.

If the screen is being encroached on by scenery, you will want to create a mask. The easiest way to do this is wait until the set is at least partially built—so you can see the shape of the projection surface—then climb up to the projector position and snap a picture. Take that digital photo into a photo-editing program like Photoshop and cut out the part of the picture that has the video screen in it. Leave all the scenic parts that are sticking into your image. Once you have the screen cut out, turn everything else black. Then, drop that photo into one of the video tracks on your editing program. Put it in the top track, the one that sits on top of all your other content. The hole that you cut in the photo will let you see the video content underneath, and the black areas will mask out the unwanted parts of your image so that you don't get stray light on your scenery.

Collect Your Images

We live in an image-rich world, so this is where you really get to overwhelm yourself with possibilities. While you are collecting images, be very aware of two things:

Resolution

Make sure that you are getting images with enough resolution to be useful. If your image is 1080 pixels tall and you pull up a photo online that is only 80 pixels tall, it is going to be a very small part of the picture. You can blow it up, of course, using either a picture-editing program or a video-editing program, but low resolution means that it will look like doo-doo when you make it bigger. This also relates to compression. An image that is already compressed will look worse if you compress it again, especially if you are going to blow it up bigger. One prime offender is DVDs, which are already highly compressed. If you are pulling content from a DVD, be aware that it "might not scale up well," which is geek speak for, "It won't look good if you make it bigger." See "Dealing with DVDs" for more information.

Copyright

Unless specifically stated, every image is owned by the creator, and you have to have permission to use it in a public place or as part of a public performance. Of course, the larger the performance venue, the greater the chance that someone will come after you, but it is best to play things safe, especially when there is so much good content around. See the sidebar.

Stock Video

Ever since film and video were created, there has been a market for stock images. These are images that were collected for various reasons with no specific project in mind, and are now available to be purchased or licensed. In the early decades of film, there were crews who were assigned to show up at fires and natural disaster sites just to grab footage of the event that would be useful someday. Many a cinematographer has supplemented his or her income by shooting generic footage of landscapes, cities, crowds, and anything else that might be useful for a project where people didn't want to take the time and trouble to film stuff themselves.

Stock footage was traditionally fairly expensive, since a photographer would have to shoot a lot of stuff in order to have a big-enough catalog of images. Each photographer had his own library, and those libraries were expensive to create; thus, they were expensive to sell. Furthermore, it took a high level of very expensive equipment to get professional-looking results. Not everybody has a 35 mm film camera sitting around.

With the advent of high-quality prosumer gear and online stock photo services, both those things have changed. These days, services like iStock allow anybody to upload still or moving images for sale to users. With thousands of contributors feeding content into the site, the variety is impressive. Photographers don't have to cover a lot of bases—with hundreds of contributors, the collected library is very diverse. Lastly, with high-quality HD cameras available at reasonable prices, the costs are low for the photographer/videographer, so the cost to the users is also low. It also helps that there are thousands of users looking for content on these sites, which helps the photographers make more money despite the low cost of the media.

Typically, the images are organized by keywords, like mountain or flames or schoolyard, so you can search quickly and efficiently for what you want. You can also browse aimlessly if you are looking for ideas.

If you go to these sites looking for content, make sure you are armed with the file format and resolution that you want. The price will vary quite a bit depending on what you want to pay for. The most expensive formats will be the ones that scale up well, like uncompressed Quicktime, as opposed to the more compressed MPEG formats that are designed for websites and mobile platforms (like phones).

The best news about these sites is that they are royalty-free, which means that once you buy the footage, you can do whatever you want with it (except sell it to someone else) without worrying about copyright.

> Google me
> **Stock Royalty-free video**

Edit the Images

Now that you have everything together, it's time to build your show. You can combine multiple images into a single image, string images together one after another, combine multiple images into a single image, add text, create effects—the list is endless.

Content should be assembled in a video-editing software program. There are dozens to choose from, including high-end standard-setting programs like Adobe Premiere, Final Cut Pro, or the Avid suite. Most computers these days come with simple video-editing software preinstalled Microsoft Movie Maker on Windows machines and iMovie on the Mac. Avid, the people who originally popularized computer-based, nonlinear video editing, even has a free version of their high-end system: Avid Free DV.

For effects, both Final Cut and Premiere have lots of stuff built in, plus you can supplement them with additional plug-in software like Adobe After Effects or Boris Continuum.

Teaching an entire class on video editing and effects is well beyond the scope of this book, but it is quite possible to start slow with a simple program like iMovie and build your knowledge and skill over time. I have personally been editing video with Final Cut Pro for more than ten years and I am still learning all the time.

If Necessary, Deal with Keystoning or Nonflat Projection Surfaces

If your projector is not directly in front of the screen (and it almost never is), you will be dealing with some degree of keystoning, the effect where your previously square image is now wider on one end than the other.

All video projectors have the ability to electronically and/or physically manipulate the image to decrease the keystone effect, but only to a point. Usually, these projectors are designed to have the projector mounted even with the top or bottom of the projection screen. Beyond that point, the projector's keystone correction can't help you. For the nonstandard world of theater projection, however, your image may be hitting at a much more oblique angle.

Software to the rescue. Both Final Cut and Premiere have plug-ins that can help you tweak the image in the opposite direction to counteract the distortion caused by keystoning. These plug-in filters are applied to the image once you are done editing.

Unfortunately, if you are playing back the media on a DVD or media player or some kind of PC-based playback program (like iTunes or PowerPoint), then you will have to create these filters based on trial and error. Take an educated guess, apply the filter, output the file, project it in the theater, take note of what it looks like, get back to the studio, and repeat. A dedicated media server can apply these filters in real time and let you make corrections on the fly in rehearsal, which is one reason they are worth the money.

There is also more sophisticated software out there that can actually correct your image, so it looks right on a curved screen. Essentially, you can feed the shape of the screen into the computer and the software will bend your image in the opposite direction. Once you show the curved-in image on the curved-out screen, it all looks right again. As of this writing, these plug-ins don't exist for Final Cut or Premiere, but there are standalone programs. Plus, the high-quality media servers can make these corrections for you.

Export the Files

Time to go back to the hardware. At this point, you will need to know the details of the compression scheme you will use. The best thing is to go straight to the specifications of your output device. Look for what formats it supports, as well as scanning systems, bit rate, standards, etc.

If you are going to play the footage back on a DVD, you need to prepare your files appropriately. DVDs are a very common and popular way to play back video these days, so let's take a moment to delve into them.

DVDs

Every once in a while, a new technology comes along that is so necessary, so timely, so user-friendly, and so cool that it is almost instantly adopted throughout the United States and then, shortly after, the rest of the world.

The DVD is such a technology. It was first used as a commercial distribution medium in 1997 and, by 2003, just six years later, was the dominant form of home video.[4]

When we say "DVD," we typically mean a DVD-Video, which is the format for, not surprisingly, putting video on a DVD.

DVD, however, is actually a family of disk formats, all of which are on 12 cm disks just like CDs. (There is an 8 cm format called a MiniDVD.) In fact, DVDs use the same kind of media as CDs, but because the laser that reads them has a shorter wavelength,[5] the grooves can be smaller, giving the DVD more room for data. A CD holds about 700 megabytes, while a standard DVD holds about 4.7 gigabytes, which is enough for a highly compressed two-hour movie. Actually, however, the "standard" DVD isn't so standard anymore and some of the newer types of media can hold even more data.

It is actually possible to lay down two layers of data on some DVDs, if you have the right kind of media and the right kind of recorder. These are called dual-layer DVDs, and they work by focusing the laser beam in two different depths in the media. A dual-layer DVD can hold almost exactly twice as much data.

But it doesn't stop there. You can also print on both sides, if you have the right media, recorder, and player. Here is a list of the various formats and their capacities:

Single-sided, single layer	4.7GB
Single-sided, dual-layer	8.5GB
Double-sided, single-layer	9.4GB
Double-sided, double-layer	17GB

If you are recording DVDs, you have a couple of different recording formats to choose from, the older DVD-R and the newer DVD+R. Theoretically,

---

[4] If you think that was fast, consider that the Japanese made the DVD the dominant form of home video distribution less than a year after it was released.

[5] 650 nm versus 780 nm where nm is a nanometer, or one billionth of a meter. So, really small.

they are both supposed to work in all DVD players, but older machines might have trouble with the + format. There are plenty of DVD writers out there. In fact, lots of computers have DVD-writing drives already installed.

When you have finished putting your program together in your video-editing program and are ready to output to a DVD, you will need to convert them into MPEG-2 elementary streams for encoding to the DVD. Your video program will have presets for DVDs in the list of output formats and should create MPEG-2 video files (.m2v) as well as AC-3 (.ac3) audio files.

Once you have written the files, you will need a DVD-authoring program, of which there are many for both Mac and Windows. Import the video and audio files into the authoring program and it will take things from there, creating a disk image with all your files in a folder called "VOB." If you want, the software can usually burn the DVD right there for you.

So, let's review: To burn a DVD, you need to choose the following:
Media (single- or double-sided, single- or double-layered)
Recording format (DVD-R or DVD+R)
File formats (almost always MPEG-2 for video and AAC or AC-3 for audio)

And, besides your video-editing program, you will need a DVD-authoring program, which might also function as your DVD-burning program. If not, then you need a separate burning program.

So that's how you put files on a DVD. Getting files *off* a DVD can be a bit more difficult. If you have ever tried to copy the contents of a DVD, especially a commercially purchased one you know that it is a pain in the tush, and that is deliberate. The distributors of commercial DVDs don't want you copying their content and handing it out for free, ya see. Copy-protected DVDs are tough, but there is software out there that can rip just about anything off of any DVD (but you didn't hear it from me). Even if the disk isn't copy-protected, you can't just take the files from a DVD and expect them to play back like normal Quicktime or AVI files. The files in that VOB folder can't be used in a video-editing program as is. If you want to use material from a DVD, you will need a DVD-ripping program that can take those VOB files and turn them into something that can be dropped into a video-editing program, like Quicktime or AVI. Even if you do get them into your editor, remember that those files are highly compressed, so they won't scale up well.

Do be very aware of copyright limitations on commercially produced DVDs. Media companies have been aggressively pursuing those who copy their material, and using the material in a public forum like a theater show is asking for trouble. With such a huge variety of royalty-free video online, it's not that hard to stay on the right side of the law.

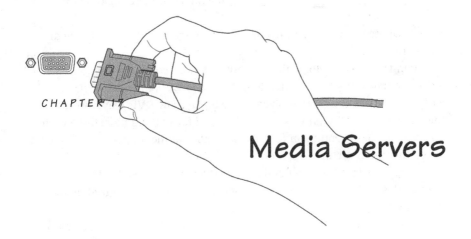

CHAPTER 17

Media Servers

Now that you have your content created, you need a place to keep it, and a way to play it back.

A media server is an electronic device that stores digital content and then "serves" it over a cable to a display device. It's actually not a new thing. In a sense, we have been using media "servers" ever since we first started using media. In the days of film, all the images were stored on photographic film. The images on those frames were the first "media files," and cellulose film was the first "storage media." You couldn't just hold up a reel of film up to a light bulb and watch it, however. You needed a device that took each of the frames, in the proper sequence, and flashed them in front of a light, at the proper speed. This device was called a film projector. Without the projector, the film was essentially useless to the viewer, just as a video file on your computer won't do you any good just sitting there. You can't pick up a roll of film in your hand and watch a movie, and you can't hold up a hard drive and watch a video. You need a device that separates out the images, arranges them in the proper order, and sends them to a display device at the right speed. In the world of film, the projector serves this function (as well as being part of the display system). In video, you need a server.

Once we switched from film to video, the playback process was actually handled by two different devices: The scanning and sequencing of the storage media was done by a tape deck, while the display of the image was done by a television monitor. The storage device was a spool of magnetic tape instead of a roll of cellulose film, but it was still a series of frames that had to be sequenced in the proper order, at the proper speed, and then sent to a display device. The monitor was just a big dumb CRT screen—it would project whatever it was sent. It was the tape deck's job to read the media correctly.

When DVDs came along, the concept was still very much the same. The video content was stored on the disk, and when we wanted to see it, we would insert it in the DVD player and push play. The DVD player would scan the images on the disk, now stored in a digital format, assemble them in the proper order, and send them to a display device at the proper speed. Here again, the brains are in the DVD player, not in the monitor.

The same is true for all other digital media files. You need a device for storing the files until they are needed, sequencing the images and feeding them to the display.

This process of taking a string of images off of a storage device, assembling them in the right order, and sending them out to a display device is called "serving." Of course, when you are talking about a digital movie file, the process is a bit more complex than shining a light through a piece of film, but at its essence, the computer that is scanning the digital file is doing the same thing that the film projector did when it slapped down a series of celluloid frames in front of a lamp. They are both serving media.

With the explosion of digital media, media servers have infiltrated our lives from every direction. If you have a TiVo or other type of digital video recorder (DVR), then you have a media server. Chances are good that you have a media server in your pocket right now. It's called an iPod.

From here on out, we are going to be discussing digital media servers. Film, videotape, and vinyl record albums were all good in their day; but for all the reasons we discussed earlier, the theater has gone completely digital, and we're going with it.

Any media server requires four things:

Inputs: The files have to come from somewhere.
Storage: The files have to be stored until you need them.
Playback: The files have to be sequenced and played back properly.
Output: The output of the files must be sent to a display device.

Inputs

Somehow you have to get the media files into the server. In some cases, the server will be digitizing the files as they arrive through audio and video inputs, but more often than not, the media will be brought to the server as a digital file, through a computer connection or removable media.

In more complex setups, your server device may need to input control information or time code from another device. See part 4 for details.

Storage

Media servers always have a storage device, which is most often an optical hard drive. The exceptions are DVD players, which use the removable DVD, and small handheld media devices (like the iPod Nano), which use solid-state flash drives with no moving parts.

Hard drives are rated in a number of different ways, including access time, read/write speed, and transfer rate, but the most common comparisons are size and rotation speed.

Size is pretty straightforward: The bigger the drive, the more files you can store. How big do you need? Ah, if only there were an easy answer to that question! The size of a video file depends on its resolution, frame rate, and compression, but just as an example, consider this. Here are some examples of the amount of space required to store *one second* of the following:

640 × 480, 30 fps standard definition video, reasonably compressed: 3.5 MB
640 × 480, 30 fps standard definition video, uncompressed: 27 MB
720 × 480, 30 fps DV camcorder video: 25 MB
1080i, 30 fps high-definition video uncompressed: 1,243 MB

If these numbers are for one second, you can start to imagine how much space you will need for hours of video, especially uncompressed HD. Media storage devices are currently measured in gigabytes (billions of bytes), but will soon be measured in terabytes (trillions of bytes).

Some systems are big enough that they require a bunch of hard drives working together. This is known as a hard drive array or a **RAID** (Redundant Array of Independent Disks).[1] A RAID is also used because it provides more reliability for data storage. With redundant drives, the inevitable failure of one drive does not lead to the loss of data. In general theatrical usage, you probably won't need a RAID, but, as previously mentioned, you *will* need to back up your drive to a second drive, for that day when the first one dies.

As far as speed goes, hard drive speed is rated in revolutions per minute, or rpm. The hard drive in your laptop is probably spinning at around 5400 rpm, while a higher-quality desktop drive is around 7200 rpm. With video servers needing to bring up media files in real time, speed is essential. If you are buying new drives, pay attention to the specifications of your server software.

---

[1] Sticklers will note that the original name, "Redundant Array of Inexpensive Disks," was updated by the drive manufacturers to remove the expectation that a RAID would be cheap.

Playback

The playback function on a server is what really separates the men from the boys, or, in this case, the DVDs from the dedicated servers. Sure, there are lots of devices out there that will play back a media file, but often we want more than simple playback. Sometimes we want to play more than one file at a time, or feed more than one projector, or play it in sync with some other event, or smoothly fade from one file to another. We may want to add text or an effect to the image or even mix in live camera footage. And of course, we want to make changes to all of it on a moment's notice, without leaving the rehearsal.

Depending on the type of server you pick, all these tasks are either a walk in the park, impossible, or somewhere in between.

Output

Once your server starts playing back the files, it needs a way to get the content out of the server box and into the display device. It needs outputs. Outputs may be analog or digital, audio or video, composite or component, point-to-point, networked, or a lot of other things. Besides media, your server device may also need to output control information or time code as well.

Let's look at four different types of media servers and how they handle these tasks.

DVD Players

The standard consumer DVD player is very good at doing what it does: playing files off a disk when you hit play. If that's all you need, there is no reason to get more complicated.

Inputs

A DVD player cannot take live inputs. It gets all of its media from the piece of removable media that you put into the tray: the DVD. Beyond that, you can't feed it any other information.

Storage

Again, the storage all happens on the DVD. Once burned, it cannot be changed. Yes, there are rewritable DVD disks, but you still have to take the DVD back to the computer and rewrite it. Plus, those rewritable disks aren't reliable enough for live performance. It's always better to just make a new disk.

Depending on the format, DVDs can store from 4.7 to 17 GB.

Playback
A DVD player has only the simplest of playback functions. It can only play one file at a time, cannot combine images, and cannot create fades between images unless they were created in the media itself and burned permanently onto the disk. There are DVD players that can be wired up for remote control, but they are expensive; and if you are going to spend that kind of money, it's better to get a dedicated media server that will have more flexibility.

One annoying thing about DVDs: Because they are consumer devices, they have consumer behaviors, like displaying the word "PLAY" in bright red letters on the screen. You may need to physically block the lens of the projector when the file starts playing so that the audience doesn't see that. Same when the file ends and the word "STOP" blares out onto the screen.

The DVD's simplicity is also its advantage. No programming, no computer connection, no training required. Drop in the disk. Push play. Showtime.

Outputs
Depending on how fancy your DVD is, the outputs will be some or all of the standard consumer connections. For video: RCA composite, RCA component, and HDMI. For audio: RCA analog audio, RCA digital audio, and Toslink digital audio.

Bottom Line
Advantages

The simplest solution. There are very few settings to mess with, and it is easy to hook the player up to your projector.

You can use commercial DVDs (as long as you obtain the rights or fall within the fair use category) or make your own with simple video-editing and DVD-burning software.

Disadvantages

DVDs cannot be edited. If you want to change a piece of video, or reorder the cues, you have to burn a new disk.

Most DVD players display the commands, like Play and Stop, on the screen.

No way to create transitions between files.

Personal Computer with Standard Presentation Software
You actually have a remarkably full-featured media server sitting on your desk: your personal computer.

Using standard presentation software, like PowerPoint for the Mac or Keynote for the PC, you can create some relatively sophisticated presentations that include transitions, a limited ability to mix files on-screen, added text, and the ability to make changes right there in rehearsal. Files can be quickly uploaded to the computer's internal hard drive, and if you have a laptop, your server is very portable.

Of course, anytime you use a computer for playback, you have to exercise standard computer rules: Don't use the computer for anything else, don't add or delete any software, don't perform any software updates once the system is stable, back up all your files, etc. The rule is, once you get the computer stable and running your show, don't change anything!

If you are going to use your computer to run the presentation, you do have to be mindful of where you are going to put it. If you are using the DVI or HDMI outputs, then your cables can't be very long, only about twenty feet. However, if you are using a desktop computer, you can add a separate video card to it that has video outputs. This is an ideal situation, as it lets you keep your regular monitor to edit files, while your extra video card feeds the projector. One common type of video card is called a **VIVO** (video in, video out), and it has several different video outputs, like S-Video, composite video, and component video.

These presentation programs won't let you mix in live video, hook up to a show control system, create sophisticated effects, or produce pixel maps—all features that professional projection designers look for—but if all you want to do is play back still images or single video files with reasonable transitions, they might be all you need.

Advantages

Can be set up with commonly available hardware and software.

Video files can be instantly added, deleted, or reordered. Text can be added on-screen.

Still images can easily be mixed with video footage.

Transitions can be cued and edited.

Disadvantages

It is only as reliable as your computer.

A standard PC only has one video output, so it can only serve video to one projector and cable lengths have to be short.

Multiple streams of video cannot be "mixed" on-screen.

PC cannot easily be controlled by a show control system.

PC cannot accept a live video feed.

Limited effects.

Personal Computer with Consumer Video Server

It is a hot market these days for consumer media players. With so much content being downloaded over the Internet, many people are installing video servers in their living room so that they can see that content on their televisions rather than their computers. Apple, always seeking the leading edge of consumer-oriented media devices, set the standard with the Apple TV server, while other companies, like Western Digital, Acer, and Iomega, followed along quickly with competing products.

A home media player is designed to be loaded up with digital media files, either over a home network (generally wireless these days) or by plugging in a USB storage device, like a hard drive or a memory stick. Then, using an on-screen interface, you choose the file you want and play it.

In many ways, this is a great solution for low-cost media playback in the theater. Consumer media servers are relatively low cost, can play a wide variety of file formats, and have projector-friendly outputs like HDMI and component video.

The disadvantages of the media servers are similar to the DVD player: no effects, no way to play multiple files or feed multiple projectors, no show control, and so on. However, they can take in new files easily, without the pain of creating new disks. They do have one major disadvantage, however. Because they are designed for on-screen interfaces, there is no front panel to allow you to choose a file for playback. You have to use the remote control to select a file from a menu on the screen. This is great for armchair screenings, but is lousy for theater playback. To use these media servers onstage, you have to figure out a way to send the video to a monitor while you select the file, then, once the file is running, switch it over to the projector. You can do this with a simple video switch, available at video equipment stores or Radio Shack, but beware the little glitch of video that can sometimes leak onto the screen when you throw the switch.

In general, while these seem like attractive options for stage playback, the downside of the interface problem can make them more trouble than they are worth.

Advantages
> Can play many different formats.
> Simple operation: just select the file and play.
> Good selection of outputs for projectors.
> Files can be quickly updated and played back in any order.

Disadvantages
> Files are selected and played from an on-screen interface only.
> No mixing of files, effects, remote control, or other sophisticated functions.

Personal Computer with Theatrical Presentation Software

If you want a bit more functionality for your presentation, like the ability to set up a cue list, create more complex timed cues, have multiple video files playing at once, or sync up your computer with other systems, like audio, lighting, or special effects, then you want to invest in one of the theatrical video playback programs. Both of the audio playback programs that we talked about in the chapter 4, Stage Research SFX and QLab, will fire off video files just like they fire off audio files, plus they can do all the things I just listed. For college or midlevel professional theaters, these are really your weapons of choice.

These two programs will still not let you mix in live video, and they have limits on what kinds of tricks they can play with the video. They are also not really set up to handle multiple video streams to multiple projectors. If you want really full-featured video processing, then you want to investigate a more fully-featured video presentation program, like Watchout, the video software from Dataton.

Watchout allows you to add live video to your video playback, as well as combine multiple video files on-screen and support multiple projectors. With Watchout, you use a single production computer to build the show, then let that computer output all the pieces of the show to a network of display computers, each of which is driving a single projector. This kind of a setup is commonly used for presentations with very wide screens, where a single image has to be broken up into several pieces and projected by several different projectors. The various Watchout display computers perform the edge blending that makes those multiple projected images look like a single image onscreen.

Advantages

Theatrical-style cue lists with timed cues, loops, and linked cues.
Multiple files playing at once.
Can be triggered by show control system.
Ability to make quick changes.
With Watchout:
Allows multiple video streams for multiple projectors and screens.
Allows you to mix multiple video and image files.
Many video effects: calculate gaps between screens, edge blend, compensate for nonsquare or nonlevel screens, warp images to fit curved screens, etc.
Can integrate live video.

Disadvantages

Additional cost.
Need to learn new software.
Requires multiple PCs and Ethernet network (for Watchout and multiple screens).

Stand-alone Media Server

If you want the highest possible level of video effects, massive control over all your images, tons of files playing at once, rock-solid stability, and the highest possible image quality, you want a stand-alone media server.

Media servers come in a wide variety, each of which is designed for a different sort of application. There are cinema servers, which are designed to play back digital movies in large movie theaters. There are broadcast servers, which are designed to provide live content for television stations. There are even slo-mo servers, which provide slow-motion replays for sporting events.

Media servers are not for casual users. While most of them have well-designed manuals and interfaces, this is an area where deep knowledge is required for setup. You can teach yourself to program a dedicated server, but you might want to set aside a couple of weeks to get the basics down. If you want to understand all the deep features of these amazing machines, you might want to set aside summer vacation.

Fortunately, there are also video servers that are designed for live performance. Choosing a server is definitely something that you want to do with a trained professional, but here are some of the features that a theatrically inclined server should have:

High-resolution outputs, up to full 1920 × 1080 HD
Keystone correction, to overcome off-center projection positions
Image warping, to compensate for curved screens
Pixel mapping to feed images to LED fixtures
Ability to control server with MIDI and DMX (see part 4)
Ability to follow or generate time code (see part 4)
Multiple outputs, to feed multiple screens or one big screen with edge-blended images
Video effects
Network capability (see "Show Control")

Advantages
Highest-quality image
Greatest variety of effects
Greatest ability to integrate with other show elements
Most stable platform

Disadvantages
Highest cost
Highest requirement for trained programmers

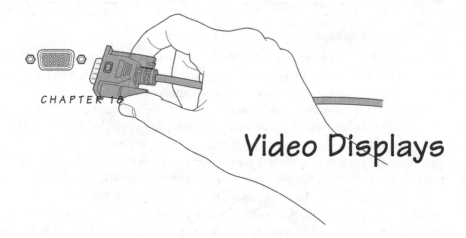

CHAPTER 18

Video Displays

The best way to look at a video image is on a **video monitor**. There is no projector in the world that can produce an image that is brighter, sharper, or more accurate than a video monitor. There are only two reasons to forgo a monitor and use a video projector and a screen. Unfortunately, they are pretty good reasons.

Reason number one: size. For the live stage, you almost always need images that are a whole lot bigger than what you can get on a video monitor. As of this writing, the largest commercially available video monitor is 103 inches from corner to corner (video monitors are always measured diagonally), and if you can afford it, then you can afford to pay someone to read this book for you. Even if you've got the money, it still probably wouldn't work. A 103-inch monitor is awesome for a home theater or a store display or a museum exhibit, but even a monitor that is just short of nine feet across can look pretty lonely on a reasonably sized stage.

For a while, there was a trend in commercial applications toward video walls: stacks of video monitors that were combined to make one giant image. Unfortunately, the edges of all those screens were clearly visible, so it looked like you were watching TV through a giant tic-tac-toe grid. The edges of the monitors got smaller in later models, and almost completely disappeared, but even then, you still had the problem of trying to match all the video screens to each other in color and brightness. Whatever you did, it still looked like a stack of monitors. Eventually, the video walls were overtaken by LED panels, which could be built without the lines and had consistent color and brightness. They are still far more expensive than the projector-and-screen combination, however, so they don't offer a good solution for the small-to-midsize theater. (They have other uses, of course, which are discussed in chapter 12.)

When it comes to size, therefore, screens offer far bigger images for the dollar.

The second reason to use a projector is if you want your projection surface to be anything other than a flat rectangle. While there are LED displays that can wrap around a curve, there is a limit to their flexibility and, again, a high cost. If your projection surface is curved or built in some strange shape, a video projector can compensate for that, while video monitors are flat and rectangular.

In order to put a video image onstage, therefore, you will almost always be using a projector and a projection screen.

Projector Technology

Welcome to another alphabet game. Should you buy LCD or DLP? Should you upgrade to LCoS or SXRD? And why can't video projector companies ever come up with a *name* for a projector technology, instead of all these letters? It's enough to PMO.

Sigh.

Okay strap in. Here we go.

Basically, almost all projectors work like this:

As you know, light is composed of three primary colors: red, blue, and green. A video projector starts with a very bright and very precise color beam of white light that is put out by a very bright projector lamp. That beam of white light is divided into three separate beams—one red, one blue, and one green—by prisms, the same way you divided sunlight into a rainbow in fourth-grade science class. Then, each one of those three beams either bounces off or filters through an electronic device that changes it from a solid beam of red, blue, or green light into the red, green, or blue portion of the video signal that you want to project. Whether it reflects off the electronic device or shines through it, the process is basically the same. The electronic device removes parts of the light beam to turn it from a solid rectangle of light to a rectangle of light with an image in it. Once that's done, those three beams of light are recombined into a single beam (prisms again) that shoots out the front of the projector and projects the full-color video image onto a screen, a wall, a dancer, or whatever it runs into.

The difference between the two main schools of thought in projectors has to do with that electronic device that imprints the video image onto the red, blue, and green beams of light.

The first way it was done was by shooting the beam of light through something called a light valve. In essence, this technique is shadow projection, just like when you held your hands up in front of a light in the shape of a bunny.

A light valve is a panel containing a grid of liquid crystal dots. These dots have the interesting property that they can turn opaque or transparent, depending on whether or not they are electrified. By turning the individual dots transparent and opaque, the projector can allow light to pass through each dot or not, just like turning a water valve on or off can allow water to pass. By doing it very fast, with a large grid of tiny valves, the light valve can create a moving picture in the beam of light, where each tiny valve is the equivalent of one pixel in the video image.

Just to put this in perspective, this liquid crystal panel is no bigger than an inch wide and may contain over a million of these tiny light valves so it's a bit more complex than your bunny projection, but the theory is the same. Remember also that there are always three of these panels, one each for red, blue, and green.

The light-valve technique is the basis of the liquid crystal display, or LCD projector. Because it has three panels of light valves, it is often listed as "3LCD."

The other school of thought in projection involves bouncing the light off a panel covered with very tiny mirrors. The mirrors can rotate to reflect the light or absorb it. Again, each mirror handles the light for one pixel. If the mirror is rotated away from the light, then no light is reflected and the pixel is dark or off. If it rotated toward the light, then the light is reflected out the front of the projector and the pixel is bright, or on.

The panel of mirrors is, of course, very, very small—millions of mirrors in less than an inch. This micromirror technology is known as Digital Light Processing or DLP, and it was invented by Texas Instruments, the folks that gave you the handheld calculator back in the 1970s.

When I said earlier that the beam of white light is divided into three beams, one each for red, green, and blue, I wasn't being exactly correct, at least when it comes to DLP. There are, in fact, two kinds of DLP: one that splits the light into three beams, like LCD, and one that sends the light through a spinning color wheel of—you guessed it—red, blue, and green panels. As the wheel turns, the beam of light is colored red, then green, then blue. A single panel of micromirrors is synchronized with the spinning wheel, so that when the light turns red, the mirrors arrange themselves to create the red video signal. When the light turns green, the mirrors rearrange themselves to reflect the green signal, followed by the blue. Because this process is happening *very* fast, your eye is none the wiser that one chip of micromirrors is doing the work of three.

As you might expect, the three-chip DLP projectors are more expensive than the one-chip-and-rotating-mirror projectors.

These two technologies competed against each other for years, spilling blood on both sides of town, until one day, Romeo LCD and Juliet DLP (not their real names) finally got together, fell in love, and had a baby. The liquid crystal on silicon, or **LCoS**, projectors, use liquid crystals to make the image, like an LCD, but they reflect the light beam, like a DLP micromirror. Sony came out with their own version of this, which they called Silicon X-tal Reflective Display, or **SXRD** because their marketing people had watched way too many science fiction movies. JVC calls theirs **D-ILA**, and you can read the footnote if you really want to know that stands for.[1] They are all LCoS.

So, which one is better?

Ha! Didn't really think it was going to be that simple, did you?

The conventional wisdom on this decision used to go like this: LCD and single-chip DLP are the cheapest. The LCoS technologies are a step up in both price and quality. The most expensive and advanced projectors are three-chip DLPs.

But, of course, technology marches on, so all the categories of projectors have kind of grown together in price and quality.

In the LCD versus DLP war at the bottom end of the price scale, it's a trade-off. LCDs are known to be brighter, creating more accurate color while generating less heat. DLPs are smaller, weigh less, have slightly better contrast, and less visible pixels.

The problem is that the comparison between projector technologies has become an arms race. When one technology declares an advantage, the other one goes back to the lab and erases it. LCDs had the edge in brightness and color quality, for example, until DLP began improving their contrast and including menus where users could tune the color balance. The fact is that all these technologies, except three-chip DLP, are converging in both price and quality, so the particular technology needs to be considered in the context of all of the features of a projector.

Bottom line: Go look. Use this chapter to understand the differences in technologies and the needs of your theater, use the Internet to gather information and read reviews, then go to the store and look at the image that comes out of the projector.

So, what other features do you need to consider when buying a projector?

Price

You get what you pay for. Period.

Projector prices vary from a hundred dollars or less for a glorified flashlight to tens of thousands for cinema-quality units.

Furthermore, things are always changing, so I can't even put numbers in print. They will change tomorrow.

---

[1] Digital Direct Drive Image Light Amplifier, so there.

The best advice is to start with a general set of features that you really want, then use the Internet to research what is available. You will rapidly zero in on a price range that suits you.

Usage

Surprise! Projectors aren't sold for use in the theater. Like every other kind of technology in the theater, we stole it from some larger market, where the need was great enough to pay for the development of the technology. Typically, projectors are organized into the following categories:

Pocket (or pico)
Home theater
Conference room
Large venue

Pocket or pico projectors aren't much good onstage, although they are very useful if you want to demonstrate projections in your set model. They are just what they sound like: projectors that fit in your pocket and are used for projecting very small images in very dark rooms.

Home theater projectors are useful in the theater, if you can live with lower levels of brightness. Home theater enthusiasts are fanatical about image quality, which is why the contrast ratings are so high, but they generally keep their theaters pretty dark, so they don't need a lot of brightness. These projectors usually do not have speakers built in, which is fine for theater because we have our own sound system to take care of that. Home theater systems have other features as well, some of which are useful, like lens shift, which allows projector placement farther off-axis. Other features, like auto iris which adjusts the brightness of the image, second by second based on the content, aren't really for us.

Conference room projectors come in various sizes, from the featherlight road warrior projectors, suitable for a room with a single conference table, to the larger-but-still-portable units that can handle a hotel conference room with a hundred people. Conference room projectors tend to be brighter than home theater projectors, because they have to compete with ambient lighting, just like a theatrical projector. They get the brightness by sacrificing on image quality and contrast, which is fine for PowerPoint slides with lots of text, but not so good for films, animation, and so forth.

Conference room projectors often have built-in speakers, large enough to fill a conference room, which, again, don't do much for us. The brightness makes them very useful for theater, however, so this is probably your go-to category. Make sure, though, that you get inputs that will work for your needs, including component video and HDMI.

Large venue projectors are just what they sound like: projectors for very big rooms. They are much brighter and they come with lenses that allow them to project from farther away, like the projection booth at the back of a large theater. Like home theater projectors, they tend to come without speakers, as large venues have their own sound systems. This category of projector is often used for large-scale theatrical projection, like Broadway shows and theme parks, but hold on to your heart when they tell you the prices. A good-quality large-format projector will cost more than your house. These are for venues with serious dough.

Brightness

As it turns out, it's not that easy to answer the question "How bright is that projector?" We have numbers to compare, of course. Projector output is measured in **ANSI lumens**, a standardized measurement from the redundantly named American National Standards Institute, a private, nonprofit organization that comes up with standard ways to do things.[2]

A typical conference room video projector puts out around 2,000 lumens, which is good for a moderately lit room where the audience is no more than about fifty feet away. The Christie Roadie HD video projector, commonly used for huge auditoriums and rock concerts, puts out 32,500 ANSI lumens, which will blast a video image to an audience more than 250 feet away. (Of course, those nice boardroom projectors will cost you less than $1,000, while the Christie Roadie retails for $159,000,[3] so you get what you pay for.) Somewhere between those two numbers is a good theatrical projector.

Lumen ratings are useful when comparing different models of projectors, but once you are in the theater, they aren't much use as a specific measurement. There are just too many things that can determine how bright a projector looks. Use them when making a decision on which projector to buy, but then set this number aside and concentrate on what you really *see* right in front of you.

Contrast

Contrast is a measurement that compares the brightest and whitest part of the image to the darkest and blackest part. In other words, if the projector has a contrast rating of 500:1, then the brightest part of the image will be five hundred times brighter than the darkest part of the image. With a projector image, there is never a part of the image with absolutely no light. Even if you are projecting a completely black image, there will be a small amount of light on the screen.

---

[2] Among other things, ANSI also standardized 8½ × 11 inch paper the height of commercial countertops, and safety standards for nuclear power plants.

[3] As of September 2010.

This is worth remembering if you want to turn the projectors on during a blackout. Even if they are projecting a completely black screen, the audience will see a slight glow on the screen. This is why more expensive theatrical projectors (like the Christie one I mentioned earlier) have a physical shutter that closes down over the lamp to create a truly blacked-out image.

In this case, paying more money doesn't necessarily get you more contrast, mostly because more is not necessarily better. A conference room projector will be between 2000:1 and 3000:1, while the Christie Roadie I mentioned earlier will be no more than 2800:1.

You will often find that home theater projectors will have much greater contrast than conference room projectors. This is because home theaters are generally much darker than conference rooms, and the enthusiasts that build them are trying to create an image that is close to the high-contrast television screen that the home theater is designed to replace. Hence, home theater projectors will trade off less brightness for more contrast.

The jury is still out (and will most likely stay out) on how much contrast the human eye can really perceive. Some opticians swear that the human eye can't see much beyond 400:1, while others will stake their professional reputations on the human eye being sensitive well beyond 100,000:1. They are not likely to lose that bet, because there really isn't a good way to test. It's all subjective, and it varies considerably depending on what your eye was doing right before the test.

Suffice to say that, for our purposes, we are going to be more concerned with brightness than contrast if our projectors are competing with any kind of live person or scenery onstage. When you are putting a projector in a location where all other ambient light is taken away, then (and only then) can you start to really push for high contrast.

Audio

Some projectors will have speakers, while others won't. Conference room projectors generally have speakers that are sufficient for a small room, so that the presenter can just plug in his laptop and go. You almost never need them for the theater, as your audio is being handled by a separate sound system.

Keystone Correction and Lens Shift

If your projector is directly in front of the center of your screen, then the image that it projects will be a perfect rectangle. If you move the projector down so that it is level with the bottom of the screen, you will need to tip the front of the projector up to keep the image centered on the screen. When you do that, you will create what projection designers call **keystoning**, an image that is wider at the top than at the bottom. The same is true in reverse if you move the projector up above the screen: The image will be wider at the bottom than the top. If you move the projector to the side, the same thing will happen, but now the keystone will be on its side.

Unfortunately, we almost never get to place the projector so that it is smack in the middle of the screen, at least not for front projection. That spot is usually out in the middle of the air somewhere. Generally, the projector is down at the audience level looking up, or hanging from the ceiling looking down, so we are almost always trying to correct some degree of keystoning.

Fortunately, almost all modern projectors have some kind of keystone correction, of one or two different varieties.

Digital keystone correction relies on a digital circuit that stretches one end of the video image, solving the geometric problem, but reducing the quality of the image. It's not a big deal for a text-based PowerPoint presentation, but it has a noticeable effect on more detailed images. Some of the fancier projectors have *automatic* keystone correction, where the projector senses what angle it is sitting at, and then adjusts the image accordingly. The more the projector is tipped up or down, the more it corrects the keystoning.

Variable lens shifting actually physically moves the lens to change the shape of the output image. Because it is altering the optics of the lens system, it does not remove any of the resolution of the image, as digital keystone correction does. For this reason, serious home theater videophiles tend to prefer lens shifting.

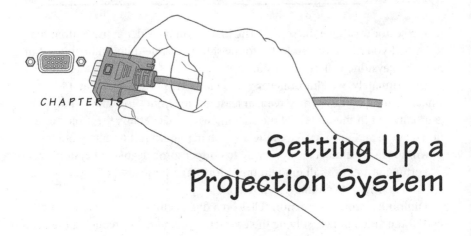

CHAPTER 19

Setting Up a Projection System

The process of setting up a projection system for live performance is about balancing a number of different issues, weighing the trade-offs, and making decisions. It isn't really a linear process, where you complete each task and then move on to the next. It requires you to consider a lot of factors simultaneously. Nevertheless, there is a step-by-step process that you can follow, as long as you realize that you may occasionally have to double back.

Figure Out the Screen Size and Throw Distance for Your Projector

If you already own a projector, then this is your first step. If you are buying a projector for a particular show or event, then do steps 2 and 3 first and then come back here.

One of the more difficult things to figure out about projection is the relationship between **throw distance**, screen size, brightness, and the length of your lens. As one of these variables changes, it drags along the others in a never-ending dance of numbers. Increase your throw and the screen size increases. Put in a longer lens and the screen size drops. Want a bigger screen? Increase your throw (but your image brightness will drop).

These four numbers—throw distance, screen size, brightness, and lens length—are related in a complex formula that used to drive the math-phobics into a dazed, catatonic state and led more than a few of us to scrap the calculations and just haul the stupid projector into the theater and "see what it looks like."

This is hardly the best approach, however, especially if you haven't bought or rented the projector yet. It really does save time and trouble if you do a little figuring before you walk into the theater with your projector.

Fortunately, the Internet has come to the rescue. If you search for "projector lens calculator," you will be presented with any number of websites that will do most or all of the calculations for you.

At the moment, my personal favorite is at *www.projectorcentral.com*. You can either start by entering the make and model of your projector, or if you haven't got the projector yet, you can enter the screen size and throw that you are after and the site will present you a list of options. You can also limit your search by any of the factors that we have talked about already, like brightness, contrast, noise level, resolution, etc.

Once you settle on a projector, the calculator will show you a graph that illustrates the size of your projected image, the throw distance, the brightness level, etc.

As I said, if you already own the projector, then do this research first. There is no purpose in designing a set with unreasonable needs if your projector can't handle it.

Decide Where You Want the Image to Appear

Now that you know how big of a screen you can fill, you can determine where that screen will go, and what it will look like. Is there a projection screen in your set, or are you using a scenic wall? Will your projection cover the entire stage or will it just fill a small screen in a window? Keep the off-axis audience members in mind. Try to place the screen so that the stage lights will not hit it. Remember that stage light can bounce off the floor and up into the screen, especially if the floor is shiny or light colored.

Decide Where the Projector Will Go

There are a number of factors to consider here, but none bigger than . . .

Will It Be Front or Rear Projection?

Probably the most fundamental decision you can make about projection is whether you are going to project from the front or the rear. And, while there are exceptions, most projection designers prefer rear projection, most of the time.

The reason is simple: You can put the projector in the perfect spot. Projections look best when the projector is directly in front of the screen, or, as projection people call it, "on-axis." This is rarely, if ever, possible with front projection in the theater. See, they got these things called "actors," who are rarely, if ever, transparent. They tend to throw their shadows all over those beautiful projections. Furthermore, putting the projector directly in front of the screen often means that the audience is looking right at it. Lastly, projectors tend to have very hot lamps, which means they have fans, and fans make noise.

In rear projection, all these problems go away. You can put the projector squarely on axis without worrying about shadows, visible projectors, or fan noise. When viewed from the front, your image will be reversed, of course, but virtually all video projectors allow you to reverse the image inside the projector, for just this reason. Sophisticated theaters are sometimes built with a **projection bay** upstage to accommodate rear projection.

The problem is, a lot of projection screens don't have enough space behind them for a projection bay. In order to get a good image, there has to be space between the projector and the screen. As a general rule, the available depth behind the screen should at least equal the width of the screen. In order to rear project, you need this amount of distance behind the screen, unobstructed by scenery, walls, or anything else.

The throw distance doesn't have to be in a straight line, however. It is possible to use mirrors to increase the throw distance, by reflecting the image sideways, up, or down. The mirror will steal some of the brightness of the image, unfortunately, although how much it takes will depend on the quality of the mirror. Also, keep in mind that the mirror will need to be as large as the projection beam, which increases in size as you move away from the projector. The farther away from the projector, the larger your mirror must be.

The second problem with rear projection is the screen itself. It has to be translucent, which means that you can't paint it with anything other than dyes or very, very thin paint. It also can't have any internal structure, because it will cause a shadow. Of course, if you are doing a play about creeping industrialism and that internal structure is part of the constructivist effect you are going for, then no problem.

In many cases, the decision will be made for you. Either your set is solid and opaque, or you don't have enough room upstage for a projection area. In this case, you are stuck with front projection, and you will have to depend on your ingenuity to solve its inherent problems.

If you have decided to go with front projection, then you will need to consider the following issues:

How Far Away Is the Projector?

The most important consideration for projector placement is distance from the screen. The effect of distance on brightness is expressed by the inverse square law, which is a bit of high school math that is worth remembering. Put into words, the inverse square law says, "The intensity of light emanating from a single source is inversely proportional to the square of the distance from the source."

Try not to close the book right now. This actually makes sense intuitively. What it means is that the intensity of a light decreases very quickly as you move away from it. If you double the distance from the light, you will actually have only one-quarter of the intensity. Two squared is four, but its an inverse relationship, so it's actually one-fourth.

Try this one: If you triple the distance from the light source (in other words, increase it by a factor of three), what fraction of the light is left? Look below for the answer.[1]

What the inverse square law means is that distance from a light source makes a huge and immediate difference. For this reason, you want to get your projector as close to the screen as possible. You will get a much brighter image from a projector that is hanging on the first electric than one that is sitting in the back of the auditorium. The inverse square law works the other way as well: If you halve the distance to the screen, your projector will appear four times brighter. So, rule number 1: Get the projector as close to the screen as possible.

Of course, the brightness of the image will also be affected by which lens you choose for the projector. If put a wider lens on your projector (or zoom it out), you will get a bigger image, but the image will be less bright. Put a longer lens on (or zoom it in) and the image will get smaller and brighter. It is tempting to move the projector farther away from the screen, zooming the lens to keep the image the same size, but beware of the loss of light. Projectors are at their brightest when that zoom is all the way out—that is, when the image is as big as possible. You can lose up to a third of your light by moving the projector back and closing down the zoom.

Distance, however, has a greater effect than the choice of lens, so the rule of thumb is, choose where the projector goes first, then choose the right lens for the size of the screen.

When choosing a place to put the projector, you will need to balance several concerns.

Can the Projector "See" the Screen?
Is your projector blocked by drapery, scenery, lighting equipment, speakers, or anything else? You've got to have a clear shot.

---

[1] You would have one-ninth of the light, or 1/9.

How Much Keystoning Will I Have?

As I said earlier, almost all projectors have built-in technology to deal with keystoning—the geometric distortion that happens when a projector is not placed squarely in front of a screen. The projector will have either digital keystone correction or variable lens shift, or both. Make sure you check the specifications to see how far off center you can put the projector and still get a square image.

Remember that projectors are generally much better at correcting vertical keystoning than horizontal keystoning. In other words, you can get away with putting the projector above or below the screen much more often than you can get away with putting it to the side.

How Much Fan Noise Does the Projector Make?

As I said before, projectors have fans. Some are louder than others. Like brightness, the volume of the fan is very subjective. Will your audience hear it? It depends on where you place the projector and what other sounds are happening. If your show is a quiet drama, then the audience will be able to hear the fan if you place it anywhere in the auditorium area. If you are doing a rock musical, you can put the projector in their laps and they won't hear it. Many projectors have noise ratings, which will give you a clue. The best way to tell if you are going to have a problem, though, is to take the projector into the theater and experiment.

You can mitigate projector noise a bit by placing it on a soft surface like a sheet of rubber or foam, or by building a box around it, but you must be very careful not to impede or defeat the fan in any way. Don't block the air vents in the projector housing! The fan is an essential part of the system. If it is blocked, your lamp will overheat and fail, sometimes explosively. Don't defeat the fan!

Building an enclosure around your fan will mitigate a lot of the noise, but take some time to design a good one. You can line the box with blankets, insulation, or other soft surfaces to absorb noise. Make sure that there is sufficient space between the insulation and the projector to allow air to circulate: at least a foot on all sides and the top. Make sure that the vents on the bottom of the projector are not blocked. Make sure that there are large openings in the box to allow fresh air to enter. Hot air rises, so put openings in the bottom and top of the enclosure. Fresh, cool air will enter the bottom and hotter air will escape out the top. Build baffles around the airhole openings so that there is no direct line of sight to the projector, but air can flow freely. Sound, especially the high-pitched sound of a projector fan, tends to travel in a straight line; so if you block that line with something absorbent, you can make a lot of progress with fan noise.

How Much Ambient Light Is There?

If you are using projections in your show, you are entering into a battleground and ambient light is the enemy. Almost any light onstage will compete with your projections, softening them or completely washing them out. You will have to work closely with the lighting designer to keep other light levels as low as possible.

One of the best ways to reduce ambient lighting is to get rid of light from the front. Even if it doesn't hit the screen directly, it will bounce off the floor and ricochet up into the screen. Light from the side will bounce harmlessly into the wings on the opposite side.

Strange as it may seem, backlight tends to wash out projections, even though the lighting instruments are pointed directly away from the screen. This is because the backlights will light up the particles of dust in the air, creating a "haze" effect. Again, sidelight creates the haze as well, but only when viewed from the side.

Painting the floor a dark color helps, but even a black floor will reflect front light into the screen, especially as people walk on it and it becomes dusty. Make sure that the paint on the floor is a matte finish, without any gloss whatsoever.

Finally, increasing the distance between the actors and the screens helps enormously. Where there are people, there will be light, so keep the actors away from the screen and you won't have to worry (as much) about keeping their light out of your projections.

How Reflective Is the Screen?

When the light from your projector gets to the screen, it has to turn around and go back out into the audience. Of course, not all of it is going to make the turn. Some of it will die in the screen. The amount of light that survives the reflection depends on the screen.

Projection screens are rated with a gain factor. The higher the number, the more reflective the screen. Unfortunately, like lumen ratings, gain factors are only useful for comparisons between screens. Gain factors are measured at the brightest point, generally straight out from the middle of the screen. As you move to the side, the light will begin to fall off. When the light has dropped to 50 percent of the maximum brightness, you have reached the half-gain viewing angle, another way in which screens are rated. A screen with a wider half-gain viewing angle will provide a better picture for people sitting out to the sides, or off-axis. High gain factors tend to produce low half-gain angles, because the screen is bouncing the light straight back out, instead of diffusing it to the sides.

In general, the whiter the screen, the brighter the image. However, a pure white screen will also make those black areas of the screen look brighter, reducing the contrast of the image. This is why many projection screens are slightly off-white or gray. It makes the blacks look blacker and sharpens the image, increasing the contrast.

You can certainly project your image onto canvas drops or flats, but be aware that they will not be as bright as a true projection screen, which is specifically designed to be reflective. Of course, the downside is, when the projections aren't on, your projection screen looks like a great big projection screen. Another downside of using a real projection screen is that it will also reflect any other light that it picks up out there, particularly if the lights are coming from the front. One classic problem is lights that come from the front bounce off the floor, hit the projection screen, and wash out the image. This problem is magnified by a highly reflective screen.

It's always fun to project your images on scenery, and this can be very effective, especially if the scenery is white or mostly white. A painted surface offers a more diffuse projection image, which is fine when you are not doing PowerPoint presentations with lots of text. Most of the projection content in the theater is images, which don't mind a more diffuse screen. Another benefit of painted surfaces is that the half-gain viewing angle is much wider, because the textured surface spreads the light around more.

If you are projecting on any kind of fabric, like drops, scrims, or cycloramas the reflectivity will also depend on the tightness of the weave. A solid canvas drop will reflect a lot more light than a loosely woven scrim. One problem with projecting on scrims is that some of the light will slip through and hit whatever is hanging behind the scrim, causing a double image. If you are projecting on scrim, it is very important to have a soft black curtain hanging behind it to "eat" the light. If you are lucky enough to have a "plaster cyc," then you have one of the all-time best projection surfaces.

Screen gain and half-gain angles are also used to compare rear projection screens. In fact, if you are buying commercial screens, you can use these numbers to compare front versus rear projection.

Rear projection screens are transmissive, rather than reflective, that is, they transmit light through the screen as opposed to reflecting back, so they are made differently. In order to avoid seeing the "hot spot" of the projector lamp, rear projection screens are often dark gray or black and made of special diffusion material that scatters the light beams. Viewing angles are smaller for rear projection than front projection, so keep that in mind if your audience is spread out wide. People sitting out toward the edges will see a dimmer, more washed-out image. Whether or not you can actually see the projector lens, rear projection can suffer from "vignetting," where the corners of the screen go dark because the light is too diffuse. You can decrease this effect by moving the projector farther away, although your overall light level will drop. It's always trade-offs. . .

Incidentally, there are a number of low-tech solutions for projection screens, but one of my favorites is using ordinary shower curtains. If your projection screens are small (like windows in the facade of a house and you can get the projector off to the side to hide the hot spot, opaque shower curtains make a great surface for rear projection.

How Will I Mount the Projector?

Finally, once you have figured out which projector and where it will go, you will need to mount it. Your method of mounting the projector should do three things: keep the projector still, keep it secure, and keep it cool.

Take a good look at what you are mounting the projector to. A common mistake is to attach a projector to a catwalk or gridwork that gets walked on during the show (typically by followspot operators or other crew). A tiny, minuscule shiver in a catwalk, multiplied over a long throw, will look like an earthquake has hit your picture. Try to attach your projector to the building itself, or if you have to use the catwalk, make sure that it is not a thoroughfare during the performance. Secondly, it is essential that your method of attachment be very, very secure so that the projector will not fall. Gravity and sensitive electronics do not get along well. Some projectors have tapped holes in the bottom that you can use to bolt it down. If you don't have those, then you can always fall back on the classic low-tech attachment—a ratchet strap like the ones used to hold down cargo in trucks or on top of cars. You can get them at hardware or auto parts stores. Try not to use bungee cords. They stretch over time. If you do use straps, don't wrap them around any of the controls that you will need, especially power, zoom, focus, and the menu key.

Finally, your method of attachment must keep the projector cool. Two things to think about here. One: Do not, under any circumstances, block any of the vents. The projector fan has to disperse a huge amount of heat, and it needs all the help it can get. Second: Don't place the projector next to, or, especially, above lighting instruments. The heat from the lights can overwhelm the fan. Maintain at least three feet between the projector and lighting instruments. When it comes to keeping a projector cool, airflow is everything.

Oh, and don't forget that you will need power for the projector, although it's nothing complicated—just a wall outlet. Do *not* put the projector into a lighting circuit unless you have a specified "nondim" dimmer module. Anything else can damage the projector's power supply.

Where Can I Put the Playback Source?

An addition to placing the projector, you also have to place the device that is playing back your video. The key thing here is control. Who will be operating the device? If it is being plugged into a show control system then it doesn't really matter where you put it, as long as it is clean, dry, cool, and relatively dust-free. If it requires a human operator, then you will want to put it somewhere accessible. Remember that there will be a video cable running up to the projector.

Get Some Test Content

At this stage, it's a good idea to get some content that is roughly similar to what you will be projecting during the show. You may want to grab a variety of things and start to project tests in the theater to see what works and what doesn't. The outcome of these tests will help you make decisions about which images you want to use. If your screen is small, you may want images with less detail. If you want to display text, you will want to make sure that it is legible. If your projector placement is too far off center for the built-in keystone correction or lens shift to solve, you will want to build distortion correction into your image.

Figure Out How You Will Connect Your Playback Device to Your Projector

If you are using a computer to drive the projector:

Best Choice: DVI

If both your laptop and your computer have DVI plugs, you are in luck! Buy a single DVI cable and plug them in. Be aware that you will probably have to place your computer fairly close to the projector. There is no official maximum length for DVI cables, but the chances of your signal degrading start to increase after twenty feet or so. It is impossible to predict exactly where the signal will become unusable, however. It depends on the particular circuitry of your laptop and your projector. In general, keep them close.

Second Choice: DVI to HDMI Conversion

If your computer has a DVI plug (common on Macs, less common on PCs) and your projector has an HDMI input (fairly common, especially on projectors designed for home theaters), then purchase a DVI-HDMI adaptor. You can use a DVI cable and convert at the projector end, or you can use an HDMI cable and convert at the laptop end. It really doesn't matter—DVI and HDMI are the same kind of signal. If you have a long cable run, DVI cables tend to protect the signal a little better, but as I mentioned above, you don't want to run these cables more than about twenty feet if you can avoid it.

Third Choice: RGB

All video projectors that are compatible with computers have an RGB port for a computer input. If you are using a PC, it will have an RGB port as well, so plug in an RGB cable and you are done. If you have a Mac, you will need a DVI to RGB adaptor.

If you are using a DVD player or consumer video server (Apple TV, etc.) to drive the projector:

Best Choice: HDMI

As I said, this is only for runs of twenty feet or less.

Second Choice: Coaxial Cable with BNC Plugs

If you are using pro or semipro gear, it will have BNC plugs on the back. These are the push-and-turn locking connector often used for pro video. An excellent choice. Coaxial cable can run up to one thousand feet with standard video, about three hundred with HD. You can use this cable with either composite or component video.

Third Choice: Coaxial Cable with RCA Plugs

You can use RCA plugs if that is what your gear has, but I recommend adapting them to a coaxial cable, either by putting the plus right onto the cable or by adapting them to the BNC plugs on the cable.

If you are using a video server to drive your projector:

It depends on the server and the type of video that you are ending, but for most applications, coaxial cable with BNC connectors is the way to go, unless you are using the digital SDI interface, in which case you use SDI plugs, or an Ethernet media network, in which case you will use Ethernet plugs.

Do a Mock-up

Do this as soon as you can. Don't wait for the set to be complete and the theater to be full of actors before you try your projection. There is nothing more helpful for the projection process than an early mock-up in the theater. You will quickly see if your plan is realistic and what changes need to be made. Set up something that resembles your final projection surface and get the projector into its actual position. Try not to cheat and get "close enough." Get it right.

Confirm the Settings on the Laptop

Once you have the screen and the projector in place and the laptop connected, you will need to get the right image on the projector. There are two ways to go when hooking up a projector: setting it up as an additional monitor or mirroring. In the first case, the projector screen operates as an extension of your computer desktop, giving you additional real estate for windows. In the second case, the projector screen shows the same thing as your computer screen. In most cases, the mirror option is what you want. Using the projector as an extension of your desktop means that all the menus, scroll bars, and other bits of computer interface will be visible. If you mirror your desktop, you can simply put the presentation software into a full-screen mode and all that other garbage disappears.

The process for setting up your computer with an external monitor differs depending on your operating system. On a Mac, you use the "System Preferences" under the Apple menu. Look for the button that says "Displays." On a PC, it depends on which version of Windows and which brand of computer you have. In some cases, the computer will automatically detect the projector and display your desktop on the projector screen. If not, then you usually use a combination of function keys to switch the screen to the projector. Hold down the Fn key and hit each of the function keys, F1 through F9, one at a time, until one of them works. If you get no love, check your manual or online.

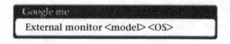

Google me

External monitor <model> <OS>

Confirm the Settings on the Projector

Once your projector is displaying your computer screen, it is time to mess with the projector settings. Depending on your projector, there may be lots of things that you can mess with, but here are the main ones:

Resolution
Focus
Size
Keystone Correction

Other than resolution (which should match the resolution that you are feeding the projector from your computer or other server), all of these adjustments should be done using your best measuring device: your eyes. Adjust it until it looks good.

Build the Presentation

What, you say? Get all this other stuff done and *then* build the presentation? Well, yes.

And no. Obviously, as soon as you start having ideas about the show, you will probably start looking around for images and throwing them in a folder on your computer. And, as previously stated, you should throw some test images up on the screen to help you make decisions. By putting the build-the-presentation step very *late*, I want to make it clear that you need to figure out the technical details of the projection system very *early*, so that you know what you are dealing with. It's a serious problem if you build your entire presentation and then go into the theater and realize it doesn't work because you used the wrong aspect ratio or the wrong colors or the wrong picture of your sainted Aunt Mary. Get the technical details figured out early on using test footage, and then get into the gritty details of the show itself.

Once you have your projection setup mocked up you can use the settings that you discovered (file format, resolution, aspect ratio, etc.) to set up a file in the video or image editing software of your choice (Final Cut Pro, Adobe Premiere, PowerPoint, iPhoto, Keynote, etc.). Then, start putting the images in the order you want, with the appropriate transitions between them. Remember to leave a blank slide where you don't want any image on the screen. It's also a good idea to put a few seconds of black on either end, just to get a clean start and stop.

Troubleshoot

Even in the simplest projection setups, there are still a host of things that can go wrong. If things don't look right, go back and check the settings again. Don't be afraid to revisit the lighting, screen angle, projection position, etc., etc., etc.

Rehearse

And make changes and changes and changes . . .

Enjoy

You have made projection happen. Congratulations!

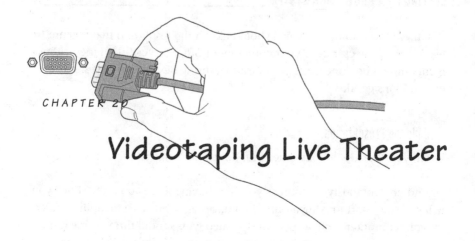

CHAPTER 20

Videotaping Live Theater

I'm always astonished when I watch videos of shows I have worked on, and not for the right reasons. There's something about committing a live performance to a video that somehow seems to suck the life out of it. It reminds me of Norma Desmond, the fading silent movie star in *Sunset Boulevard*, when an admirer says, "You used to be big!" and she replies, "I am big. It's the pictures that got small."

Unfortunately, taking a performance out of the immersive, immediate environment of the theater and putting it on a relatively small screen leaves us with a flat imitation of a rich three-dimensional event.

In order to combat this, video producers have fallen back on a number of tricks over the years, all intended to make up for the shortcomings of a video performance by providing enhancements that the live audience didn't enjoy.

Probably the most effective compensation that producers provide is the close-up. In all but the very smallest theater, there is a fair amount of distance between the audience member and the performer. Your eyes and your brain are very good at concentrating your attention on a specific performer; but when the performance is rendered on a screen, it robs your visual systems of the ability to "zoom in" on a particular performer. A camera can push in close, getting rid of extraneous visuals and giving a sense of intimacy and connection, drawing the observer into the performance. When shooting live performance, remember the importance of getting close, and remember that a good close-up always requires a tripod. Zooming in on a distant subject magnifies the effect of a shaky hand. Movements that might be acceptable in long shots will feel like earthquakes in close-ups.

The bad news about close-ups, however, is that you might miss events that are not within the frame. Further, there are times that you want to see the entire stage in order to get a sense of the whole spectacle. Sometimes you want to give up the individual connection in favor of getting a look at the group as a whole, like when the stage fills with dancers, or a choir, or acrobats. And if that weren't enough, sometimes you want to split the difference, showing a small group of two or three people. And sometimes you want it all, so you can constantly switch between different viewpoints. The solution? Multiple cameras with multiple angles.

There are two ways to shoot an event with multiple cameras. The first is to use a live video switcher that takes all the video feeds from the cameras and plugs them into a box where the director can choose what he wants to see, moment by moment. The switcher doesn't just switch—depending on its quality and cost, it might offer the ability to dissolve, wipe, fade, spin, twist, window-shade or dozens of other transitions. More complicated systems might offer slow-motion replay special graphics and effects, and on-screen titles. And of course, this is to say nothing of the audio, which must be mixed and switched to match the pictures. A first-class live shoot, like a sporting event or a live event show, has dozens of people who are concerned with creating a seamless stream of video, smoothly switching from one angle to the next.

There are smaller multicamera switchers that are made for lower-cost productions. Companies like NewTek make switchers that are designed for live mobile productions, and they will run you a lot less than that multimillion-dollar semi full o' gear that is sitting outside Monday Night Football. But you are still talking tens of thousands of dollars in cameras, switchers, and associated hardware; plus, you will need a director that knows the show well and can create a smooth series of shots of a live production. The live show is an unrepeatable event.

Another way of approaching multiple cameras that generally appeals to lower-cost productions is to just shoot the whole thing on several different camcorders and then edit the different angles together later on. This process got a whole lot easier when Final Cut Pro added the multicamera editing function to its software. Other software manufacturers now have versions of this feature as well.

The multicamera approach is to shoot the show on a number of different camcorders, with each one recording the entire show, beginning to end, without stopping.

Generally, one camera is assigned the job of covering the entire stage in a master shot. This gives you a go-to shot that you can always cut to and prevents you from missing anything. The other two cameras should be given as specific assignments as you can. One of them could be assigned to close-ups, while another one could be told to cover small groups, or to pick up reactions from other performers. It never hurts to have one camera shooting the audience, if there is enough light out there. An audience cutaway shot showing them laughing or crying or applauding is always a crowd pleaser.

Once you have all the footage from the different angles, you import it into your video program. Place each of the files into a different track in your new sequence, lining them up so that they are all in sync with each other. The common trick to this is to have someone walk up to the stage when all cameras are rolling before the show and take a flash photo, facing the cameras. Because the flash is very short (less than a single frame of video) and quite bright, it's easy to find the one frame in all the video streams that shows it. Line up that frame in all the tracks in your software and you are ready to go. At this point, you will need to identify the tracks as "multicamera," which will link them together and open up some new functions.

When you play back all those streams in multicamera mode, FCP allows you to switch between them, using keys on the keyboard. As you switch between them, FCP keeps track of where those cuts are. When you play back the file, FCP cuts between the angles, producing a finished product with multiple angles. Of course, if you miss something or change your mind later, the software lets you change your mind and move cuts around until you are satisfied.

If you are shooting video, remember that video cameras are not as sensitive to light as the human eye, so try to get the light levels as high as possible on stage.

Also, it is *highly* worth the time and effort to pay attention to sound. Great video loses much of its impact without decent sound.

The single most important thing is to get the mic as close to the stage as possible. I highly recommend buying a stereo microphone, mounting it right in front of the stage and feeding that microphone into one of the cameras. Use that one feed for the entire program and ignore the audio from the cameras that are farther away.

Even better than that is to put several mics on the front of the stage and run them to a small mixer. Use that mixer to mix the entire show down to one stereo mix, and run *that* into one of the cameras. Camcorders these days record at CD quality or better, so the recording will be quite good quality if you get the mics up close enough.

Of course, if you are planning on videotaping any theatrical event, make sure that you have the right to do so. No professional theater will ever allow you to videotape a performance without permission, so don't try. Ushers are trained to spot clandestine cameras in the audience, and at the very least, it will earn you an unceremonius exit from the space. Experienced theatrical stars are very sensitive about being taped without their knowledge and permission. Broadway legend Patti LuPone recently stopped a performance of her phenomenal Broadway revival of *Gypsy* right in the middle of a song to forcibly berate an audience member who was taping the show. She strode out to the edge of the apron, demanding his immediate removal, and lemme tell you, what Ms. LuPone wants, Ms. LuPone gets. As I heard it, the removal of the offending individual was greeted with thunderous applause as the Broadway legend nodded to the conductor to "take it from the bridge."

Bottom line, if you are going to videotape a show, never assume that it is acceptable to do so. Get permission before you start.

Part 4: Show Control

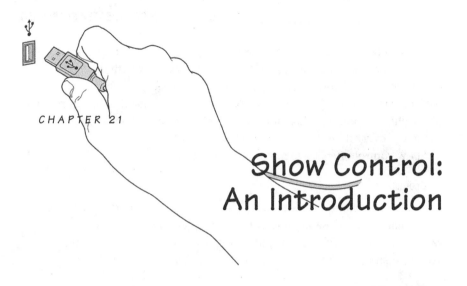

CHAPTER 21

Show Control: An Introduction

Show control has now replaced audio as the most mysterious and unknown of all the technical theater arts. For one thing, it isn't immediately obvious what show control *is*. Lighting, video, and audio are all fairly recognizable to the casual theater observer, to say nothing of scenery and costumes. Show control is clearly the most abstract of all the theatrical systems. What does it *do*? In fact, it's not really a system; it's a metasystem— a system that controls other systems.

Show control ties together all the systems that we have talked about so far. It is the system that makes the lighting synchronize with the sound, the scenery start with the music, the projection screen land before the video turns on. Show control systems create coordination, synchronization, and timing between the different disciplines.

Just in case you've had some show control training, here's the test to see if you need to read this intro:

"The lighting controller is chasing time code from the audio playback, while sending a MIDI note onto the video server to fire cues."

You are not alone if the above sentence is nonsense to you. Read on! If the test sentence was child's play to you, skip to the next chapter.

General Concepts of Show Control

Show control systems exist to coordinate two or more other systems backstage allowing them to run in parallel, or "sync up." When Bart Blackey takes a shot at Cowboy Joe, the sound of a ricocheting bullet needs to sync up with the tin can being blown off the hitching post, to give a simple example. To give a complex example, imagine a theme park show with dozens of explosions, collapsing scenery, a fast-paced soundtrack, live flames, stunts, lighting cues, sound effects, and video. Now imagine that all of this is packed into eighteen minutes of nonstop excitement that has to happen the exact same way every time. C'mon down, show control!

Show control offers three major backstage advantages:

Coordination

As I said, show control is a way of synchronizing one or more systems, so that events happen at the same time or in a particular order. Anytime you have two operators with their hands poised to push two buttons simultaneously, you have an opportunity for show control.

Consistency

Sure, the show might run perfectly tonight, when everyone has their opening night face on. But some shows run for months, if not years, and the crew may change. For complicated shows that will run for long periods of time, with multiple performances in a single day and/or multiple crews, show control can help the show maintain the same timing and quality over time. If there is one thing that a computer is good at, it is doing the same damn thing over and over.

Complication

In the "complicated" example above, we had eight different systems, all of which are creating multiple effects, one after another, for a blisteringly fast show. Some things are really beyond the capability of a human being. When shows start to get really complicated, show control can get hundreds of tasks done quickly and accurately by preprogramming them into computers and letting the lightning-fast electronics do their thing.

Show control systems, whether simple or complex, are always custom designed for each show. The needs of each production are different, and in show control, it is always difficult to generalize. Nevertheless, there are concepts that run throughout the world of show control that will help you talk through it with programmers, technicians, and money people, so here are the big picture concepts you really need to know:

Synchronous versus Asynchronous

Does your show run in the same order every time, or does it need to be flexible, to accommodate guest interactivity?

Sometimes the events of a show run in order, with all elements following a prearranged script. This situation is most familiar to theater people, who generally live in an environment where scene 1 always follows scene 2 and this light cue always goes with that sound cue. Technical events always happen in a particular order. This is known as synchronous show control. In a synchronous situation, there is usually some sort of schedule, which keeps all the events in order. That schedule might be a paper script, followed by a stage manager, who calls all the cues in the right order. "Lighting 49 and sound 17 . . . *go.*" The schedule might also be an electronic cue list, which automatically knows which cue comes next in the sequence.

An asynchronous show allows events to happen in any order. A system of interactive displays in a museum is asynchronous, for example. If a guest pushes a button on a touch screen, the earthquake simulation begins. The show control system sends a message to the floor shakers to start shaking, while also telling the sound system to play a rumbling sound, the lighting system to simulate a power outage, and the video to show clips of falling buildings. It doesn't matter if the cue for the earthquake comes before or after the cue for the tornado in the next room. The cues can happen in any order, whenever they need to happen for the show.

Event-based versus Time-based

Do the cues in your show follow a precise timeline, or do they follow certain events, like an actor's actions or lines?

Most theatrical show control systems are event-based. In other words, each cue is tied to a certain event, like an actor saying his line. When that event happens, the operator pushes GO on the machine and we're off. Nice and simple.

But what if there are too many things happening in a short amount of time for an operator to keep up? Or what if the "show" continues all day long, like a museum display or an automated fountain? In this case, it might be better to set up a timeline and tell all the machines to do their thing at a particular moment in time. This is known as a time-based764 system.

Some time-based systems actually use the time of day as their clock. In other words, the machines are told to do their thing at a particular time of day, say 3:00 PM or every hour on the hour. This works well for museum displays and fountains, but not for theaters. Theatrical time-based systems often make use of **time code**, a very precise timer that ticks along during the show, providing a time reference for all the control devices.

In this scenario, the only time that the operator hits the GO button is at the beginning of the show. From that point on, the machines are in charge.

One of the machines generates time code, sending out an electronic timing signal that counts off seconds (and fractions of seconds) to the other machines in the system. Each machine has a set of cues, each of which runs when the clock reaches a certain value. The system starts counting when the operator pushes GO so all time code values are relative to the moment that the show started. If something happens at four minutes and sixteen seconds on the time code scale, that means that it has been four minutes and sixteen seconds since the operator pushed GO.

Many systems use some of each. For example, when you hit the GO button on the light board, it might run several cues in sequence. It might run the first cue to completion, then wait five seconds and start a second cue, then wait three seconds and start a third cue before the second one is complete. After all the cues are complete, it sits quietly until the operator pushes the button again. In this way, the lighting board combines an event (you pushing the button) with a timeline (the preprogrammed length of the entire sequence of cues). The Universal Studios *Waterworld* show is time-based; the show control system runs a clock and all the cues are timed to that clock. However, the clock does not run continuously from beginning to end. The show is actually broken down into five timed segments and the system stops completely after each section, waiting for the operator to push GO for the next section. These pauses allow for sections of actor dialogue that do not have to be timed to the clock. In general, actors don't like to deliver their lines on a timer.[1]

Anytime you have time code, you have a device that is generating it and one or more devices that are **chasing** it. Chasing time code means that one device is watching a clock that is being run by another device. A show control computer, for example, might be generating time code, which is being chased by a lighting console, an audio console, a pyrotechnics console, and a video server. In this scenario, the lighting console has a series of cues, each of which is programmed to happen at a particular time code number. The lighting console chases the time code, and when the time code number equals the console's preprogrammed cue, the console runs the proper cue. When time code is in use, it is generated by one machine and chased by all the rest.

We'll be talking more about time code in chapter 23.

---

[1] Just for the record, *Waterworld* does not use time code. The show control system runs its own internal clock and then sends out cues to the other devices at the proper time. The devices themselves (audio, pyrotechnics, special effects, etc.) do not track the time code; they just wait for the show control system to say GO.

Masters and Slaves

Show control is about machines controlling other machines, and just like humans, the one that is in control is called the master and the other one is called the slave. The master controller is the one with the GO button—the one where the human being tells the system that it is time to start. The master sends out commands and the slaves follow them without complaint (which is where the comparison with humans ends). There is no rule, however, that says that any particular machine in a system has to be the master. In a system with a dedicated show control computer, that machine is almost always the master. When there is no dedicated show control machine, however, all bets are off. You might recall that in the Broadway production of *Wicked*, one of the lighting consoles controls the other two, as well as the captioning system. In many pyrotechnic shows, the audio system acts as the master, playing back the time code as it plays back the music, and the pyro controller is slaved to the time code being generated by the audio device (with a human being holding down an Enable button to ensure that it is safe to fire).

The decision about which machine will be the master and which will be slaves is based on the circumstances of each show. Sometimes, the audiotape will be the master because the music playback is continuous, making it the most time sensitive of all the devices. Sometimes the lighting controller will be the master because it has the most cues, and therefore it makes sense to gather all the nonlighting cues there as well. Sometimes, there will be a dedicated show control computer that does nothing but generate show control commands, making it the most logical master. There are even cases where the master and slave labels change during the show. For the Blue Man Group show in Las Vegas, the lighting controller sends cues to the video server when it calls up video clips to enhance the lighting. Later on, the video server turns the tables and sends cues to the lighting system when it needs to broadcast video footage through the moving lights. It's all very democratic.

Interfaces

The interface is the place where the computer and the human communicate with each other. It may be the screen and mouse of a personal computer, or it may be a custom-designed panel full of buttons. Besides the main interface where the system operator sits, there may also be other interfaces around the set where cast and crew can communicate with the system. For example, many systems have the following:

Enable Buttons

An Enable button is used to tell the computer that it is okay to do something. They are most common in time-based systems, where the computer is just rolling merrily along, running cues, and sending out commands, but needs to know if it is safe to do something. For example, if the computer is going to move a platform onstage, there may be an Enable button placed where a backstage crew person can see if everything is clear around the effect. If everything is good, the crew person holds the button down. When it is time for the effect, the computer checks the status of the Enable button. If the button is down, the effect can happen. If not, the effect is aborted. This is often called a **dead man's switch**. If the stage manager is dead (or distracted by a costume change gone wrong) and no one is watching the effect, it doesn't happen and no one gets hurt.

Contact Closures

When an operator or a guest pushes a button, it creates a **contact closure**. Contact closure means that two pieces of wire have been brought together and are in contact with one another, thereby completing an electrical circuit. These contact closures can be buttons, door switches, floor mats, anything where a physical object is moving and bringing two wires together.

To make a contact closure work, the computer sends out a low-voltage electrical current on a wire. When the closure happens, the signal jumps to the other wire and then comes back to the computer on that wire. When the computer sees that the circuit is closed, it does whatever it is supposed to do. For example, a carnival fun house may have a contact closure wired to a particular section of floor. When the guest steps on it, the floor moves down, closes the circuit, and tells the computer to play the sound of a werewolf howl.

Contact closures comes in two varieties: **normally open** (NO) and **normally closed** (NC). These are just what they sound like. A normally open contact closure is normally not connected—the electrical signal is not being transmitted. When the switch is closed, the signal is connected, and the computer does whatever it has been told to do. A normally closed circuit starts the show with a complete circuit and doesn't do anything until the circuit is broken. These are often used for emergency stop circuits. That way, all of the normally closed stop buttons can be on a single circuit. If any one of the buttons is pushed, breaking the circuit, the computer halts the show.

Limit Switches

This is a special case of a contact closure. When a piece of scenery is designed to move, the system designer always wants to control how far it goes. The technicians may place half of a small switch on a motorized wagon and the other half at the wagon's destination. When the wagon gets where it's going, the two halves of the switch come together, close the circuit, and the computer gets a signal to stop the motor. Limit switches are used to keep the stagecoach wagon from crashing into the saloon platform. Besides the standard limit switch, there are several variations. A **decel limit switch** tells the system that the platform is approaching the end of its travel and should start decelerating. An **over-travel switch** is a safety device that tells the system that the platform missed its limit for some reason and went too far. In this case, something is wrong with the system. Shut it down, boys.

Emergency Stop

Also referred to as an **E-stop**, this is the big red button that tells the system to stop what it is doing and I mean right now. This shuts down the entire system to prevent injury to people, equipment, and corporate lawyer's stomach lining. There is always one on the main show control console, and there may be others around the set, depending on the needs of the show. Stopping the show by hitting the E-stop button accidentally is a fifteen-beer penalty.

Protocols

When a plane is getting ready to land at an international airport, it's important that the pilot and the air traffic controller communicate clearly. The regulatory agencies that run the world's air travel system have decided that English will be used for all air traffic control, but that's not enough. There has to be a set of rules for *how* English is used in this situation. For example, the controller always identifies which plane he is talking to before giving directions: "United Flight 227, turn right to 120 degrees." If he were to start with the directions, "Turn right to 120 degrees," before identifying United Flight 227, he might have a sky full of planes turning right before they realized which one he was talking to. Communication requires both a vocabulary and a set of rules for using those words. This set of rules is called a **protocol.**

In the world of show control, there are a number of protocols in use, some of which cover commands and some of which cover the systems that transmit those commands. If you are going to use show control, then you are going to need two machines that both speak the same protocol.

For amateur users, the three most common protocols are the following:

MIDI: The Musical Instrument Digital Interface

Originally developed to allow electronic synthesizers to control each other, MIDI really hit its stride with the introduction of personal computers. Musicians were able to use their PCs to record musical notes, edit them, then play them back automatically on their keyboard. Show control has taken MIDI from the musical world and used it in all manner of devices, especially lighting controllers and audio playback systems.

DMX: Digital Multiplexing

We've already covered DMX in a lighting context, but it is also another tool in the show control toolbox, particularly with lighting-related devices and special effects like fog and smoke.

MIDI Show Control

MIDI was borrowed from music, and DMX was borrowed from lighting—as such, they both could only do so much for show control. In 1989, a working group of theater pros dove into the problem and created MIDI Show Control, a protocol designed specifically for theatrical show control. MSC provides commands for many common show control applications, like stop, go, and Next as well as more sophisticated commands for devices like video servers.

MIDI Show Control has become quite popular around amateur, academic, and semipro theaters because it is easy to work with and generally uses the English language instead of technospeak. If you are willing to put in a few evenings with a manual, you can actually do quite a bit with MSC without a degree from MIT.

We'll go deeper into all of these protocols in the chapter 23.

PC versus PLC

In many cases, theatrical control programs run on garden-variety personal computers, or PCs. This is fine when you are sending commands to lighting consoles, audio systems, and other nonlethal devices. When it comes to devices that have an element of danger, however, you don't want a machine that is designed for e-mail, word processing, and digital jukeboxes to be flying scenery or blowing up fireworks. For these devices, you want a box that is dedicated to that task alone. You want a PLC.

A **programmable logic controller** is a computer that controls something— generally something that moves or blows up. This type of device used to be called a programmable controller, until the personal computer revolution came along and stole their acronym. Wishing to avoid an unpleasant scene, the engineers quietly changed the term and the abbreviation.

A PLC is a dedicated piece of hardware that is designed solely to control machines. PLCs can be found in factory automation, streetlights, escalators, elevators, and hundreds of other devices. You are surrounded by them. It is a requirement for any type of system that involves **life safety**. In other words, if your system is the kind of thing that could hurt someone, like an automated rigging system or flame effects or hydraulic lifts, it must be controlled by a machine that doesn't do anything else. As my grandmother would say, "Stick to your knitting." Do what you do best and don't get complicated.

PLC programming, however, should be done by a trained programmer. They will know best how to maintain a safe and sane stage. In some cases, once the original programming is done, the programmer can create an interface where a casual operator can change aspects of the system. For example, an automated rigging system has an interface that allows you to set things like trims and speeds. The essential brains of the system, however, is a PLC, and the programmer has set it up in such a way that, no matter what stupid thing you try to tell it to do, the system will keep you from hurting yourself.

At the End of the Day: The Human Element

Some people think that show control takes away a job backstage and gives it to a machine. In my experience, however, show control never reduces the number of people necessary to run a show—it only makes that show more reliable and consistent, allowing a greater level of complication and creating new ways of interacting with devices. All show control systems are still created and maintained by people. In fact, a good show control programmer may occasionally decide *not* to automate something. Computers, after all, only do what they are told. They cannot deal with unexpected circumstances, nor can they be taught to be "reasonable." The best show control in the world—the best way to keep any show under control—is still a human being.

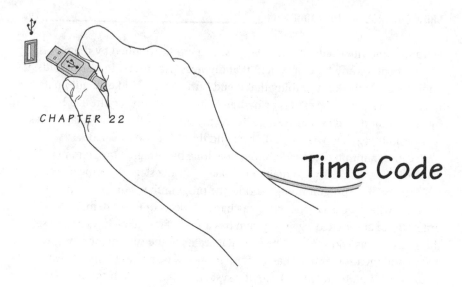

CHAPTER 22

Time Code

Sometimes, when setting up a show control system, the designers need a "clock" that all the devices can use to synchronize their watches. You could use the time of day, of course, but then you could only run the show once a day and at a specific time. No, we need a standardized clock that we can start at any time and stop whenever we want. I've said it before and I will say it again: Theater technicians don't invent technologies if they can steal it from another industry, and the clock is no exception. This time, they went to the television industry.

When videotape was invented, the engineers needed a way to identify each individual frame of video on the tape. This was important because the engineers wanted a way that they could grab a particular piece of that video and copy it to another tape. In short, they wanted to invent video editing. In order to pull that off, they needed a way to say, "Start at this exact frame and go to that exact frame." This numbering system became known as time code, and it has since spread past the video world into film, music, and live theater, where is operates as a standardized clock that helps everyone stay in sync with everyone else.

The organization that spearheaded this effort is called the Society of Motion Picture and Television Engineers, and thus the time code they invented is called SMPTE (pronounced "SIMP-tee") time code.

Because SMPTE time code was born from video, it doesn't just count hours, minutes, and seconds—it also counts frames. The standard format for SMPTE time code is as follows:

HH:MM:SS:FF

So,

01:24:45:18

. . . means 1 hour, 24 minutes, 45 seconds, and 18 frames.

The original frame rate for video in the United States was thirty frames per second, so standard time code uses that same number.

There are other frame rates in use, however, including twenty-four frames per second for film and twenty-five frames per second for European video. If you are in the United States and there are no indications to the contrary, however, you can pretty much bet that you are using 30 fps time code–with one exception:

Drop Frame Time Code

The exception is a quirk that came about when color video appeared. The engineers discovered that, for a number of head-spinning reasons, the color signal actually ran very, very slightly slower than everything else, which caused an hour of color video to actually run long by 3.59 seconds, which added up to almost a minute and a half a day. And that, ladies and gentlemen, is three 30-second revenue-producing commercials lost per day, and *that* will never do.

In order to solve the problem, those clever engineers invented **drop frame time code**. In spite of the name, no frames are actually dropped with this kind of video. Rather, the time code skips numbers every now and then: specifically, two frames per minute,[1] every minute except the minutes that are divisible by ten. This adds up to eighteen frame numbers skipped every ten minutes, which almost exactly compensates for the problem. This bit of mathematical skullduggery results in a slightly slower frame rate of 29.97 fps. We only do this in the United States, and only for video, so there is no drop frame time code for PAL or film.

Some systems indicate that drop frame time code is in use by replacing the colons between the numbers with semicolons like this:

00;01;02;29

But it's not consistent between systems, darn it.

The only thing you really need to know about drop frame is that all the devices in your system need to be set for the same frame rate. The following are the most common:

30 fps	NTSC non-drop-frame (also HD)
29.97 fps	NTSC drop-frame
25 fps	PAL
24 fps	Film

---

[1] Frame 0 and frame 1 of the first second of every minute are skipped–so, for example, the clock would count like this as it reached two minutes: 01:59:28, 01:59:29, 02:00:02, 02:00:03, etc.

Using SMPTE Time Code for Audio Sync (A Head)

One of the places that SMPTE time code went after the video guys invented it was into the audio studio. Back in the eighties, many musicians started using their PCs to compose music, using a new technology called MIDI (Musical Instrument Digital Interface). MIDI didn't record actual audio—it was a way of playing electronic keyboards remotely by sending them commands to play certain notes at certain times. At that stage in the game, computers were quite capable of sending out commands to keyboards or other software-based instruments, but they weren't powerful enough to record audio at a high-enough resolution to keep musicians happy. Therefore, a hybrid studio appeared: The keyboard tracks were recorded to a computer using MIDI, and the rest of the instruments and the vocals were recorded to multi-track tape. In order to keep everything in sync, the SMPTE time code was recorded as an audible signal on one of the tracks of the tape. Whenever the tape started rolling, the computer would listen for the time code and then snap to the right place in its own recorded sequence of notes. From that point on, the tape and the computer would stay in sync with one another. Later on, tape decks and computers were equipped with special time code inputs and outputs, so the time code didn't have to be played as an audio track. This was a good thing, because time code is incredibly loud and annoying to listen to, and if any technician ever mistakenly routed that track to a speaker, it would deafen everyone in the studio.

Using SMPTE Time Code for Video Sync

Eventually, of course, computers grew bigger drives and faster processors and took over all the recording tasks, including recording all the analog instruments and voices. These days, most professional audio recording is done on software, like Digidesign Pro Tools, Apple Logic, Steinberg Nuendo, and Mark of the Unicorn Digital Performer. If the recording is done on external recorders, they are almost always digital recorders.[2] However, this did not remove the need for synchronization. Au contraire, the studio began filling up with even more digital gear, all of which needed to be synchronized.

---

[2] Even though the digital revolution put most tape decks out of business, there is an interesting phenomenon in the audio recording industry where hybrid analog/digital systems are being used to record audio onto a tape, immediately pull it off again, and feed it into a digital audio workstation. Many engineers and musicians swear that putting the audio on tape, however briefly, gives it an attractive warmth and compression that digital systems cannot match. The Endless Analog CLASP system is one example of these systems.

There was one group of composers that had a particular need for synchronization—soundtrack composers. The composers were sent a videotape of
a film or television show, and they needed to synchronize it to their digital
soundtrack, which was recorded on their computer. Since time code was
already being used in the film and television production, it was only natural
that it be used to synchronize the pictures with the soundtracks. In the beginning, the time code was recorded on one of the audio tracks of the videotape,
so that the computer software could "listen" to it, just as it had with the audiotape. Later, sync signals were fed to the computer through dedicated time
code inputs. With tape slipping away, modern film and television content is
often delivered to the composer electronically, in the form of digital video
files. Modern audio recording programs allow you to drop in a video to play
along with your recorded sequence, but time code is still used to keep everything organized.

Professional film crews are using time code more and more on set these
days, supplementing the time-honored technique of the clapboard, that
ubiquitous black-and-white board with the guillotine-like stick on the top.
Previously, postproduction houses used the snap of the clapboard to sync up
audio and video clips. Find the frame where the stick hits the board and line
it up with the snapping sound on the audio track, and you are in sync. With
time code, however, it can be much simpler; all you do is record the picture
and the audio with the same time code and presto, they link up automatically
when they are both uploaded into the editing software. Film crews still snap
the clapboard at the beginning of every take, partly as a backup and partly
because some traditions should never die.

If you enter a postproduction house these days, you will see SMPTE time
code everywhere, providing accurate sync between picture and audio.

Using SMPTE Time Code for Show Control

With time code being used so commonly for audio and video production, it
wasn't long before it got to the stage. Time code is used in many situations
where several different devices have to be in sync throughout a show and
they need a common clock.

For example, imagine a musical show with a complicated lighting system
and lots of special effects. The audio system is playing the music back from a
multi-track tape, the lighting system is controlling a large rig of moving lights,
and the show control system is managing the pyro, automated rigging, and
moving scenery systems.

Because the audio system is both playing continuously and very intolerant
of discontinuity (i.e., we don't want it to skip), we could decide to have the

audio deck generate the time code. After making sure that all the devices in the system are set to the same variety of time code (same frame rate, drop or nondrop, we take the time code output from the audio playback deck and run it to the lighting console and the show control computer. Each of these slave controllers has a playlist of cues, each of which is assigned a certain time code value. When the show starts, the operator hits PLAY on the audio deck, which immediately begins to generate time code. The other devices immediately begin to chase the time code, so that within a fraction of a second, all the devices are running in sync with one another. When the time code gets to the value assigned to a certain cue, that cue happens. By linking all the cues to time code, the lighting, pyro, and scenery all do the exact same thing at the exact same moment in the musical soundtrack every time (assuming that the operators have their hands on the appropriate Enable buttons at the right time).

This kind of approach is very programming intensive and it takes a long time to set up. It's worth it, however, if the show is complicated, running for an extended period, or expecting a lot of changeover in the crew. Note that time code is far less useful if the music is performed live, because live musicians will not follow the clock as accurately as a recorded soundtrack. In fact, most shows with live orchestras have very little use for time code.

Other Flavors of Time Code

LTC versus VITC

Originally, when video was only on tape, the time code was printed along the edge of the videotape in a straight line, just like the audio tracks. The video signal, however, was printed on the tape by a spinning head that cut across the tape diagonally, in order to sandwich in more information. It's a bit like the difference between parallel parking and diagonal parking. You can fit more cars with diagonal. Also, the spinning head increases the apparent speed of the head past the tape, and faster head speed means more data can be laid down.

The time code that was printed along the edge was known as **linear time code**, or LTC, and it worked fine, with one exception. You couldn't read it if the tape was stopped. To address this issue (and to make space for more data), some systems started using **vertical interval time code**, or VITC (pronounced "VIT-see") which is laid down by the spinning video head, mixed in with the video data. The time code actually appears in the black space between the frames, and thus an editing system can read it even when the tape is stopped. LTC and VITC code weren't just printed in different places on the tape. They were also different electrically, and for various reasons, some engineers prefer one or the other. Consequently, even though they were originally intended to address a problem with tape, these two formats persist in the nontape digital world. As with all types of time code, the most important thing is that all the devices are set up to send and receive the same thing.

MIDI Time Code

MIDI Time Code is an extension of the MIDI standard (see part 1) and is often used with musical or audio devices. Basically, it's SMPTE time code adapted to go down a MIDI cable. MTC actually sends a time signal every quarter frame so the resolution is a bit higher than regular SMPTE, but for all practical purposes, it's the same thing—it's just coming down a different cable.

If you have a SMPTE signal coming into a MIDI system (if, for example, you are using a video playback device to sync with a computer MIDI program), you might need a converter box that takes SMPTE in one side and sends MTC out the other.

AES/EBU Time Code

It is also possible to embed time code in an AES/EBU digital audio signal, so if you are using this protocol, you are also sending time code.

Proprietary Sync Signals

Of course, despite all the attention paid to standardization, many manufacturers have come out with their own proprietary ways to synchronize equipment that is made by the same manufacturer. Alesis, for example, maker of the popular HD24 line of digital recorder/players, uses Alesis Sync to tie together multiple decks and remote controls. Even when a system uses a proprietary interface for its own equipment, however, it is extremely rare for any piece of reputable gear to eschew the common time code standards. Alesis, for example, supports SMPTE, AES/EBU time code, and MTC in addition to its own standard.

Word Clock

As audio studios get more complex and more digital devices come in, there is a danger that SMPTE or MIDI time code, with their frame-accurate timing, will not be enough to keep all the devices perfectly in sync with one another. After all, a thirtieth of a second can be a long time, and even the tiniest of drift can lead to audio pops, clicks, and noise.

Hence, some studios have a **master clock**, a device that puts out a *sample-accurate* timing signal, known as a **word clock**. If your sample rate is, for example, 48 kHz, then the master clock will put out a signal forty-eight thousand times per second, which will allow all the devices to lock together perfectly.

This is a feature that you will probably never, ever need onstage, but I mention it just in case you wonder what that word "clock input" is on the back of your digital device.

As I said in the introductory chapter, if you are going to have a conversation with someone (or something), you have to have a common language and a protocol that defines how to use that language. Over the years, the theater industry has stolen, altered, and, if truly necessary, created a host of different ways for machines to talk to each other. With its opportunistic talent for stealing technologies from other industries, theater has begged, borrowed, and stolen show control technologies from music, lighting, industrial fabrication, and computer networking, among others. Some of these technologies have been so-called open standards that were agreed upon by industry working groups, which included representatives from several different companies, while others were proprietary technologies that were developed by a single company and (sometimes) licensed to others.

All of these protocols have their uses and their problems. All of them are good for something, and none of them is good for everything. The same is true of show control software. As one show control programmer said to me, "No one has made a single piece of software that does everything well."

As you read through these different communication protocols, then, take note of the specific quirks of each one and the kinds of jobs that it does well. However, it's also a good idea to take these descriptions with a grain of salt. The theater industry (and the world) is full of people who are using technologies in wonderfully unusual ways. Just because no one has ever tried to control a bubble machine with smoke signals doesn't mean it isn't worth a try.

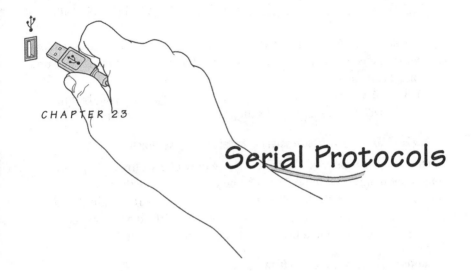

CHAPTER 23

Serial Protocols

Some kinds of control protocols involve a single stream of communication over a dedicated cable in a setup known as **serial control**. In this type of system, a master controller sends commands over a wire that originates at the master and terminates at the slaves. The wire is only used for that one purpose and doesn't carry any other kind of data. The slave devices that plug into the cable must be set to receive the data on a particular channel and cannot be "discovered" by the master controller any more than your television can be discovered by the folks at your cable company. They just broadcast reruns of *Knight Rider*. Whether you watch it is your business, and the cable company won't know one way or the other.[1] This is why some people refer to serial control as a "broadcast" style of data transmission.

There are various kinds of serial control in the entertainment industry, but there are three particular kinds that are of interest to those of us without degrees in computer programming.

DMX

We've already had a long talk about digital multiplexing, so if you skipped over the lighting section, go back there now and review. Suffice to say that, for the purposes of show control, DMX is still mostly used for lighting-related devices like moving lights, autoyokes, and color changers. There is, however, a smattering of other nonlighting devices that use DMX and can be controlled by a light-

---

[1] Of course, there are the Nielsen ratings, but that data is collected by specially designed boxes that are connected to a small number of televisions, and they don't use serial control—they are networked.

ing console. Chief among these are fog machines and smoke machines, which are not hampered by DMX's limitations (limited number of channels, only one kind of data set, etc.).

Whatever device you are controlling with DMX, the process is fairly simple. Each device will have a slightly different process, but the basic steps are the same:

Plug in a DMX Cable from the Master Controller to the Slave Device

Use five-pin DMX cables unless your device only offers a three-pin plug. Remember that DMX can be daisy-chained by connecting the "DMX OUT" of each device to the "DMX IN" of the next device. Remember also that the last device should be terminated, either internally (if the device has such a feature) or by plugging in a DMX terminator to the DMX OUT.

Set Your Device to Receive DMX Data

Depending on the device, it may first have to be told to accept DMX control instead of manual or local control. Follow the instructions in the user manual.

Decide Which Channel of DMX You Want to Use for This Device

Obviously, pick a channel that you are not using for something else. It is quite possible to set more than one device to the same channel, of course, if you want both of them to get the exact same information at the same time. For example, if you have two smoke machines and you want them to be controlled the same way, it is just fine to put them on the same DMX channel. All things being equal, it is better to keep them on different channels, if you have enough. You never know when you might want to have a bit less smoke onstage left than stage right.

Note that some devices will use more than one channel. A smoke machine, for example, might use one channel to regulate the amount of smoke and one channel to set the fan speed.

Set the Device to That Channel

Each machine will have its own method. Older machines might use tiny DIP switches buried inside a panel some place. Newer machines will have an LED readout and some buttons. Follow the instructions in the manual to set the channel. If the device uses more than one channel, it will almost certainly have a base channel, which is the lowest number that it will use. If the device uses three channels, for example, it will use whatever base channel you set and the next two highest numbers.

Set Any Additional DMX Parameters

Some devices will let you set additional parameters for DMX control. One common setting is a "DMX Fail" mode. This tells the device what to do if the

DMX signal is interrupted. For a smoke machine, you might want to specify "Go to zero." In other words, if it loses the signal, it stops putting out smoke. Check the manual for any other necessary DMX settings.

Use Your Lighting Controller to Send DMX Data to the Device

The numbers will have different effects depending on the device. A smoke machine, for example, might regulate the amount of smoke it produces based on what value you send. If you send "0," it doesn't send out any smoke. If you send "100%," then it turns on full blast. Remember that the DMX scale is actually 0 to128, and your lighting controller is translating that into a 0 to 100 percent scale.

Enjoy

One of the nice features of DMX is that unlike many show control protocols (including MIDI), it operates quite well in a wireless application. One reason is because DMX continually rebroadcasts the data. If a DMX number gets dropped due to wireless interference, it's not a problem. Another one will be along in a fraction of a second.

MIDI

The musical instrument digital interface (MIDI) was born in the world of keyboard synthesizer players. Back in the 1980s, it was quite common for rock keyboard players to appear onstage (and work in the studio) behind a wall of keyboards. Every synthesizer produced unique sounds, and any keyboard player worth his imitation ivory keys had a battery of electronics that allowed him to wail like a wolf or purr like a house cat as necessary.

Problem was, all those keyboards took up a lot of space. Second problem was, many keyboard players wanted to combine the sounds of different keyboards together. Solution? A standardized digital protocol that allowed one keyboard to be controlled from another keyboard. When two keyboards are hooked together with a MIDI cable, the master keyboard sends commands to the slave keyboard. Thus a keyboard player could use one keyboard to control many others. Once that became possible, synthesizer manufacturers started to make electronic instruments without a physical keyboard, known as sound modules. These instruments could be rack-mounted and connected to the master keyboard through MIDI, clearing them from the stage or studio and letting everyone see the keyboard player.

Like DMX, MIDI is a one-way protocol. A single cable can only carry information in one direction. Like DMX, MIDI devices can be daisy-chained. Most MIDI devices have three ports: a MIDI OUT to transmit information, a

MIDI IN to receive it, and a MIDI THRU, which outputs a copy of whatever comes in the MIDI IN port. Connect one cable from the MIDI OUT on the master unit to the MIDI IN on the first slave then connect a second cable from the slave's MIDI THRU to the next slave's MIDI IN. Repeat for as many slaves as necessary, although musicians will probably stop after three because after that, all those THRUs start adding latency that is musically unacceptable. Some devices, particularly those that are primarily designed to be used as slaves, combine the OUT and THRU ports into a single port.

You cannot use Y cables to split a MIDI cable into two outputs. You must use a MIDI THRU box with one input and multiple outputs. Larger setups use MIDI distribution boxes, which often include other features, like synchronization. As a rule, MIDI cables should not exceed fifty feet.

MIDI uses a five-pin DIN-style plug. This cable is unique (at least in the theater) and makes it virtually impossible to hook up something other than MIDI into a MIDI port. The plugs use **opto-isolators**, which mean that the signals coming in through the cable never electrically enter the unit. The signals are stopped at the plug and transmitted over a purely optical connection, which removes interference and prevents **ground loops**, the scourge of audio setups.

MIDI also resembles DMX in that it transmits information on a number of different channels, in this case, sixteen of them. In a now-familiar story, sixteen channels seemed like a lot at the time, but that number is now seen as woefully inadequate. When plugging your system together, you will need to set each slave unit to receive information on its own channel.

The thing to remember about MIDI is that despite the fact that it was invented to play music, it does not actually transmit *sound*. It transmits *commands* to play sounds.

In the world of MIDI, all the keys on a standard piano keyboard are numbered from the lowest to the highest, first with the letter of the note then the number of the octave. Thus the lowest key is A0 and the highest is C8. The key that all piano students know as "middle C" is C4.

When a MIDI-compatible keyboard is played, it sends a string of messages out of the MIDI OUT port that describe which keys are being struck and released, as well as how hard they were hit. It is possible to record these messages on a time line and then play them back, either to the same keyboard that recorded them or to another sound-playing device. These messages are known as **channel messages**, because they are sent out on a particular channel.

Channel messages come in many different forms, but the most common are note-on messages, which tell the device to start playing a note, and note-off messages, which tell the device to stop playing the note. You can immediately see a difference from DMX, where the data is sent continuously until it changes. In MIDI, a message is only sent when the status of a note changes.

This is good news, because it doesn't clog the data line with a lot of unnecessary repeated data, and bad news, because if the device misses the note-off command, the note may get "stuck" and never stop playing. This is one reason why many MIDI systems have an "ALL NOTES OFF" panic button that sends an immediate note-off message to every possible note.

Note-on messages are always accompanied by a velocity value, which tells the device how loudly to play the note. You might wonder why velocity was used to determine volume of a note, but remember, MIDI was developed for keyboard players who know that the harder you hit a key, the faster it travels from top to bottom. It is a lot easier to measure the velocity that a key is traveling than the pressure with which it was hit, so velocity was chosen as a way to measure volume.

Note-off messages also have a velocity, known as the release velocity, that measures how fast the key travels back to its resting position, but this message is rarely used for anything.

Besides note-on and note-off, there are several other kinds of channel messages in MIDI, such as the following:

Aftertouch: a type of message that is sent when the keyboard player presses down harder on a key that has already been pushed down.

Control change: a message that changes attributes of nonkey controllers, like pedals and sliders on the keyboard.

Program change: a message that changes the sound program for a channel, e.g., changing from a piano sound to a horn sound.

Pitch wheel: messages that are sent when the keyboard player messes with the little wheel on the keyboard that slides the pitch of a note up and down.

As you can see, MIDI is heavily designed for the needs of the performing musician. As show controllers, we are almost always interested in the note-on messages, which are used as Go commands for our theatrical devices.

A channel message contains several parts, so let's dissect one. If you were to hit, for example, the C4 key on a MIDI-compatible keyboard set to transmit on channel one, it would send out a MIDI message with four parts:

1. Type of message (note-on)
2. Channel number (1)
3. Note number (C4)
4. Velocity (however hard you hit it)

Of course, the actual message is nowhere near this verbose. Read the sidebar if you really want to know what is actually being sent.

MIDI: Bit by Bit

Like everything else in the computer world, MIDI is transmitted in binary form, meaning a string of 1s and 0s. These "bits" of data are organized into "bytes" of data, which contain 8 bits each. MIDI messages are composed of three bytes: one status byte and two data bytes. The status byte describes what kind of message is being sent and what channel it is being sent on. The data bytes describe what note is being played and how hard it is being played.

Every status byte begins with a "1," so there are 3 bits left to identify which command is being sent and 4 bits left to identify the channel. For example, the note-on command is given the identifying number 1 in the MIDI specification. In binary form, that is 001. If that note is being sent on channel three, then the status byte would be 10010010, where the first bit identifies this as a status byte (1), the next 3 bits identify this as a note-on (001), and the last 4 bits refer to channel 3 (0010). If you are getting good with binary, you may notice that the binary code for MIDI channel 3 is actually the number 2. This is because computer programmers start counting at zero, while the rest of us humans start counting at one. Thus, MIDI channel 1 is actually sent as zero channel 2 is sent as one channel 3 is sent as two etc.

Every data byte begins with a "0." With 1 bit used up, that leaves you 7 more bits to describe the number of the note. Seven bits means that you can use numbers from 0 to127, so now you know why there are 128 possible notes. We previously said that in MIDI, each note is designated with a letter and a number. Middle C, for example, is C4. This is only for the musicians on the front end, however. The programmers assign a number to each note from 00 (note C1) to 127 (note G9). Middle C (C4) is note 60 to the programmers. In binary, that's 00111100. Likewise, the velocity is also numbered from 0 to127. Let's say you hit the key sort of medium hard, producing a velocity of 65. In binary, that is 01000001.

Put it all together and you get the following:

Status Byte (note-on, channel 3)   Data Byte (C4)   Data Byte (velocity of 65)
10010010   00111100   01000001

This is what is actually sent down the MIDI cable when you push C4 kinda hard.

As I said in the introduction, staring at binary numbers all day is pretty headache inducing, so programmers often use hexadecimal numbers to represent these bytes of data. I mention it here because if you ever start digging into the programming of a MIDI device, you will often find commands being listed in hex format. In the world of hex we count from one to sixteen using both numbers and letters:

0 1 2 3 4 5 6 7 8 9 A B C D E F

This technique is often useful in computer applications where we are often representing numbers in multiples of sixteen. The above message, in hex format, would be 93 3C 41, which is marginally easier to take than the binary version, if you understand hexadecimal thinking. If you do get into the system at this level, I recommend one of the many number conversion websites, widgets, or phone applications to help you translate decimal numbers to hex and vice versa.

Using MIDI for Theatrical Show Control

So why do we care about this in theatrical show control? Well, let's face it, we are the original technology thieves, and when we are presented with a simple, cheap, straightforward way of controlling one device from another device, we pay attention real quick, even if the language and structure of the protocol is based on music.

So what is MIDI good for in the theater?

Remote Control

One of the most common uses of MIDI in the theater is to operate one device from the front panel of another. For example, a lighting controller can be set to take commands from an audio playback device. The audio playback device (the master in this scenario) sends note-on commands to tell the lighting controller to run cues. Note-on commands always have a note number attached to them, so the note number is used to tell the lighting controller which cue to run. There is a limitation here because there are only 128 note numbers and you may have more than 128 cues. System designers solve this by using controller messages (another type of channel messages, like a note-on) for cue numbers above 128. It's a bit awkward, but it works.

This kind of setup is very useful for things like synchronizing a sound cue and a light cue. Let's say that you have a great big blast of thunder coming from your audio system and you want to synchronize it with a flash of lighting from your lighting system.

If you are using a PC-based audio playback system, like QLab or SFX, this is quite easy. Computers do not automatically come with MIDI outputs so you must add a USB-MIDI hardware interface that gives you plugs for MIDI IN and OUT. Also, your lighting controller must be compatible with MIDI, which is quite common these days.

While the specifics of each setup are different, here is the general process for setting this up. You will need to consult the manuals of your devices to complete each step as each manufacturer organizes their user interface differently.

Once you have the hardware MIDI interface installed in your computer, run a cable from the computer MIDI OUT to the lighting controller MIDI IN. Configure your audio playback device to send MIDI data and your lighting controller to receive it.

The process for configuring the audio playback and the lighting controller for MIDI is not complex, but it is different for each device, so follow the manual. Here, for example, is the MIDI setup sequence for the ETC Express lighting console, as listed in the manual:[2]

[2] Express 125 and 250 lighting control system. Express 125/250 User Manual, v.3.1

Press [Setup].	Go to the setup display
Press [6] [Enter].	Select the Options Settings menu
Press [1] [Enter].	Prompt reads:
	Select MIDI channel (#1 through 16), or press DISABLE MIDI to disable MIDI
Enter a number between 1 and 16.	Specifies MIDI channel
Press [Enter]	Completes the ETC MIDI setup

Make sure that your controller is transmitting MIDI data on the same channel that the slave is receiving it.

Set up a cue on the audio playback system.

The cue will have two parts that will happen at the same time: a MIDI message will be sent to the lighting controller to play the appropriate cue number (the flash of lightning and a sound file will play with the clap of thunder).

Once you have this link established, all you have to do it hit Go on the audio software, and *ka-WHAMMO*, a flash of brilliant lightning is perfectly lined up with a deafening peal of thunder.

Sample Playback

Another popular use of MIDI onstage is for controlling **sample playback**. A sample is a small chunk of recorded sound, anywhere from a fraction of a second to several minutes. A **sampler** is a device that records these small bits of sound and assigns them to specific MIDI notes. By mapping a bunch of sounds to a bunch of different notes and then playing those notes from a MIDI-compatible keyboard, you have instant access to as many different sounds as you have keys on your keyboard. This is highly useful for a show where specific sound effects are tied to precise actions by the actors. Live stunt shows use these kinds of setups for the sounds of punches and kicks being delivered by the actors onstage. When the hero smacks down the villain with a blow to the body then a blow to the head then a kick on his butt to send him on his way, the sound operator can follow the action quickly and accurately by playing the sounds on a MIDI keyboard attached to a sample playback machine.

You can also get sample playback software for your computer.

You can use this software to record or import sound files, assign them to MIDI notes, and then play them back using an external MIDI-compatible key-

board. If you don't have a lot of cues, or if your cues play in a nice, predictable order with pauses between them for you to find your place, then using
MIDI and sample playback is more trouble than it is worth.

However, if your show is extremely audio-heavy and the cues need to
happen quickly, in random order and/or be tied to specific actions, then this
approach might be just the ticket.

MIDI Triggers

If you think about it, the MIDI keyboard we talked about above is just an array of switches. Each key on the keyboard has a tiny switch under it, which is
connected to a tiny brain that maps that switch to a specific MIDI note. When
you play the key, the switch is activated and the brain inside the keyboard
sends out the MIDI note that goes with that key.

The key and the tiny brain together operate as a **MIDI trigger**, a device
that triggers a specific MIDI note. MIDI triggers don't have to be keys on a
keyboard, however. They can be anything that moves enough to activate a
switch. This small switch can be attached to a button, a lever, a drum pad,
the seat of a chair, or anything else that will move far enough to trigger the
switch.

Once you have the switch set up, the next step is to convert the contact
closure of the switch to a MIDI note that can be sent to your playback software. There are a number of different options here, including buying a used
electronic drum kit. Connect the MIDI OUT from the drum kit controller to
your computer. Each of the pads of the drum kit puts out note-on messages
for particular notes. Assign those notes to whatever sounds you want in your
computer and you are ready to go with a bunch of MIDI triggers that can be
assigned to any sound you like.

There are also commercially available solutions for this and other MIDI
setups. A clever company called MIDI Solutions,[3] for example, puts out a
MIDI switch controller called the F8, which takes eight inputs from contact
closures of any type and turns them into MIDI notes that can be fed into your
MIDI software. If that weren't enough, they also make the R8, which is the
exact opposite: it takes MIDI notes and turns them into contact closures. This
is useful if you want to use MIDI to turn on a light or some other electrical

---

[3] www.midisolutions.com

device, which is useful if you want your audio playback software to operate indicator lights for those switches. Endless possibilities . . .

MIDI Show Control: The Protocol for the Rest of Us

As show control became a higher priority backstage, the need grew for a protocol that was specifically dedicated to the theater. DMX and MIDI were good as far as they went, but the theater needed a more developed, more specific protocol that wasn't being forced to be something that it wasn't.

What system designers wanted was a standard list of commands, similar to the cueing commands that lighting control consoles used, like GO, STOP, and RESUME. They wanted to be able to set up multiple cue lists and networks with lots of different devices. They wanted to control all manner of media devices, from slide projectors (this was the early nineties, when we still used such ancient technology) to video projectors to lasers. And they wanted time code, so sequences could be locked together in a preprogrammed sequence.

To address all this (and more), a team of people from the United States Institute for Theater Technology (USITT) got together in 1990 to propose a new standard of theatrical show control.

Rather than completely invent the wheel, the show control team decided to build this dedicated show control protocol on the back of an existing protocol: MIDI. Despite its flaws as a show control protocol, the MIDI protocol was already widely implemented in the entertainment industry, and many devices already had MIDI hardware ports. It's always harder to change hardware than software, so the fact that there was already an established standard for MIDI cables, plugs, and ports was a big selling point. It's a lot easier to upgrade the software in a lighting controller than it is to install new plugs on the back panel.

MIDI had another tremendous advantage. A portion of the specification had basically been left wide open by the original creators: the MIDI System Exclusive or SysEx message. Normally, MIDI messages, like the channel messages I described earlier, had to follow strict rules on format so they could be read by any MIDI-compatible device. This structure ensured that all the devices that plugged into a MIDI system could, at some level, talk to each other. The writers of the MIDI spec, however, had left a place in the communication protocol where manufacturers could include data that was specific to a particular device—data that could have a different format than the rest of the MIDI spec. They created the SysEx message as a kind of empty bucket that could contain any type of message.

The theatrical show controllers pounced on this opening like grizzly bears on salmon, creating an entire show control protocol that is transmitted inside this SysEx bucket.

Using the transmission protocols of MIDI and adding their own set of commands embedded in SysEx messages, the designers created MIDI Show Control, or MSC, thus creating a tech geek's dream: a protocol wrapped up inside another protocol.

Seen from the front end, however, MSC is a very straightforward and simple language that sounds remarkably like the language we speak backstage every day.

If, for example, you want to tell the lighting controller to run cue 81, you don't have to figure out that note 81 is actually note A5, then send a message that looks like "note-on, channel 3, note A5, velocity 60" to run light cue 81.

MSC allows you send a message that just says "GO light cue 81," which makes a lot more sense.

Rather than assigning different MIDI channels to different devices, MSC requires that each device have a discrete number: a device ID. That way, you just address the cue to the device that needs to hear about it.

Commands are formatted to match the needs of each discipline, such as lighting, sound, video, etc., so each message contains a number that tells the device which format to follow. Lighting controllers, for example, follow the lighting format, which is numbered 01.

When a device receives a message, it first checks to see if the device ID and the command format match its own. If not, the message is ignored. If they do match, then the device sits up, takes notice, and tries to run the command that comes next.

So put it all together and an MSC message looks like this:
Device ID number
Command format
Command
Data

Let's say that our lighting controller above is device #2. The MSC message then looks like this:
Device 02 - Lighting - GO - Cue 81

Just like any other show control system, an MSC system has a controller device, which stores and sends out the commands, and one or more controlled devices. It is possible for a device to be both a controller and a controlled device. Controllers can be connected by MIDI cables in the same way as standard MIDI devices, or if they have the capability, they can be connected via an Ethernet network using a MIDI-over-Ethernet protocol. For this reason, it is not unusual to see lighting controllers with Ethernet ports these days.

Besides using a more familiar syntax, MSC has a number of advantages over regular MIDI. For one thing, MSC is designed to make full use of MIDI time code. For example, it includes commands to tell devices when to start chasing MTC and when to stop, and it can reset the clock to a particular value or to zero. MSC also allows the use of multiple cue lists, which can be quite useful. In our thunder-and-lighting example above, all of the lighting cues could be set up on a separate cue list in the lighting controller, out of the way of the rest of the show, but easily identifiable by MSC.

Like MIDI, MSC does not send the actual media over the wire, just a command to play it. In this way, it operates as a classic show control device: a system that controls other systems.

MSC also suffers from some of the same limitations as MIDI and DMX, however. It is still an open-loop interface, which does not require or acknowledge any feedback from the devices. It can tell the light board to GO, but the light board isn't going to tell you that it WENT. If someone kicked out the power cord for the lighting board, an MSC system will never know about it. For this reason, MSC is still not a good protocol for life-safety applications. MSC can certainly be used to tell a pyro controller that it is time to fire, but the controller itself must have all the necessary safety controls (enable buttons, E-stop buttons, etc.) to guarantee that it is safe to fire.

Beyond safety issues, however, these open-loop, serial interfaces (DMX, MIDI, and MSC) are useful for what they do, but often disappointing to the serious show control programmer. It just isn't enough to send commands out into the ether and never get anything back. Show control, like marriage, really works best when there is two-way communication. And for that, we need another set of protocols entirely.

CHAPTER 24

Network Protocols

The serial control protocols that we discussed in the last chapter are useful things, and chances are very good that most theaters will be perfectly happy using them for the foreseeable future. They are where the theater industry is at right now. They are not, however, where the theater industry is going.

The key word in almost any technology these days is *interactivity*—that is, the ability for any piece of technology to interact, to have a two-way conversation with users, databases, other machines, and the world at large. Once you have invoked the I word the logical next step is *network*. Serial protocols are very good at sending small amounts of data from point A to point B with a minimum of fuss, but they have several problems:

The Conversation Is Unidirectional

As I've said, these kinds of systems allow a master to talk to a slave, but not the reverse. A controlled device cannot report its current condition, position, status, direction, etc. It can't even tell the master that it has been *turned on*. Even more significantly, it cannot report if it is working correctly or whether it carried out the action it was told to do.

Each Protocol Requires Its Own Network

You cannot run DMX over a MIDI line or vice versa, and you can't send media over either one of them. It is not uncommon for theaters to have multiple control lines, operating with multiple protocols, running all over the grid.

The Machinery to Run These Task-Specific Protocols Is Expensive

Because these are niche industries, the type of equipment required, from MIDI cables to DMX opto-splitters, is more expensive than commonly available network devices based on more common protocols, like Ethernet.

Every Device Must Be Controlled the Same Way

Protocols like DMX and MIDI present their control information in a specific way, and the device must comply. There is no room to send control information in a way that is specific to that device. On a DMX network, you do it the DMX way. On a MIDI network, you do it the MIDI way. Programmers and equipment designers are clever people, of course, so you will see lots of clever tricks that allow these serial protocols to do things they were never intended to do (MIDI Show Control is a prime example), but at the end of the day, these protocols are quite inflexible.

A Single Device Failure Can Harm the Network

Because many of these networks depend on a daisy chain of cables and devices, the loss of one of those devices can hurt the reliability of the network.

Data Is Not Checked for Errors

When a MIDI or DMX message goes out, there is no way to check if it arrived intact. DMX solves this problem by continuing to send the same information continuously, but that creates a lot of unnecessary traffic on the network, which starts to be problematic when you are updating hundreds, if not thousands of channels. MIDI users deal with this problem by, well, dealing with it.

They Don't Scale Up Well

Sure, it's really easy to run a single DMX cable from your lighting console to your dimmer rack. If you put in a few moving lights, it's easy to run a second cable from your console to the lighting rig. The problem starts when your dimmer rack grows past 512 dimmers and you start putting in a whole lot of moving lights, or LEDs, or fog machines. All of a sudden, your single DMX cable has mushroomed into dozens of cables, along with racks of opto-splitters. You've got one set of boxes merging data and another set splitting it back up again. Every new device means a new connection back to the control console, and before you know it, you are singing the "Calgon, Take Me Away!" song.

Compare this situation to a control protocol you use every day: the Internet. Strictly speaking, the Internet is not a control protocol—it's a combination of a bunch of different protocols—but imagine if your Internet connection operated like DMX or MIDI. It would be . . .

Unidirectional

Forget about being able to call up a website. You would have to sit and wait for the person running the network to consult a list of users and then send you the websites they thought you needed. If you had a problem, you couldn't tell anyone. You would have to wait until someone from the head office happened to notice that they hadn't seen anything from you for a while and hope that they stop by to check on you, like an elderly shut-in lying face down among your cats. And you can also forget about your computer being discovered. That's the process that happens every time you log into the Internet. The Ethernet switch or router in your home, office, or coffee shop "sees" your machine come online and promptly identifies it, giving it an electronic address (known as an IP address) so that it can send and receive data. If your computer worked like DMX, you would assign it an address yourself and hope that no one else was using the same one. If someone else was already using that address, that's too bad. Now you are going to get all the websites that they are getting, so you better hope they don't have any strange, um . . . habits.

Fortunately, the Internet protocols allow two-way communication. You can ask for the information you need, and it is sent over the network with your address stamped on it. Internet protocols also discover your machine and can automatically configure it to connect to the network, without you having to do anything.

Protocol-Specific

If your PC worked like a serial protocol, you would have one Internet for e-mail another to download music, another to look at websites, and so on. Because each network had a different task, it would have a different protocol and different equipment.

On the Internet, the protocols can send information without needing to know what it is for. They don't care what kind of information they are sending; all they do is chop it up into small pieces, send it to the right address, and put it all back together again. It could be control information, music, an order form for new shoes—doesn't matter.

Equipped with Unique Materials

"You need a network cable? That will be fifty dollars."

Better get used to paying high prices for even the smallest of items, like network cables. Every time you buy an Ethernet cable or a router or even a computer, you benefit from enormous economies of scale. That is, your cable or router or computer is cheaper for you because the networking technologies you are using are also being used by millions of other users. If the technologies you wanted were only being used by a small group, it will be a much bigger hit to your wallet.

Device-Specific

In this scenario, you would not only have different networks for e-mail music, and so forth, you would have different computers for each one as well, because each network would only know how to talk to one kind of machine.

Because the protocols are broadly written, released to the public, and easy to implement, the Internet can be used to connect all kinds of computers, as well as phones, cash registers, and tracking devices on trucks. Even the copier in my office is on the Internet.

Dependent on Other Devices to Function

Did your neighbor's computer crash? You might be out of luck if your connection to the network went through his computer. That daisy chain of cables that saved you those long cable runs might have put your own computer at risk.

On the Internet, each device has its own connection to the network router, so if the computer on the next desk dies, it doesn't affect your own connection. Of course, if the router dies, you're out of luck, but the router is smaller, less complicated, and more reliable than your buddy's laptop.

Not Error-Checked

Internet data travels on a *very* crowded network. It may be traveling for thousands of miles, over copper cable, microwave signals, under oceans, or bounced off satellites. With that kind of travel, errors are inevitable. To you, the user, that means that photos are corrupted, text is lost, videos crash, and there's no guarantee that you are looking at the data that was sent.

Internet protocols use various kinds of error checking to make sure that the data that arrives is the same data that left.

Not Scaleable

Want to connect with a new website? You will now need to run a physical cable from your computer all the way to that website server in Nigeria. If the Internet worked like a serial protocol, every new machine would require a new connection back to you.

On the Internet, however, it is easy to add more machines; you just run a new cable into your local router, enter some new settings into your computer, and boom, you are online. Of course, as more machines come online, the transmission lines and assorted hardware will eventually need to be upsized to handle the increase in traffic, but you don't need to lay more cables, just bigger ones. Furthermore, this upsizing process can be done a little at a time, as necessary. You don't have to reconfigure the entire network to bring a new person onto it.

For all of these reasons and more, show control technicians have been trying to get all of our devices onto networks—preferably generic Ethernet networks—for as long as there have been networks. Most of those efforts have been specific to a single company or a small group of companies. All of the major lighting manufacturers have tried, at one time or another, to create Ethernet-based networks for sending DMX data, like ETCNet designed by ETC, or MA-Net, designed by MA Lighting, and these work just fine. In fact, these networks can save a lot of money for a large installation, as Ethernet cable is not only cheaper, it can send a lot more data. A single DMX cable can only carry one DMX universe of 512 channels, whereas an Ethernet cable can carry dozens of networks. Furthermore, with its star configuration, it can be more reliable than the daisy-chain layout of DMX. See the sidebar for more info about Ethernet.

What exactly is Ethernet?

First popularized in the 1980s by Digital Equipment Corporation, Intel, Xerox, and 3Com, Ethernet is now an international standard for LANs, or local area networks. These are networks that run inside a single facility, like an office, school, or home.

Ethernet is constantly evolving, but as of this writing, it is generally carried on an unshielded cable with eight wires in four twisted pairs, the **Category 5** or "Cat5" cable, which is usually blue. It uses an eight-wire connector, known as an **RJ45** plug, which is slightly wider than a telephone plug.

Every device on an Ethernet network is given a MAC address when it joins the network. This address is used to send small amounts of data, known as packets, back and forth over the network. You should not confuse these with IP addresses, which are used to communicate with the Internet at large. MAC addresses only relate to the LAN.

Ethernet networks are constructed in a star pattern, (techs call it a "star topology"), meaning that each machine is at the end of a wire that runs back to a central **switch**. This way, the demise of any one machine doesn't take any other machine off the network. The switch keeps track of which machines are on which legs of the star and examines the address on each packet of data as it goes by. By only sending data down the leg of the star where it needs to go, the switch greatly reduces traffic on the network. Older Ethernet **hubs** connected machines together but didn't look at the addresses on the data—they just repeated it throughout the entire network. Every single machine saw every piece of data, which produced a lot of unnecessary traffic.

Ethernet switches improve this situation mightily, and now that they have gotten ridiculously cheap, switched Ethernet has become the network structure of choice.

Ethernet networks can run at various speeds, which keep getting faster all the time. When it was first standardized, Ethernet could run at 10 megabits/second, which was known as 10-BASE-T. In 1995, a version known as Fast Ethernet, which ran ten times faster, pushed the original format aside and ruled for three whole years until it was overtaken by Gigabit Ethernet, which was ten times faster than Fast. Then 10 Gigabit Ethernet had its moment in the sun, but as I write this, 40 Gigabit and 100 Gigabit Ethernet are being standardized. From the ways things are going, the world will be into Terrabit Ethernet before this book is into a second edition.

Setting up an Ethernet network is fairly simple, assuming that each one of your devices already has an Ethernet plug. (If not, you will need to install a network card, so follow the directions in the manual or consult a pro.) Go to the office supply store and choose an Ethernet switch that has enough plugs for all the computers or other devices that you want to plug in. Put that switch somewhere that is fairly central to all the devices. Run a cable from the switch to each one of the devices. You may have to adjust some settings on the switch by accessing it through one of the connected computers. Follow the directions in the manual. If you are not hooking up your network to the outside world, however, you may not have to change anything.

If you *are* hooking up your computer to the outside world, then you need a **router**. This device connects your Ethernet network to the Internet, generally through a coaxial cable. The router assigns each of your devices an IP address, which helps it connect with the outside world. Again, in many cases, a router is plug-and-play, but you may have to configure a few things by contacting the router through one of the computers on the network. It will usually have an IP address that you can enter into your web browser, just like you would enter a website address like *www.google.com*. This will bring up the router's interface on your computer and you can follow the instructions from your Internet service provider in-house IT person, or standard-issue teenager to configure it.

In fact, there are lots of options for putting DMX on Ethernet, including public domain software and DMX-to-Ethernet hardware gateways that help you use an Ethernet backbone to transmit DMX signals.

Audio companies have been getting into the network game as well. As we saw in the audio chapter, the privately owned and licensed CobraNet protocol has become well known as a way to perform audio over Ethernet or **AoE**. Other audio companies have also had varying degrees of success with using networks to send specific kinds of control information or media.

Beyond these proprietary efforts, however, there have been two major efforts in the public domain to create control systems that can operate on Ethernet networks.

Art-Net

Originally designed by Artistic License, a lighting design and hardware company based in the U.K., Art-Net is a method of transmitting DMX over Ethernet. What makes it unique among DMX-over-Ethernet protocols is that once they got done designing it, Artistic License released Art-Net into the public domain. That meant that anyone designing the Art-Net capability into their equipment could do it for free—they don't have to pay a licensing fee to Artistic License.

Besides the upfront increase in data capacity and reliability offered by Ethernet, Art-Net also has a few advantages over a regular DMX network. It allows some degree of two-way communication, including remote patching of DMX devices, and allows you to transmit the contents of the control console video screens to screens in remote locations. It is also compatible with a lot of remote controls so you can operate some features of your control console from far away. This is useful stuff if you are climbing around in the grid and you want to turn on a channel at the light board.

As of this writing, Artistic License claims that "over twenty companies"[1] are now designing equipment that is compatible with Art-Net and there is every reason to do so, especially as the protocol is in the public domain.

It bears repeating that, as I said in part 2, there is a time and a place to put your lighting data on an Ethernet network. Ethernet cables are still more fragile than DMX cable, and they have a shorter range (three hundred feet versus nine hundred feet for DMX). You don't want Cat5 cables running down an electric pipe and getting tied up with sash cord. Furthermore, setting up an Ethernet network requires a certain amount of knowledge (but nothing that you can't get from a few hours of Internet browsing or a conversation with an IT-savvy person).

The best solutions are combinations. Many installations run Ethernet from the control console up to the lighting position then break out into standard DMX cables which can withstand the rigors of a theatrical lighting grid.

With all its benefits, however, Art-Net is still just a control network for DMX information. The theatrical world has been waiting for an all-around performer, a flexible, configurable, scalable network protocol that is specifically designed with the needs of the theater in mind. And we may have found it.

ACN

By now it should be pretty clear what we want in a network control protocol. It should allow two-way communication with almost any type of device. It should handle large amounts of data of various types. It should be scalable,

---

[1] "What is Art-Net?", appnote016.pdf, downloaded from artisticlicense.com on 15 Nov 2010.

reliable, and perhaps most importantly, the networking hardware and software should be easy to use with logical interfaces and plug-and-play setup. If it takes a degree in electrical engineering to set it up or operate it, it isn't going to catch on in this fast-moving, wild-and-woolly community of theater artists, most of whom are what Apple Computer used to call "the rest of us."

The Architecture for Control Networks might be that protocol. ACN is the product of years of effort by the Control Protocol Working Group (CPWG) of the Entertainment Services and Technology Association (ESTA), although in a larger sense, it is the result of decades of research, development, and trial and error.

Let's say that you want to tell all your moving lights to follow a moving platform as it slides on-and offstage. This is not unprecedented. Previously, however, the problem was solved, like digging the Chunnel, from both ends at once. Using a motorized platform and special software, the scenery guys would create a control program that would run the motors and put the platform where you wanted it, when you wanted it there. At the same time, the lighting guys would program their moving lights to follow the same pre-programmed path. The show control system would give both systems a Go at the same time, and assuming that nothing went wrong, the moving lights would follow the same path as the platform and everything would be ducky. The scenery software would track the path of the platform by using **encoders**, electronic devices on the platform and/or the motors that tell the system the precise location of the platform from moment to moment. The lighting guys don't have that advantage—they just keep sending new positioning information to the lights and hope for the best. Like I said, if nothing goes wrong, the lights will follow the platform.

The problem is, the lights aren't really following the platform—they are just following a preprogrammed path that happens to be the same pre-programmed path that the platform is following. If the platform slows down for some reason, or pauses for a moment before starting its cue, the lights don't know about it. They just go on their merry way, following their pre-programmed path, blithely ignoring the real position of the platform.

Let's say, however, that you want to lock the position of those lights to that platform so they follow wherever it goes, whenever it goes there. Previously, you would need an electrical engineering major from MIT to write you custom software that would take the positioning information provided by the encoders, translate it through a complicated algorithm into positioning information for the lights, translate that into DMX commands, and send those to the lights. It's possible, but who has that kind of time or expertise?

The problem is, you've got two different kinds of systems—a moving scenery system and a moving lighting system—that can't talk to each other.

Sure, you can use DMX/RDM to get the light to report its position to the lighting controller. And yes, you've got the encoders on the platforms to tell you where the scenery is. But without a good network protocol, you will never be able to pass this information between the two systems.

Enter ACN.

Because this network is designed with a much more flexible structure, it can handle data from lots of different kinds of systems.

It achieves this flexibility in much the same way as the Internet connection on your home or office computer.

As we saw previously, the Internet protocols we use every day do a pretty good job of moving information around a network. They can handle lots of different types of data and devices, they check for errors, they are, all in all pretty solid.

The Internet works with several different protocols, all lying on top of each other and taking care of different parts of the process. The low-level protocol describes the physical structure of the network, the next layer describes how data is transported on the network, the next one handles error checking and other more sophisticated functions, etc., etc. Each successive layer takes on more specific tasks.

If you follow the popular "information superhighway" analogy, the low-level protocol defines how to build roads (how big, what materials, etc.), while the next one defines the traffic laws that keep people from crashing (what side you drive on, red means stop and green means go, speed limits, etc.), while another one defines what kinds of cars will be allowed to drive on those roads (size and weight, headlights, seat belts, emissions, etc.).

To loosely follow this analogy: on the Internet, the physical Ethernet network is the road. Ethernet specifications cover things like what kind of cables and plugs are used and how fast the network runs. The traffic laws that define how to use those roads are known in the Internet world as TCP/IP,[2] which is actually a whole suite of protocols. TCP/IP describes how the data is broken up into pieces and sent to remote addresses. The cars, of course, are the packets of data that travel around the globe on those Internet wires. As with real cars, there are also rules about what form that data takes.

The designers of ACN borrowed quite a bit of this structure. The network can be carried on Ethernet cable and uses a portion of the TCP/IP suite of protocols to address and move the data. On top of those protocols, however, sits a set of protocols that are unique to ACN. These protocols define a host of different tasks, including how devices are identified and how the network deals with the different behaviors of each device. In fact, each device can maintain

---

[2] Transmission Control Protocol/Internet Protocol.

a behavior library that helps the other devices on the network address the capabilities of that device. These protocols also handle the error-checking functions so data is transmitted reliably.

Because the network structure follows the standard Internet structure at the lower levels, however, it can run on a network that is connected to the Internet. This may sound like something that only level five geek lords would be interested in, but imagine calling a repair technician when your lighting controller goes funky and watching him operate the console from his desk in Wisconsin. Or London.

Of course, hooking up to the net is both good news and bad news. If your control network is connected, technicians can check up on their gear from a remote location, but you must also protect your gear with firewalls and virus protection.

ACN also makes use of an important Ethernet functionality called multicasting, which solves the problem of how to address data to a lot of users without clogging the network. Let's say that you have three smoke machines on a DMX network. The first question you ask is, do you want them all to fire at the same time, and at the same intensity? If the answer is yes and yes, then you put them all on the same DMX address, and you only send out one set of data on one channel. However, if you want them to operate at different times or intensities, *even just once*, then you have to give them all a separate DMX address and transmit three sets of data, even if it's the same data most of the time.

Multicasting allows you to send the data to all the users that need it, even if the list of users changes. Furthermore, multicasting uses the capabilities of the network hardware in such a way that each data packet only passes through the network once. This keeps the volume of traffic way down.

So how do you use ACN?

First of all, you need an ACN-capable device.

Back in the early days of DMX and MIDI, computer processors were expensive, so it's no wonder that the protocols were designed with a brain on only one end. Lighting controllers had the brains; dimmers were dumb and did what they were told. Now that there is more processing power in your washing machine than the Apollo spacecraft,[3] it is far more cost-effective to put a brain on both ends of the network. In order to take advantage of ACN, the controlled device must have enough processing power to communicate effectively with the network, and the manufacturer must invest in programming time for their devices. ACN devices must not only be able to read the information from the network but also respond to it correctly. This, of course, is

---

[3] If you have one of the new "fuzzy logic" washing machines, this is actually true.

the great fear of the proponents of ACN—that manufacturers will not see the financial gain in making these investments.

Second, you need something you want to do with it. This is where the immense creativity of theater artists comes in. How do you want to interact with lighting, with media, with audience members, with other performers? How do you want to connect various elements of your show together? It is a waste of time to use any technology just to use it, so go back to the stories that you want to tell, and when you get that grand idea that requires interactive, interconnected technology, start asking around at your theatrical supply company or at trade shows where manufacturers meet their customers or on their websites.

The future of ACN is still a bit precarious. If the network protocol continues to catch on, you will see more and more devices sporting the ACN-compatible label. Also, as the technology develops, you will see more elegant interfaces, just as more Internet usage spawned more elegant user interfaces, like web browsers, e-mail programs, smartphones and iTunes. As ACN spreads, it is the users who will determine how it gets implemented, through the power of the marketplace. A similar situation existed years ago with MIDI Show Control. Because a lot of users expressed their desire to connect lighting boards to other devices, MSC is now standard on most lighting consoles.

Stay tuned. The future is out there.[4]

---

[4] I am greatly indebted to John Huntington, the show control wizard, for writing his article "The ACN Future is Here" for *Lighting and Sound* magazine in 2007, from which much of this information is excerpted. John's book *Control Systems for Live Entertainment*, now in its third edition, continues to be the bible of show control.

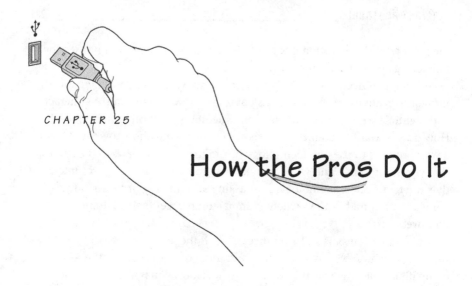

CHAPTER 25

How the Pros Do It

The Best of All Worlds: Studio Nick at Nickelodeon Suites, Orlando

With so many show control programs floating around, one of the most common questions is, "Which software should I use?"

According to many show control experts, the answer is, all of them. The truth is, no system can do it all, and each system has areas in which it excels. Stage Research SFX, for example, is well known for its extensive scripting language, which allows programmers to create complex functions. Medialon is known for flexible timelines and scheduling. As we saw in the *House of Dancing Water* setup, LCS provides excellent support for complex audio systems, while QLab is highly respected as a video playback device. Other devices, like Richmond ShowMan or the Alcorn McBride V16, are used for more complex permanent installations, where reliability is key and budgets are more generous.

In fact, in some cases, a show control programmer may combine two or more systems in a single installation, as Drew Dalzell did for the Studio Nick theater at the Nickelodeon Suites Resort in Orlando, Florida.

"To me," says Dalzell, of Diablo Sound, "none of these systems are complete." What he means is that no one system can cover all of the show control bases. That's why when designing the system for the multipurpose theater space at the Nickelodeon resort, he mixed it up a little.

Studio Nick is a flexible stage that is used for several different shows, all derived from Nickelodeon television channel properties. Most of the shows are interactive, and some, including the popular *Slime Time Live*, are actually done in a game show format, using audience volunteers who compete in games like the Hula Shake and Slime Bob. The rear of the set is a large rear-projection screen, while each team has an LCD monitor on their side of the stage to display their score. There are numerous lighting and sound cues that accompany the games, cover set changes, and underscore the host's trips to the audience for volunteers.

All of this makes for a messy show, not only because of the multicolored slime that finds its way into every game, but also because of the unpredictable nature of the performance. With volunteers being egged on by enthusiastic hosts and a screaming audience, anything can happen. Games may be rearranged, timings may change, cleanups are inevitable, and the scoreboards must change depending on who actually wins. With dozens of high-energy lighting, sound, and video cues, as well as a packed show schedule, Dalzell needed a show control system that was flexible, reliable, and could be operated by an untrained crew.

Solution? Two show control systems.

At Studio Nick, the master controller is a Stage Research SFX system, which is operated through a custom touch screen operated by a crew member. The touch screen allows the operator to choose the game then displays on-screen buttons for game-related events, like "Red Team Wins Round."

The SFX system calls up lighting cues by sending MIDI Show Control commands to a High End Systems Hog 2 lighting controller.

For the video clips, Dalzell chose the reliable video functions of another show control program: QLab from Figure 53. SFX and QLab were connected by MIDI commands, but not a MIDI cable. In order to avoid a long MIDI cable from the control booth to the backstage video position, Dalzell chose to network the two machines over Cat5 network cable. By installing a software program called ipMIDI on both computers, Dalzell created a virtual sixteen-channel MIDI line between them, allowing SFX to select different video clips from the QLab library. QLab then sends the video clips to a Crestron video switcher.

With several different video streams coming from QLab and several different monitors onstage, SFX also must control the Crestron audio switcher over a serial cable, sending it information on which video stream goes to which video screen.

For the video scoreboards, Dalzell's team created a video clip for every possible score number. Then, using the SFX scripting language, Dalzell created a program that keeps track of the score throughout the game and calls up the correct video clips from QLab, thereby using SFX's excellent scripting language and QLab's reliable video serving.

In practice, most of the above is invisible to the operator and the audience. The operator starts the game by selecting the current game from a list on the touch screen. The screen changes to the custom interface for that game. As each event happens in the game, the operator selects the appropriate button from the screen. Dalzell's programming then kicks in, providing the right light cues, sound cues, and video clips.

The Nickelodeon stage reminds us that every production is different and one size doesn't fit all. That's why good show controllers keep a lot of different tools in their toolbox, both hardware and software. After all, slime waits for no man, and a programmer has to be ready for anything.

Outro: What Really Matters

"**A**ny intelligent fool can make things bigger, more complex, and more violent. It takes a touch of genius—and a lot of courage—to move in the opposite direction."

—E. F. Schumacher

The writer of the seminal economic text *Small Is Beautiful* reminds us all that beauty is often found in the simple places, bigger is not necessarily better, and adding high technology will not necessarily raise your show to a higher level. As David Mamet writes, "The audience only has one question: 'And then what happened?'"[1]

In other words, more is not necessarily more.

The vast majority of the technology covered in this book is the technology of the image—technology that can create vivid pictures (and sound) beyond what can be done with human actors, wood, fabric, and paint. If you know what those images are, and why they are there onstage, these technologies can add incredible power and scale to your show. Of course, sometimes you're just having fun. No one needs a reason to put big fat moving lights on a rock show, but the best use of *any* technology is to reveal the inner workings of the story (even the story of a big fat rock show). As you explore the wonders of digital theater, with all its vast possibilities, always ask yourself, "How can I use this technology to reach my audience's heart?" How can you use these devices to communicate the emotional core of your story—the part that is simple, straightforward, and powerful?

How can you tell the audience what happened next?

---

[1] *On Directing Film*, David Mamet, Penguin, 1992.

Twenty Digital Terms that All Theater People Should Know

The amount of technical information that digital theater techs throw around is completely frightening. If you want to have a useful conversation with one of those "digi-techs," however, you can do quite a bit if you have the following twenty terms under your belt. All of these terms are explained in greater detail in their respective sections.

Lighting

Moving Head versus Moving Mirror

The two kinds of moving lights. Moving headlights allow the entire lighting unit to pan and tilt. Moving mirror units keep the lighting unit still and redirect the light beam with a moving mirror.

DMX

The standard control protocol used to create networks of lighting equipment, such as control boards, dimmers, and moving lights as well as some special effect equipment like fog and smoke machines. In DMX networks, all devices have a DMX address. There can be up to 512 different addresses in one DMX universe.

LED

An LED is basically a tiny computer chip that radiates light. They are packed together in LED video screens and also in light sources that can replace incandescent bulbs.

Conventionals

Any theatrical lighting instruments that are not moving lights. Also known as "what we used to use before you kids came along."

Video

Pixel

A pixel (short for picture element) is a single dot on your television screen. They are the points of light that make up a video image, and they are usually how video image sizes are measured. For example, a standard-definition video screen in the United States is 640 pixels wide by 480 pixels high.

Composite versus Component

Composite video uses a single cable to send all three video colors (red, green, blue). Component cable uses separate cables for each color (and sometimes additional cable for synchronization data).

High Definition versus Standard Definition

There is no firm definition about the difference between high and standard definition, but generally, any video signal that is larger than 1,080 by 720 pixels is considered high definition. Of course, some day there will be much larger images, and we will consider the current high-definition video to be boringly standard.

Four-Three versus Sixteen-Nine

These are both terms that refer to aspect ratio, the ratio between the width and the height of a video image. Four-three or 4:3 is the standard aspect ratio of non-high-definition video in the United States. Sixteen-nine or 16:9 is considered wide-screen video because, surprise, it's wider than 4:3. Note that 16:9 is always wide-screen, but is *not* always high definition.

Codec

A codec is a computer program that allows you to compress a video file and thereby make it small enough to fit on a storage device (such as a hard drive, video server, or DVD) or be sent over a network. The same program allows you to decompress the file in order to display the video. "Co" = compress, "dec" = decompress, therefore: codec. A large variety of codecs is generally included inside video editing software programs.

Audio

Sampling

Sampling is the process by which analog audio (like the sounds we hear with our ears) becomes digital audio (which can be stored and played back in a computer). Any time you are recording digitally, using your computer, a digital audio recorder, or even a digital video camera, you are sampling.

Sample Rate

The number of samples that are being recorded every second as a file is being digitally recorded. The standard sample rate for CDs is 44.1 kHz or 44,100 samples per second. Pro audio is generally recorded at 48 kHz or 48,000 samples per second.

Audio File Formats: AIFF, WAV, AAC, MP3

These are the four most popular file formats for digital devices. AIFF and WAV were created by Apple and Microsoft, respectively, and are for non-compressed audio. They are functionally identical, but each one tends to be preferred by their respective communities: Apple people like AIFF, while Microsoft people prefer WAV. AAC and MP3 are for compressed audio files, which makes the files smaller and somewhat lower quality. AAC is newer and better.

Show Control

Serial versus Network Control

Show control systems can operate in one of two ways: either by running dedicated control lines from master devices to slaves (serial) or by plugging all the control devices into a network that freely passes information among all of them (network).

MIDI

Originally a protocol for controlling electronic musical devices, MIDI is now used to control many different types of theatrical devices, including lighting control boards and digital audio players.

Time Code

A standardized internal clock used in some show control systems to synchro-nize operations and assign Go times. The most common is called SMPTE ("simp-tee") time code. If time code is being used in a system, there is one device generating it while the other devices chase it.

E-Stop

The big red button that makes the show control system stop everything it is doing right this very minute. A common safety device.

Computers

USB

USB refers to a particular type of cable and plug as well as a communication protocol. It is the standard way of hooking up peripheral equipment (such a hard drive, thumb drive, printer, or audio interface) to a single computer. USB is currently moving from version 2.0 to version 3.0, which will be faster than any other commercial interface Goodbye, FireWire).

Ethernet

Ethernet also refers to a communication protocol. It is the standard way of creating a computer network that links multiple computers and other devices, such as printers, routers, and many types of theatrical equipment. Ethernet networks usually use Cat5 cables (see below).

Kilobytes versus Megabytes versus Gigabytes

These are the standard measurements for computer file sizes, and each one is much, much bigger than the last. There are one thousand kilobytes (KB) in one megabyte (MB). There are one thousand megabytes (MB) in one gigabyte (GB). For extra credit, there are one thousand gigabytes (GB) in one terabyte (TB).

Cat5

A style of communication cable, used for Ethernet networks (among other things). Usually colored blue and carrying four twisted pairs of cables.

Glossary

AAC: Advanced Audio Coding. A form of lossy audio compression popularized by Apple Computer. The successor to MP3.

AC: Alternating Current. The kind of electricity found in the walls of all buildings in the United States. So-called because the electrons switch direction in the cable, many times per second.

ACL: Aircraft Landing Lights. Very tightly focused lamps that produce a sharp beam of light.

ACN: Architecture for Control Networks, a network protocol created by ESTA to allow various kinds of entertainment data to be sent over digital networks.

ADAT Lightpipe: A form of digital plug and cable used to connect audio devices.

ADAT: Alesis Digital Audio Tape. Originally created as a tape-based digital tape, now used as a form of digital interface to connect all kinds of audio devices.

ADC: Analog Digital Conversion. The piece of electronics that converts an incoming analog audio signal into a digital signal that can be routed and processed by electronic equipment.

AES/EBU: Audio Engineering Society / European Broadcasting Union. A digital standard that was created by these two organizations. It covers digital audio signals that are being carried between two digital devices. It defaults to 48 kHz but can actually run audio at any rate.

AES/EBU Time Code: SMPTE time code that has been embedded into AES/EBU audio signals. Identical to regular SMPTE code, except that it runs inside the digital audio signal.

Aftertouch: In MIDI, a type of message that is sent when the keyboard player presses down harder on a key that has already been pushed down.

AIFF: Audio Interchange File Format. An uncompressed audio format codeveloped by Apple Computer and used extensively on Apple's machines.

Ambient Light: Any light source that is present onstage along with a video image. Ambient lighting is the best way to reduce the visibility of a video projection or monitor.

Amperage: The strength of an electrical current, expressed in Amperes (or amps). Also known as "current."

Amplifier: A device that raises the level of an audio signal so it is powerful enough to drive a speaker.

Analog Signal: Any electrical signal that is continuous in time and has continuous changes in strength, as opposed to a digital signal, which is composed of discontinuous values.

AoE: Audio over Ethernet. Any process that sends digital audio signals over Ethernet networks in real time, such as CobraNet, MADI, or QLAN.

Apple Lossless: A form of lossless audio compression created by Apple Computer.

Art-Net: Originally developed by the Artistic License company, a method of transmitting DMX over Ethernet networks.

ASIO: Audio Stream Input/Output. Audio driver software for the Windows computer.

Aspect Ratio: The ratio of the width of a video image to its height. Because it is a ratio, not a measurement, the numbers do not refer to specific measurements, but only to the relationship between the two measurements.

Audio Interface: A physical device that plugs into a computer and allows the user to plug in microphones and other kinds of audio inputs, as well as output devices like amplifiers and speakers. Sometimes known as a sound card.

Auxiliary Send (often aux): A mixer output that can be fed from any or all of the input channels without affecting the levels of those channels in the master outputs. Often used for effects or monitors.

AVI: Audio Video Interleave. A digital multimedia container format created by Microsoft and used extensively in Windows computers. Being replaced these days by more flexible formats like Ogg and MP4.

Balanced Signals: Audio signals that are sent on two wires simultaneously, reducing interference and distortion.

Ballast: An electronic device that stabilizes current in certain types of lights, such as florescent bulbs and short-art lamps.

Beam Shapers: A mechanical device in a moving light that changes the shape of the output light beam.

Bit Rate: In video, the amount of data being transmitted over a digital video line, usually measured in bits per second, or bps.

BNC: Bayonet Neill-Concelman, but absolutely no one ever calls it that. Style of video coaxial plug.

BWF: Broadcast Wave Format: a version of Microsoft's WAV audio format, standardized by the European Broadcasting Union. Common in motion picture, radio, and television production.

C-clamp: A metal, C-shaped clamp that is commonly used to suspend theatrical lighting equipment.

Category 5: A type of network cable commonly used for Ethernet networks. Often called Cat5, usually colored blue and carrying four twisted pairs of wires. Equipped with rectangular Eight-wire connectors commonly (but technically wrongly) called RJ45.

CCD: Charge Coupled Device. The computer chip in a video camera that captures the video image and turns it into an electronic signal.

Channel Messages: In MIDI, the messages that are generated by the user playing notes. Channel messages cover notes, velocity, and aftertouch, among other things.

Channels: How lighting control consoles organize the devices that it is controlling. The designer can assign any devices (dimmers, fog machines, etc.) to any channels so that the overall picture makes more sense.

Chasing (Time Code): When any electronic device is following (and synchronized to) a time code signal that is being generated by another device.

Circuit Breaker: An electronic device that monitors the amount of current running through a circuit and shuts it down if the current goes too high.

Circuits: In lighting, one or more plugs that are permanently wired together in the theater, carrying power from the dimmers to the lighting instruments.

Coaxial Cable: An electrical cable consisting of (1) an inner conducting wire, (2) a layer of insulation, (3) a conducting shield, and (4) an outer sheath. Commonly used for video transmission as well as Internet signals.

CobraNet: A set of software, hardware, and network protocols that produce a form of Audio over Ethernet. First created by Peak Audio, now owned by Cirrus Logic.

Codec: Software that provides compression and decompression for video signals.

Color Depth: In video, the number of bits used to describe the color of a pixel.

Color Temperature: A measurement of the color of a light, stated in degrees Kelvin (K). Generally used to compare the various kinds of white light, from warm (around 2800K) to cool (around 5000K).

Color Wheel: In a moving light, a round glass filter with various colors on it. Spinning the wheel creates different colors in the beam of light.

Component Video: Video signals that run on several different cables, at least one each for the red, green, and blue signals. Component video cables may have up to five different cables.

Composite Video: Video signals that put all the colors and all the brightness information on one cable.

Compression: In audio, the process of reducing the dynamic range of an audio signal. In video or audio, the process of reducing the file size of a digital file, usually by removing data that the human ear and eye cannot hear or see.

Contact Closure: A physical switch that sends an on/off signal to an electronic circuit. They come in two varieties: normally open and normally closed.

Contrast Ratio: The difference in brightness between the brightest and darkest parts of a video image.

Control Change: In MIDI, a message that changes the attributes of nonkey devices, like pedals or sliders.

Conventional Lights: Theatrical lights that do not move during the performance.

Cue Stacks: A series of cues in a lighting control program.

Cue-Only: A lighting control style where changes to channels are made to one cue only and not to any other cues. The opposite of tracking, where changes to channels are automatically carried into past and future cues.

Cycles per Second: The speed at which an electrical voltage is alternating, measured in Hertz (Hz).

CYM Color Mixing: A method of creating colors in lights by combining three different color wheels or scrolls: cyan, yellow, and magenta.

D-ILA: Digital Direct Drive Image Light Amplifier. A video display technology that uses liquid crystals to make images, like LCD, but reflects the light beams, like a DLP (JVC's version of LCoS).

DAC: Digital Analog Conversion. An electronic device that converts a digital signal from an electronic device into an analog signal that can be sent through speakers or headphones.

Data Byte: In MIDI, the portion of the data string that describes what note is being played and how hard it is being played.

DAW: digital audio workstation. A computer system that collects, mixes, and outputs audio programs.

DC: Direct Current. Any electrical current that flows continuously in one direction, as opposed to alternating current (AC), which rapidly switches directions.

Decel Switch: In a mechanical show system, a switch that is thrown when a moving piece is approaching the end of its travel and needs to slow down.

Diaphragm: The delicate part of a microphone that vibrates when struck by changes in air pressure.

Dichroic filter: A glass filter that creates color in a light beam by reflecting unwanted color frequencies (as opposed to absorbing them, like a standard filter).

Digital: Any electrical signal that is discontinuous in time and strength and composed of a string of numbered values. Opposite of an analog signal, which has a continuous signal.

Digital Keystone Correction: Electronic correction of keystoned images by stretching one side of the image and shrinking the other.

Dipless Fading: A lighting control device that fades between two sets of channels numbers (two cues) without allowing the level of the light to fall below the starting or finishing level.

Direct LEDs: LED devices that act like standard lighting instruments. We see the light coming out of the unit, but not the unit itself.

DLP: Digital Lighting Processing. A method of turning a video signal into a visible image by using a matrix of microscopic micromirrors.

DMX: Digital Multiplexing. A communication protocol that allows a single lighting controller to control hundreds of dimmers over a single cable.

DMX Address: On a DMX universe, the identification number of a single device.

DMX Dongle: A device that plugs into a computer through a USB port, allowing the computer to control a DMX network (with proper software installed).

DMX Fail Mode: How a DMX system acts if the DMX signal is lost.

DMX Splitter: An electronic device that splits one DMX signal into more than one universe.

DMX Universe: A single set of devices that can be connected to a DMX control console through a single cable. One universe can handle up to 512 DMX addresses in up to thirty-two different devices.

DMX512: The official name of the DMX standard, which shows that each universe can handle 512 channels.

Driver: In the world of audio, a software program that connects a hardware interface (like a microphone input or headphone output) with audio software.

Drop Frame Time Code: A type of time code that was developed to accommodate certain requirements of color video, by skipping eighteen frame numbers every ten minutes. No longer necessary but still occasionally seen.

DVD: Digital Versatile Disk or Digital Video Disk. First term is actually more accurate, as not all DVDs are video.

DVI: Digital Visual Interface. A video standard for computer and projector video signals.

Dynamics: The description of an audio signal's volume over time.

E-Stop: See Emergency Stop.

Edge Blending: The process of blending two video images together on a screen to create a single, seamless image. Generally used to create brighter images than would ordinarily be possible.

Edison plug: The household plug seen in all American homes, containing two parallel blades and sometimes a U-shaped grounding pin. Technically known as a 5-15 non-locking NEMA connector, but you will never hear that term on any stage anywhere.

Effects Loop: An audio signal circuit that comes out of an aux output, goes through an effects box (e.g. reverb), then reenters to the mixer through a return plug.

Effects Processor: An audio device that processes an audio signal, adding effects like echo, reverb, and delay.

Ellipsoidals: Theatrical lighting instruments with ellipsoidal reflectors, shutters, and gobo slots.

Emergency Stop: Any device that immediately and completely shuts down an electronic or mechanical show device, usually as a safety feature.

Enable Button: A button that is pressed by an actor or crew member to let the show control system know that it is safe to run an effect.

Encoders: Electronic devices that track the movement of physical devices, like winches, wagons, and motors.

EQ: Equalization. Any device that adjusts the strength of different audio frequencies to produce a different tone of sound.

Error Checking: A technique that allows more reliable transmission and reception of digital data over networks.

Ethernet: A set of hardware and software standards that allows for high-speed transmission of data over local area networks (LANs), like those in homes, schools, businesses, and theaters.

Fields: In video, a set of video scan lines that contains every other line. Two fields (one even and one odd) together make up one frame.

Filament Hum: The effect produced when power from SCR dimmers at less than full power flows through standard theatrical lighting lamps. The sharp-edged electrical current literally causes the filaments to vibrate and hum.

Fixture Library: On a lighting control board, the list of settings for particular moving lights, containing such information as color numbers, template numbers, etc.

Fixtures: See Lighting Instruments.

Flash Video: A form of digital video container file, extremely common for video content on the Internet. Originally used for the Adobe Flash Player but now used just about everywhere.

Focal Length: In a video projector lens, the length of the lens system, while defines how much an image is converged (made smaller) or diverged (made larger). A longer focal length produces a narrower image.

Frame Rate: The number of frames of video that are drawn per second, measured in fps, or frames per second.

Frame Size: The outside dimensions of a frame of video, measured in pixels, width by height.

Frame: In video, a complete image of a single, static picture. Video works by playing a string of frames in sequence, which your eye sees as a moving image.

Fresnels: Theatrical lighting instruments with a grooved lens and no shutters or gobo slots.

Gain Factor: A measurement of the amount of reflectivity in a projection screen. Also known as screen gain. Higher numbers mean that a screen will reflect higher amounts of light.

Gobo: A metal template, into which a design is carved, placed inside a lighting instrument to create a shadow pattern in the beam of light.

Ground Loops: In an audio system, a form of unwelcome noise, caused by the system having several different connections to ground.

H.264: Compression format that is part of the MPEG standard. Generally used for downloaded formats due to its smaller size.

Half-Gain Viewing Angle: A measurement that shows how visible a projection image is when viewed from off-center. At the half-gain viewing angle, the projected image is 50 percent as bright as when viewed from directly in front (at 0 degrees).

HDMI: High-Definition Multimedia Interface. A style of digital cables and plugs designed to transmit uncompressed audio and video. It is the same as DVI, but unlike DVI, can also transmit audio.

Hexadecimal: A numbering styles that uses the numbers zero to nine plus the letters A through F to create a base-16 numbering system. Very useful in the world of computers where computer chips often store data in groups of 16 bits.

HID: High-Intensity Discharge Lamp. A style of lamp that generates light by jumping electricity across a tiny gap inside a gas-filled glass envelope.

High Definition: A video signal that has a higher resolution than standard definition video. While there is no specific number for high definition, these days the signals are either 1,280 by 720 pixels (known as 720p) or 1,920 by 1,080 pixels (known as either 1080i or 1080p).

HTP: Highest Takes Precedence. A setting inside a lighting control console. When the console is confronted with two different level settings for the same device, an HTP console will take the higher of the two settings. Opposite of latest takes precedence (LTP).

Image Capturing: In the video world, how a digital device scans a visual image and records it as a digital file.

Indirect LEDs: LED devices that act like video screens. We do not see a beam of light, we see flashing lights as pixels in a video image.

Interface: Any electronic device that connects two different kinds of devices, such as audio microphones and computers. Also used in the term "User Interface," the control portion of an device that allows a human being to control the inner workings of the device.

Interframe Compression: Video compression that works by removing data that is repeated in subsequent frames.

Interlacing: The creation of video images by scanning all the odd lines of an image followed by the even lines. The opposite of progressive, where all the lines are scanned in order.

Intraframe Compression: Video compression that works by removing data in a single frame that is not necessary for the human eye.

JPEG: Joint Photographic Experts Group. Images that use the standards created by the JPEG group to compress the image down to a smaller file size.

Keystoning: The distortion of a video image caused by placing the projector off-center of the screen. Generally, the image takes on a trapezoidal shape.

Latency: Delays that are introduced into an audio playback system by electronic processing.

LCD: Liquid Crystal Display. A video display technology that uses the light modulating properties of liquid crystals to create a passive display, like a television, or a projected image, like a video projector.

LCoS: Liquid Crystal on Silicon: A video display technology that uses liquid crystals to make images, like LCD, but reflects the light beams off micromirrors, like a DLP.

Life Safety System: Any show system that, were it to fail, would cause serious harm or loss of life to a human being.

Light Valve: A digital device that creates a visible video projection by sending a beam of light through microscopic LCD crystals, each of which can be opaque or transparent.

Lighting Control Console: An electronic device that allows a user to control theatrical lighting and special effect equipment, generally using the DMX512 control protocol.

Lighting Instruments: Theatrical lighting devices, known erroneously to rookies and theatrical outsiders as "lights."

Limit Switch: A physical switch on a theatrical show device that is tripped when the device reaches the end of its travel distance.

Limiter: In the audio world, a device that sets a maximum volume for an audio signal.

Line-Level Signal: An audio signal level that is commonly used to process audio signals in mixers, effects units, computers, interfaces, and amplifiers. Stronger than microphone level but well below speaker level.

Lossless Compression: A form of audio compression that reduces the size of an audio file without reducing the quality of the sound. Also known as "magic."

Lossy Compression: Audio or video compression that reduces file sizes by permanently removing information that is seen to be less important.

LTC: Linear Time Code. A form of time code first used on video tape where it was written in a linear stripe along the edge of the tape. Replaced by VITC (see below).

LTP: Latest Takes Precedence. A setting inside a lighting control console. When the console is confronted with two different level settings for the same device, an LTP console will take the most recent of the two settings. Opposite of highest takes precedence (HTP).

Manual Preset Boards: Manually operated lighting control boards with multiple scenes, each of which has a string of sliders or wheels that control dimmers. The forerunners of computer-based memory consoles.

Master Device: In a show control system, the device that is "in charge." Generally the device that is outputting time code or Go commands to the other devices.

Matrix: In the audio world, a grid where inputs are assigned to outputs. The matrix is usually an on-screen interface, not a physical grid. The matrix format allows any number of inputs to be assigned to any number of outputs.

Media Container Files: Digital media files that contain one or more other files and allow those files to be played simultaneously in sync with each other.

Media Server: Any electronic device that stores digital media files and plays them back (or "serves" them) to a display device. Some servers have display devices built into them.

Memory Consoles: Computer-based lighting control consoles that store all the cues in a computer memory that can be called up in any order and edited.

Metadata: Information about data that is included in a data file, e.g. date of recording, sample rates, type of recorder, etc.

Metal-Halide Lamp: See High-Intensity Discharge Lamp.

Mic-Level Signal: The level of audio signal that comes out of a microphone. An extremely low-level signal that must be boosted up to line level in order to be processed or mixed.

MIDI: Musical Instrument Digital Interface. A standard industry interface that allows suitably equipped musical instruments to control and be controlled by computers and other musical devices.

MIDI IN: The plug on a MIDI-compatible device where the MIDI signal enters. The MIDI device listens and responds to data that enters here.

MIDI OUT: The plug on a MIDI-compatible device where the MIDI signal leaves. Any MIDI information generated by that device is sent out here.

MIDI Sequencer: A device that records and plays back MIDI notes, either as a standalone device or as software on a computer.

MIDI Show Control: An industry-standard protocol, based on the MIDI standard, used to control theatrical devices such as lighting, audio, and special effects.

MIDI THRU: The plug on a MIDI-compatible device where the MIDI IN signal is copied and re-outputted. Used to daisy-chain devices together. Any MIDI information generated by the device itself is sent out the MIDI OUT port, *not* the MIDI THRU, which is only used to copy the data from the MIDI IN.

MIDI Time Code: A form of time code that is compatible with the MIDI standard. It has four times the resolution of SMPTE time code, but is otherwise similar.

MIDI Triggers: Physical switches that send MIDI notes to MIDI controllers and sequencers.

Mixer Channel: A single input on an audio mixer, which usually allows the user to route a single audio signal, as well as set volume level and equalization.

Moving Head Light: An automated moving light where the entire light is panned and rotated by several motors. Opposite of moving mirror light.

Moving Light Profiles: See Fixture Library.

Moving Lights: Theatrical lighting instruments that allow the user to pan and tilt the light as well as change color, templates, and other features during a live performance. Opposite of conventional lights.

Moving Mirror light: An automated moving light where the light-outputting portion stays in one place and the beam of light is directed around the stage by a moving mirror. Opposite of moving head light.

Moving Yoke light: See Moving Head Light.

MP3: MPEG-2 Audio Layer 3. An audio encoding format that uses lossy compression to greatly reduces file size by removing audio information that is thought to be unnecessary.

MP4: A multimedia container format for digital audio and video files. Technically known as MPEG-4 Part 14, it uses the file extension "mp4," which is now used as its common name. It is directly related to QuickTime and is essentially identical to the "mov" format, with some additional features.

MPEG Program Stream: The common digital container file format for DVDs. Generally contains video and audio files which are played in sync with each other.

MPEG: Motion Picture Experts Group. Files that follow the standards created by this industry working group. MPEG files comes in many varieties and may be container files or specific video or audio files.

MSC: See MIDI Show Control.

Mute: A control button that silences an audio input.

Network Hub: A device that sends network data out to multiple arms of a LAN. Unlike a network switch, it does not determine which data should go to which arm of the network.

Network Router: A device that connects a LAN network to the outside world.

Network Switch: A device that sends network data out to multiple arms of a LAN. Unlike a network hub, it only sends data out to the arm of the network where the data is headed, thus reducing network traffic and increasing network speed.

Network Topology: The general design of the shape of a network. Common topologies include ring and star.

Non-Dim Circuit: A lighting circuit that only has two settings: on and off. Commonly used for projectors, fog machines, and other electronic or motorized devices that would be damaged by dimmed power.

Normally Closed: A contact-closure circuit that transmits the voltage of the control circuit until the switch is triggered, at which point the control voltage is cut off.

Normally Open: A contact-closure circuit that does not transmit the voltage of the control circuit until the switch is triggered, at which point the control voltage is sent back through the wires.

NTSC: National Television System Committee. The common video standard used in North America.

Opto-isolator: An electronic device used for data inputs on some devices, like DMX circuits. The opto-isolator keeps the actual electric signal on the cable from entering the electronic device, thus protecting the device from interference. The electric signal crosses an internal barrier as a beam of light and is then recreated inside the device.

Outboard Gear: Audio equipment that is not built into a mixer, but connected externally.

Over-Travel Switch: A physical switch on a show device that is triggered if a moving unit overshoots its normal limit. Used as a safety device.

PAL: Phase Alternate Line. The common video standard for Europe (except France) and Asia.

Pan: The side-to-side movement of a moving light.

PAR Can: A theatrical lighting instrument based on a sealed-beam lamp with an internal reflector, similar to a car headlight.

Patch Panel: A physical panel where lighting circuits are connected to dimmers.

Pattern: See Gobo.

Perceptual Coding: The practice of reducing accuracy of certain parts of digital audio files that are thought to be beyond the capacity of most people to hear.

Phono Plug: Type of audio plug. Also known as a 1/4" plug. Can be mono or stereo. Stereo version sometimes known as a TRS (tip-ring-sleeve) plug.

Pitch Wheel: On a MIDI keyboard, a control device that shifts the pitch of a note up or down. Also refers to the messages that are generated by the wheel.

Pixel: Short for picture element, a single point on a video monitor or video projector.

Pixel Mapping: The computer-based process of breaking a video image down into parts and mapping those parts on to the pixels available in a video image.

PLC: See Programmable Logic Controller.

Power Supply: A device that takes power from the wall and converts it into the voltage and amperage required by an electronic device. If the power supply is plugged into the power outlet directly, it is often called a wall wart.

Powered Speakers: Audio speakers with internal amplifiers. They must be plugged into a power source to operate.

Program Change: In MIDI, a message that changes the sound program for a channel, e.g. changing from a piano sound to a horn sound.

Progressive Scanning: A video image that is constructed by scanning all the lines of the image in order, from top to bottom. Opposite of interlacing.

Projection Bay: Space created upstage of the set to allow the projector to have an adequate throw distance for rear projection.

Protocol: A set of rules that determine standards for communication.

QuickTime: A multimedia format created by Apple Computer. It is used for a wide variety of different file formats including video, audio, still pictures, and interactivity. Normal QuickTime functions are fairly limited and generally users must buy a QuickTime Pro license from Apple to do anything significant. Apple's multimedia editing software programs come with QuickTime Pro installed.

RAID: Redundant Array of Independent Disks. A group of disks that work together to provide large amounts of storage space where the data is backed up in redundant drives.

RCA: Radio Corporation of America. These days, it most commonly refers to a style of audio plug used for consumer video and audio.

RDM: Remote Device Management. A protocol created for DMX to allow two-way communication between DMX-compatible devices.

RealMedia: A media container format used for various kinds of streaming media formats from the RealNetworks company, including RealVideo and RealAudio. Streaming formats are played on your computer in real time and are not stored permanently on your machine.

Refresh Rate: See Frame Rate.

Resolution: A measurement of the detail of a still image or video frame. Higher resolution means more pixels, which means, in general, better quality. Resolution is often stated in frame size i.e., the number of pixels in the image.

Return: A mixer input where an audio signal that has previously been sent to an outboard device returns to the mixer.

Reverb: The addition of a timed echo sound to an audio signal, to provide the illusion that the sound is coming from a larger space.

RFU: Remote Focus Unit. A remote control device for a lighting control console.

RGB: Red Green Blue. A video monitor or signal that is composed of three separate signals, one red, one green, and one blue.

RJ45: A jack originally designed for telephone plugs, but later used for computer network cables. Often used (erroneously) to describe the plugs on the end of Cat5 computer network cables.

RMVB: RealMedia Variable Bitrate. A variable bitrate version of the RealMedia container format. Very popular in Asia.

S/PDIF: Sony/Philips Digital Interconnect Format. A digital audio format, created primarily for the consumer audience.

Sample Playback: The process of playing digital audio samples on a sound system.

Sampler: A device that records short audio recordings (samples) and assigns them to particular musical notes so they can be played back in any order.

Sampling: The process of recording analog audio signals as digital files. How digital audio is created from analog sounds.

Sampling Rate: The number of samples that a sampler records or plays back per second. Usually listed as thousands of samples per second.

Scan Lines: The horizontal lines of pixels on a video screen.

Scanners: In lighting, the British term for a moving mirror light.

Scanning System: Definition of the type of scanning used for a video file, i.e., progressive or interlaced.

SCR: Silicon Controlled Rectifier. The most common form of theatrical dimmer. Uses two fast computer chips to turn electrical circuits on and off sixty times per second.

SDI: Serial Digital Interface. High-quality digital video interfaces, often used in broadcast video applications.

SECAM: Sequential Couleur Avec Memoire. The French video standard, like PAL in the rest of Europe or NTSC in America.

Serial Control: A control system where a dedicated control line runs directly from a control device to one or more slave devices. Opposite of a network control system.

Short-Arc Lamp: See High-Intensity Discharge Lamp.

Shutters: Metal sliders on an ellipsoidal lighting instrument that can cut off a portion of the light beam.

Signal Chain: In audio, the path that an audio signal takes from the source, through mixer and processors, to the output device.

Slave Device: In a control system, any unit that is taking commands or receiving timing from a master device.

SMPTE: Society of Motion Picture and Television Engineers. The organization that came up with the first television standards in the United States. Also, the name of those standards.

Soft Patch: A method of connecting inputs and outputs inside a computer or lighting control console. Opposite of a hard patch or a patch panel, which is a physical set of connections.

Solo: Control button that turns off all outputs except the one under the Solo button.

Sound Card: See Audio Interface.

Speaker Cone: The portion of a speaker that vibrates back and forth when an audio signal is fed into a speaker. The part that actually creates real sound.

Speaker Level Signal: An audio signal that is strong enough to drive a speaker. Usually comes from an amplifier.

Stage Pin Plug: A rectangular, nonlocking electrical connector used in theaters. Usually has three pins, although older models may have two.

Standard Definition: Video signals that are less than 1,280 by 720 pixels.

Star Topology: A form of network topology that has a switch or hub at the center and separate network lines radiating outward to each network device.

Starting Channel: When assigning DMX channels to a device with multiple channels, the lowest number that will be used by the device.

Status Byte: In MIDI, the portion of a data string that describes what kind of message is being sent and what channel it is being played on.

Stepper Motors: In moving lights and other theatrical devices, motors with highly accurate placement controls that can be precisely rotated into a specific position.

Strobe: A lighting effect where the lamp turns on and off quickly. Generally not possible with incandescent lamps unless physical shutters are used.

Submaster: On lighting and audio control consoles, a slider that can be assigned to control a certain number of channels.

Switched Ethernet: A computer network that uses switches (as opposed to hubs) to route data to various parts of the network, thereby reducing network traffic.

SXRD: Silicon X-tal Reflective Display: A video display technology that uses liquid crystals to make images, like LCD, but reflects the light beams, like a DLP (Sony's version of LCoS).

Sync: See Synchronization.

Synchronization: The process of making two or more signals play back in the proper relationship to each other. For example, getting a video file to play at the same time and speed as the audio file that goes with it.

System Exclusive Message: In MIDI, a message that is designed to be understood only by a specific kind of device.

TCP/IP: Transmission Control Protocol / Internet Protocol. The protocol used by the Internet to route data packages to the appropriate location.

Templates: See Gobos.

Three-fer Cable: A power cable with three female plugs and one male plug. Used to combine three different electric devices into the same circuit.

Throw Distance: Distance from the video projector to the video screen.

Time Code: A standardized timing signal used by electronic devices (such as video or audio players) to play back files at the correct speed. Also used to provide timing information for show control and media playback devices.

Toslink: A digital audio plug for optical connections. Used most commonly for ADAT and S/PIDF connections.

Tracking Console: A lighting console that takes any channel changes and copies them to all other adjacent cues, so that changes will not have to be made repeatedly. Opposite of cue-only console.

Transformer: Electronic device that changes the voltage of an electrical signal.

Twist-lock Plug: A three-pin theatrical plug that locks male and female plugs together by, surprise! Twisting them.

Two-fer Cable: A power cable with two female plugs and one male plug. Used to combine two different electric devices into the same circuit.

Two-Scene Preset Board: See Manual Preset Board.

USB: Universal Serial Bus. A specification designed to connect various electronic devices to a computer. USB refers to specific kinds of plugs and cables that are used to plug items such as hard drives and audio interfaces into computers. There have been several versions of USB, including 1.0, 2.0, and the current state of the art: 3.0.

Variable Lens Shifting: On a video projector, the device that corrects for keystoning by moving the position of the projector lens.

VBR: Variable Bit Rate. A way of compressing video that allows the bit rate to fluctuate depending on the needs of the file.

Velocity: In MIDI, the speed that a key travels from its resting position to its bottom position. Usually controls volume.

Video Monitor: A screen that displays video images. Previously known as a "TV."

Video Standards: The various sets of video specifications that are used to make all video in a certain country compatible, e.g., NTSC (North America), PAL (Europe and Asia), and SECAM (France).

Video Sync: The signal that ensures that all video signals are scanning the screen at the same time and in the same direction.

VITC: Vertical interval Time Code. A style of time code originally created for video tape, where the time was printed and read by the spinning video head.

Voltage: The amount of force being used to transmit electrical power, measured in volts.

Wattage: The amount of power required to operate an electrical device, measured in watts.

WAV: Waveform Audio File Format. Computer file format created by Microsoft and IBM for storing uncompressed audio.

Word Clock: A form of synchronization found in high-end audio studios, where all devices follow a centralized clock operating at a particular sampling speed, e.g., 48 kHz.

XLR: A popular form of audio plug, commonly used for microphone and live level signals, originally having three plugs but now available with four or five pins as well. The initials in the name refer to the original plug, called a Cannon XL after the company that first popularized them: Cannon Electric. Some people still call it a Cannon plug.

Zoom Ellipsoidal: An ellipsoidal lighting instrument with a changeable focal length.

Index

Books from Allworth Press

Allworth Press is an imprint of Skyhorse Publishing, Inc. Selected titles are listed below.

Technical Theater for Nontechnical People, Second Edition
by Drew Campbell (6 × 9, 272 pages, paperback, $19.95)

Technical Film and TV for Nontechnical People
by Drew Campbell (6 × 9, 256 pages, paperback, $24.95)

Careers in Technical Theater
by Mike Lawler (6 × 9, 288 pages, paperback, $19.95)

Running Theaters: Best Practices for Leaders and Managers
by Duncan M. Webb (6 × 9, 256 pages, paperback, $19.95)

The Stage Producer's Business and Legal Guide
by Charles Grippo (6 × 9, 256 pages, paperback, $19.95)

Performing Arts Management: A Handbook of Professional Practices
by Tobie S. Stein and Jessica Bathurst (8 ½ × 11, 552 pages, paperback, $50.00)

Business and Legal Forms for Theater
by Charles Grippo (8 ½ × 11, 192 pages (includes CD-ROM), paperback, $29.95)

Fundamentals of Theatrical Design
by Karen Brewster and Melissa Shafer (6 × 9, 288 pages, paperback, $27.50)

The Health & Safety Guide for Film, TV & Theater, Second Edition
by Monona Rossol (6 × 9, 288 pages, paperback, $27.50)

The Perfect Stage Crew: The Compleat Technical Guide for High School, College, and Community Theater
by John Kaluta (6 × 9, 256 pages, paperback, $19.95)

Stage Combat: Fisticuffs, Stunts, and Swordplay for Theater and Film
by Jenn Zuko Boughn (7 ¾ × 9 ⅜, 240 pages, paperback, $19.95)

Great Producers: Visionaries of the American Theater
by Iris Dorbian (6 × 9, 212 pages, paperback, $19.95)

Building the Successful Theater Company, Second Edition
by Lisa Mulcahy (6 × 9, 256 pages, paperback, $24.95)

To see our complete catalog or to order online, please visit ***www.allworth.com***.